Around the World in Fifty Years

Travel Tales from a Not So Innocent Abroad

Elayne Clift

Copyright © 2019 by Elayne Clift. All rights reserved.

This book or any portion thereof may not be reproduced or used in any manner whatsoever without the express written permission of the publisher except for the use of brief quotations in a scholarly work or book review. For permissions or further information contact Braughler Books LLC at:

info@braughlerbooks.com

Printed in the United States of America
Published by Braughler Books LLC., Springboro, Ohio

First printing, 2019

ISBN: 978-1-945091-98-8

Library of Congress Control Number: 2018957730

Ordering information: Special discounts are available on quantity purchases by bookstores, corporations, associations, and others. For details, contact the publisher at:

sales@braughlerbooks.com
or at 937-58-BOOKS

For questions or comments about this book, please write to:

info@braughlerbooks.com

Braughler™
Books
braughlerbooks.com

Table of Contents

Preface vii

Introduction   1

Counting Cats in Zanzibar: Reflections on Travel
Through a 7 Decade Lens 3

Africa   7

An African Odyssey. 9
Cape Town and the Bush. 13
A Doula in Somaliland 27
Kenya and Tanzania. 41
Khartoum Nights 47
The Medieval Magic of Morocco 51

Asia   55

A Cook, a Driver and a Train Station 57
Images of India. 60
A Twelve Mile Trek in Nepal 63
This is Thailand, Silly! The Reality of Living in a Land
You Love, Frustrations and All. 71
Vietnam: From Hanoi to Saigon: Visions of Vietnam. 77
Laos Lite: Three Days in Luang Prabang. 83
Cambodia: Beyond Angkor Wat, Sadness In Cambodia 87

Tiennanmen Square 90

Caribbean, Central and South America	91

Dominican Republic 93
Panama 99
Guatemala Revisited 101
A South American Journey 107
Galapagos Waters 117
Cuba: A Journey Back in Time and Toward the Future 119

Europe	141

Turkish Delights: Two Weeks of Treasures
and Topography 143
The Pleasures of Portugal 153
Stockholm: City of Surprises on the Sea 161
Norway: A Tale of Two Cities, and a Ship 165
A Balkan Reprise 175
A Greek Journal 189
Iceland: Nice Place to Transit but
Would You Want to Live There? 207
Tortura Pura: A Diary of Driving in Italy 211
Culinary Crossings 215
Falling in Love Again: France Revisited 221
An Italian Romance 227
In Search of My Grandmother's Shtetl:
A Romanian Pilgrimage 231
Gypsy Girl in Bucharest 239

Paris Blues 241

Land o' Lakes: England's Glorious North Country 245

Middle East	249

Dubai Desert Wish. 251

Israel. 255

Jordan: A Post-Feminist Era? Not By a Long Shot 261

North America	265

Shadows and Stars 267

A Soft Adventure for the Hale and Hearty 273

Images of Alaska. 279

Everglades 280

Signs of Vermont 281

Misty Mountain Night. 282

Winter Curse in New England 283

Day Four in the Land of Enchantment 284

Global Perspectives In Poetry	287

All the Starving Children 288

Getting Religion 290

I Listen and My Heart is Breaking. 292

Aboriginal Man 294

Beyond The Veil 295

Queen Maeve's Grave. 296

Epilogue	**297**
Longings	299

End Matter	
Acknowledgments	303
Photo Credits	305
About the Author	307

Preface

As someone who has loved travel since childhood trips led me across the border to Canada, I have been blessed to have visited more than 90 countries around the world (and every state in America) over the course of a long career in public health education and advocacy. That career took me to many countries, as did my husband's work as an international civil servant.

Fortunately, he is as addicted to travel as I am and we were often able to accompany each other on business trips, or to meet up in enticing places in the course of our work-related travels. We were equally fortunate that being British, he, our children and I all got "home leave" to England bi-annually. That provided a great jumping off point for some of our explorations. At other times, we just saved up our airline points and our pennies and went where the spirit took us, often staying in what are now called Air BnBs or with friends who were kind enough to host us.

I began writing travel journals somewhere along the line, and then, as I grew into journalism, I started publishing travel articles in various publications. Then I began sharing my journals and published pieces with friends and soon they couldn't seem to get enough of them. "I can't wait to see your travel tales!" they said as I was about to set off. "I feel like I've been right there when I read them!"

Not long ago, I realized that I did have stories to tell that would interest others bitten by the travel bug so I began to put together a somewhat random collection of my writings, add a few pictures, and short footnotes, and Voila! This book.

Some of these pieces were archived on floppy discs so I had to retype them into the manuscript. (Not fun.) Other memories were in my more recent "Travel" file (much easier to include). There are pieces that read like straightforward travel writing and others that are more personal and conversational. Most of them include a picture I've taken while a few rely on stock photos. There's a personal note at the end of each piece.

The stories included in this collection are not complete in terms of my travel experiences by any means. I've chosen them as representative of a region, or because they hold fond memories for me, or because they are humorous, and may be helpful to future travelers.

The material is shared in no particular order. Rather, the collection is a kind of walkabout: Just go where the path takes you. I have, however, provided regional designations for structure.

Some of the writing goes back quite a long time while other pieces are relatively recent. I realize that some places I've written about are likely to have changed enormously since I was there. They'd probably be unrecognizable to me now, and I expect I'd be glad that I saw them when I did. I hope readers will not find it necessary to chastise me for that. Finally, I have not dated the pieces because I couldn't always remember what year a particular trip occurred.

I hope you will sit back and simply enjoy this book as a bit of armchair travel. Please savor what you will, forgive my sins of omission, and feel free to be in touch if you have any comments or questions. Enjoy and Bon Voyage!

Introduction

Counting Cats in Zanzibar:
Reflections on Travel Through a 7 Decade Lens

All my life I have disagreed with Henry David Thoreau: Unlike him, I definitely think it is "worthwhile to go around the world to count the cats in Zanzibar."

The joy of travel has been in my blood since I was a young child when the high point of summer was the family trip to Toronto to visit my father's relatives. On the eve of the journey my sister and I would lay out our new shorts, halter tops, and primary color sandals in order to be ready when the alarm went off at 6:00 a.m. Teeth brushed and hair combed, we ran to the car (a big, black Buick) and for once did not argue with our brother for the window seat. We were too busy savoring breakfast at Howard Johnson's, part of the annual ritual that would begin our trip to another country!

Every year we took a different route in order to "enjoy the scenery." Pre-interstate and Holiday Inn days, we drove through Pennsylvania Dutch country or New England or New York State, where we visited Ithaca's gorges, the 1,000 islands, and of course, Niagara Falls. Every night, we looked for AAA-approved cabins in which to sleep, with their worn linoleum floors, chenille bedspreads, and inevitable spiders. We thought it was pure heaven (except for the spiders.)

Once in Toronto we checked into the Royal York Hotel where a little man who looked just like the Phillip Morris icon roamed the lobby calling out, "Call for Mr. Smith!" or "Call for Mr. Jones!" The next morning, before heading to my grandfather's house, we ate breakfast in The Honeydew Restaurant and stopped at Simpson's or Eaton's so that my mother could add another bone china tea cup and saucer to her collection. Only then were we ready for the obligatory visits where our cheeks would be pinched as this aunt or that said, "Look how you've grown!"

In 1964 I traveled solo to Europe for the first time. I thought I'd died and gone to Heaven as I experienced Amsterdam, London, Paris, Rome, and the Swiss Alps. Relishing every moment of my Eurorail Pass train rides, every conversation with fellow travelers from different cultures, every museum and cathedral, I thought I'd go mad with the excitement of it all. I stopped breathing at the sight of Michelangelo's David, wept in San Marco Square, thrilled at the sound of Big Ben and the pageantry of the Changing of the Guard, ate *prix fixe* three-course meals on the Left Bank, and smiled back at Mona Lisa. I even fell in love, but that is a story for another time. In short, I knew that my life had changed and that as part of my metamorphosis, I would never stop traveling.

And I haven't. I returned two more times to Europe on my own, married a Brit who loves traveling as much as I do and with whom I was able to circle the globe because of his work, then mine. That work took us to countries in Africa, Asia, Central America and the Middle East. Together we have been to more than 90 countries (and all 50 states) for work and/or pleasure. I even managed a teaching gig in Thailand for a year.

While in Thailand and then after that we traveled like mad cockroaches, scurrying from Southeast Asia to South America with a few European and Middle Eastern countries thrown in.

Then we had a hiatus and something strange started to happen. We began to realize that we no longer wished to be in big, busy cities. We didn't want to "do" cathedrals and museums and ruins. The thought of double-digit hours in flight grew increasingly off-putting. Renting apartments and eating dinner "at home" became more appealing than staying in hotels. Three weeks away seemed like an awfully long time.

I knew I was in trouble when I penned an essay called "Paris Blues" in which I wrote:

"There is something ludicrous about standing on the Pont Neuf asking yourself why you're there. Most people would give anything to stand on that iconic bridge overlooking the Seine. But on a recent trip I felt like a jilted lover. I asked myself terrible questions: Why did I come back? What am I supposed to do here, now, this time? I asked myself an even more ominous question: Is it possible for an inveterate traveler to lose the thrill of reprise? Is there such a thing as traveler's ennui? Do I need larger fixes and only new places to feel again the thrill of people and place? I would feel utterly deprived not to see Paris again. But the fact is I stood on a bridge in Paris and wondered what I was doing there."

Shortly after writing that, I found myself telling friends that I seem to be more into "purposeful" travel now, wanting to go places where I can contribute something and better understand the culture. A few years ago, I spent two weeks volunteering at a hospital in Somaliland. Recently, I went to Greece to volunteer with pregnant refugees. Shortly after this book was published I volunteered at a rural hospital in Peru.

I'd also like to revisit some of my favorite places, like England's Lake District, or venues that have changed enormously since I was there, like Bangladesh. (I did make it back to the Balkans recently). Sometimes I can't believe how much my travel tastes have changed.

The British author Penelope Lively wrote about her diminished desire for travel in her memoir, <u>Dancing Fish and Amonites</u>. "There are things I no longer want, things I no longer do," she noted, travel being among them. She also surprised herself. "What? No further desire? You who crossed the Atlantic twice a year or so? Who was happy to hop off pretty well anywhere?" Lively never wanted to see another airport, she said, never wanted to "brave Terminal Four" or "sit squashed in a metal canister with hundreds of others for hours on end."

Attempting to explain the change in her attitude toward travel the much-loved writer pondered whether "there is some benign mechanism that aligns diminished capacity with diminished desire." I'm not quite ready to go there yet – thankfully my capacity is not yet diminished and I still look forward to traveling - but her interpretation does begin to make a certain sense.

For now, my somewhat altered travel tastes notwithstanding, I continue to agree with Mark Twain: Travel is still enticing, not least because it is "fatal to prejudice, bigotry and narrow-mindedness." Like Mr. Twain, whose account of one trip gave us <u>Innocents Abroad,</u> I think "it would be well if such an excursion could be got up every year and the system regularly inaugurated."

Extended trips may not be the thing anymore. I may find myself changing priorities, venues, schedules, and accommodations – more café crawls, less cathedral gaping; fewer sightseeing excursions, more chatting with the locals. But I am definitely not ready to let my passport expire. After all, I never know when I might have a fierce urge to weep once more in Venice, to visit Mongolia, or to count cats in Zanzibar.

Africa

"You know you are truly alive when
you are living among lions."

KAREN BLIXEN

An African Odyssey

Let's Get Going

Once checked in at New York's JFK Emirates Airways desk, I have hours to kill before boarding my plane to Dubai so I decide to try talking my way into the 1st Class Lounge. The host says "Sorry," he absolutely cannot admit me despite pleas based on the long wait, length of trip, and finally my age, so I wait outside the lounge and ask the first man who shows up if he will take me in as his guest. "Sure" he says, telling the host "she's with me." But alas, he is not a Gold Card member so I must find another date. It doesn't take long before a Gold Card Sugar Daddy cheerfully informs the host that I am his guest. "Where I come from we call it chutzpah," I say, smiling at the lounge hostess. Sugar Daddy and the host laugh, I'm in and spend the next 4+ hours sipping Pinot Noir, noshing on smoked salmon and assorted other goodies, reading email and the New York Times.

The Airbus 380 is one amazing airplane – two complete decks accommodate 550 passengers (we are 400 that night); first and business passengers inhabit the upstairs and economy the lower deck. There is a spa in first class along with showers and private cabins. You cannot see from one end of this baby to the other; it requires 26 crew, and I wonder how the hell they get this load of metal off the ground but they do and it's a smooth if long flight.

Arriving in Dubai, the largest airport I've ever seen, I catch the courtesy bus to the Millennium Hotel for a complementary layover. The temperature feels like 90+ with humidity 120 even though it is evening. In addition to the heat, I'm tired so in no mood for what comes next. Standing in line to check in so that I can grab four hours sleep and a shower before another long flight, I realize that every time it is my turn to approach the desk clerk, a man from the line to my left or right rushes up to the counter. This is clearly "No Country for Old Women," or women of any age. Finally, I nudge a guy to my left out of my way, check in, and collapse in bed. The next morning, I understand without a doubt that women in Dubai are nothing more than "potted plants with vaginas" as I email my friends. No one opens a door or offers help with luggage and I note that on disembarking from the shuttle bus at the airport the women in the van don't even try to exit before every male is off the vehicle. At the gate, boarding pass in hand, I approach the Emirates ground crew at the counter.

"I have a question…" I begin.

"You must get in line," the man barks at me, pointing to a long queue leading to another waiting area.

"But I would like to ask…"

"Madam, join the line."

"Do all those people have questions too?" I ask.

"You must join the line Madam. You can ask question inside."

"But there is no one there; it's a waiting room!"

"You must get in the line, Madam."

"Is J an aisle seat?" I ask. "That's all I want to know."

"Yes, aisle seat."

"There now, that wasn't too difficult, was it?" I snarl, giving the Emirates woman at the counter a What-is-it-with-these-men look. As I pass by her I whisper, "How do women manage to live here?"

"You must be very strong," she whispers back.

"I don't let them get away with it," I say. "I am not a potted plant."

"I can see that, Madam," she says smiling in sisterhood.

Nearly twelve hours, two "low fat" meals, three bad movies and one backache later, I disembark in Cape Town.

Beaded Elephant, South Africa

Cape Town and the Bush

Day One

My Meet-and-Greet and a driver (Victor) await me with a comforting sign that says CLIFT as I exit Customs. I am even more comforted when we leave the airport and I feel cool morning air. On the drive to our wonderfully situated apartment near the Waterfront area of Cape Town, Victor and I chat about South Africa's history. Near the airport we pass a shanty town before heading into modern, inviting downtown Cape Town with Table Mountain looming as the city's central icon. I'm excited to be here, but all I want is a bed and a shower.

After a nap, shower and change of clothes, I walk to the Waterfront, a happening place. It's a working harbor but mostly it's a fun venue with lots of restaurants, shops, street entertainers, and a huge mall. There are hotels, boats, a lovely statue of South Africa's four Nobel Peace Prize winners (Sisulu, Tutu, DeKlerk, Mandela) and a huge Lego-looking man made from red Coke crates. There's an Aquarium and a craft market, which of course, I peruse with due diligence, stopping to chat with some of the artists. Completely forgetting that Yom Kippur begins at sundown, I sit in a café enjoying a Castle beer and a delicious panini while watching a group of street musicians with painted faces sing and jive. Then I head for the mall and Woolworth's, which I'm told has a food court like Marks & Spencer's. I buy wine, salads for dinner, and breakfast food and head back to the apartment to change. Victor fetches me to return to the airport to Meet-and-Greet my husband, Arnold, arriving from Amsterdam. We watch the KLM plane touch down, park, and are in the waiting area as he exits Customs. Back at the apartment we eat, drink and count our blessings in being here.

Day Two

Our guide Kelly, originally from Uganda, collects us promptly at 8:00 a.m. and we set off for the city tour, beginning with a brief history of District Six where in the 1960s forcible removal began. It is here that the full human disaster of Apartheid begins to be real and horrific. Black and "coloured" families were torn asunder as the government designated the area "for whites only". Homes were demolished, people who refused to leave were beaten into obedience, door to door evictions took place. Laws went into effect to end mixed race marriage and families were forever broken apart as mothers and children were separated from their husbands/fathers. (We learn more about this later when we visit the District Six museum.)

Our drive through the city reveals a mix of architectures (Dutch, Victorian, modern) in this casual, laid-back small city. We see Desmond Tutu's church, Parliament and City Hall, the city gardens, the Slave Lodge, the university, the hospital where Christian Barnard performed the first heart transplant; then we head to the Castle, a 17th century fort established by the Dutch. Unfortunately, the changing of the guard doesn't take place on Sundays but we enjoy coffee and the small museum before queuing at Table Mt. for the cable car. There we talk with a group of African mamas, pensioners on a day's outing. When Arnold corrects them about how many provinces there are in South Africa (12, not 11) they howl with laughter and give me big hugs and high-fives for being married to a smart guy who knows more about their country than they do! Then we talk with a young black family whose toddler son is so gorgeous I want to take home with me (until his mom tells me what a handful he is).

Table Mountain is the central icon of the city, visible from everywhere like a kind of urban Ayers Rock. It takes its name from appearing flat on top and because the fog rolls over it as if a huge tablecloth were being thrown over it in preparation for a feast. The views of the city below are spectacular.

After descending we drive through the cobblestoned streets of the Malay Quarter, an old Muslim neighborhood with colorfully painted houses, mosques, and an emerging tourist flavor. The "ice cream colors of the quaint Bo-Kaap homes" are surely on their way to becoming the Georgetown (DC) of Cape Town.

We have talked along the way with Kelly about South African history and race relations. He tells us that the younger generation has moved beyond racism; for them, Apartheid is a part of their history that has no meaning based on personal experience (similar to our younger generation's attitude toward the Civil Rights era or the Vietnam War experience). There are no remaining social barriers and intermarriage is now accepted, he says. But some in the older generation still harbor strong feelings. It's hard for blacks who lived through Apartheid to forget what was done to them, while some Afrikaners still hold racist beliefs. We experience this first-hand later in the day.

But first we say our goodbyes to Kelly when he drops us off downtown at the Greenpointe Market. We eat lunch in an outdoor café in front of the colorful street vendors reminiscent of Thailand's Night Markets where everything is "same, same but different." (Here you quickly learn it is "same same and same" and that souvenir items are quite expensive.) We buy two paintings and a few trinkets, then, exhausted, hail a taxi to return home. The driver is an Afrikaner full of himself. We are stunned when he tells us he's been driving for years and his least favorite fares are "American Niggers." I want to tell him to stop and let us out but worry that Arnold will think I'm causing an incident. Later he says he wishes I had; we should not have remained silent. Our guide the next day concurs. "It's important to let them know such behavior is unacceptable."

Day Three

Craig picks us up at 8:15 for our Full Day Peninsula Tour and we meet our traveling companions: a couple from California, two gay couples from the Midwest and Boston, and a Dutch couple. The coastline is truly exquisite, the weather perfect, Craig delightful. (We soon become fast friends who can tease each other; turns out he is a great Jewish guy who wants to meet my daughter "if the apple doesn't fall far from the tree," he says, since he likes my sense of humor.)

As the program promises, "we cruise along the exquisite stretch of coastline known as Millionaire's Paradise from Clifton to Camps Bay to the exclusive beach hamlet of Llandudno" but our first stop is Houts Bay where we graze the souvenir kiosks and have coffee while the others take a 40-minute boat trip to Seal Island. (We've already seen seals and Arnold doesn't want to risk getting seasick.) We then drive Chapman's Peak, hugging the magnificent coastline for spectacular ocean views. We lunch overlooking the sea at a restaurant in the Cape of Good Hope section of Table Mountain National Park, a part of the famous Cape Floral Kingdom. The landscape is fabulous, especially as we luck out and see three wild zebras, some eland (like elk), ostriches, and the ubiquitous baboons that inhabit the cape. Making our way slowly back to town, we pass through the old naval port of Simon's Town, then stop at the penguin colony at Boulders Beach. Our final treat is seeing half a dozen Southern White whales up close and personal – a rare sighting!

Upon our return to town, we rest then set out for traditional (if somewhat gourmet-ed) pan-African fare at the Gold Museum. A set menu starts with an assortment of starters ranging from a beautifully spiced tomato soup to delicately flavored prawns, meatballs, and other hors d'oeuvres. These treats are followed by a mild chicken curry, African dal, spinach with tomato and onion, and of course South African wine. Dessert is a fried pastry ball and a huge basket of fruit. While we eat, we enjoy singing, drumming, and dancing; the evening concludes with the waitstaff serenading us in an African choir.

Day Four

Titus fetches us at 8.45 for our Walk to Freedom Tour and we are joined by young French, Dutch and American couples – the latter, living in England, are honeymooning. As it happens, she is "a Jersey girl" like me and spent eight years of her youth in Ocean City!

Our day begins at the District Six Museum and what an extraordinary place it is – reminiscent of any Holocaust Museum or the museum we visited in Vietnam that captures what happened there during the war. There are photographs, recaptured oral histories, street signs, commemorative tapestries, a replica of a black "house" – one narrow room in which there is a sideboard, a small square table & two chairs, two single beds, an armoire, a radio, oil lamps, pails for fetching water. Sections of the museum, put together by people who were forceably removed from District Six, reveal pass cards, political machinations, punishments, and poverty such as most Americans have never seen. It is a deeply moving place, especially when you read the captioned photographs and the diary and journal entries.

We follow the museum with a walkabout in Langa, the oldest township in Cape Town. What we see there is a shocking reminder of how much is still to be done in South Africa before decent housing and dignified work is available to all its citizens. Never have we seen a more dramatic dichotomy between rich and poor as in this country. Along the coast and in the Cape Town suburbs abundant wealth is evidenced by gorgeous homes, luxury boats, fantastically expensive seaside apartments, while the conditions millions of black people still live with here are nearly indescribable. In the townships there are corregated shacks one on top of the other. Hovels with no privacy, no proper bathroom or kitchen facilities, no furniture other than broken tables, benches and beds are shared by several families.

Still, we are warmly welcomed by women smiling in welcome as we take pictures. When I motion to ask if I may sit next to the Mama in what passes for a communal kitchen she rushes to provide me with newsprint to sit on; then she lays a piece for Arnold. "Papa! Papa!" she says waving her hand for the elder of the group to rest. Further on, we visit a nursery school where gorgeous smiling children sing to us. Then we make our way to the local pub, or Shebeen, a shack where a bucket of local brew (beer that looks like soap) is passed around; everyone sips from the bucket, which traditionally is emptied by men who congregate in Shebeens after work.

The experience of this place is sobering because of its abject poverty but there is also a sense of courage and hope among the people (many of whom invariably suffer from TB, HIV/AIDS and other chronic diseases.) We are struck by the friendliness of all Cape Towners, but here there is a sense of dignity that is hard to explain but easy to embrace.

Leaving Langa Township we learn that our scheduled trip to Robbens Island that afternoon has been cancelled because the ferry has broken down. Initially disappointed we regroup and end up with a marvelous afternoon (probably better than visiting the famous prison where Nelson Mandela and many other ANC heroes spent so many years). At our request, Titus drops us at the world-famous botanical gardens of Cape Town (Kirschenboesch) where we lunch on Baboties (a traditional dish of minced meat with raisins and spices overlaid with an omelette-like egg on top, peaked with chutney) before taking the guided golf cart ride around 90 hectares of magnificent plants, trees, and flowers; we also meet a family of owls and see some fascinating birdlife.

Instead of taking a cab back to town we decide to jump on the red City Bus, a double-decker, partially open-air narrated tour bus which turns out to be a brilliant move; instead of returning directly to the city, the bus takes us on a picturesque journey back to Houts Bay, Camp Town and other seaside resort towns before returning us an hour later to the Waterfront.

Day Five

There is only one other guest on our full day Winelands Tour and we get off to a good start at 8:00. Thomas is an odd fellow but our guide, Mohammad, is a hoot and a friend of Craig's so we are immediately on the same (informal) page. We decide to have no real fixed plan but to meander once we reach wine country. We begin with a leisurely coffee overlooking a gorgeous valley. (The region is reminiscent of Chile's wine country with its mountains and valley vistas; some say it resembles California wine country.) Then we make for the Taal Monument near Paarl, an extraordinary, symbolic monolith of abstractions representing South Africa's historical and geographic influences. We also stop at the prison gate where Nelson Mandela walked to freedom after his final 18 months in jail (he was sent here to secretly negotiate his release and to prepare for life "outside"). A marvelous, larger-than-life statue captures the moment as he strides forward, fisted hand raised in solidarity, broad smile on his gentle face. His words, inscribed on the base of the stature, speak volumes about peaceful reconciliation and reveal what a magnificent leader he is.

Stopping for wine tasting before lunch, we then head to an old Dutch estate for an informal, outdoor meal before moving on to visit the Huguenot Monument in the delightful small French town of Franschhoek. From there we cross the verdant Helshoogte Mountain Pass arriving at the charming town of Stellenbosch in time to visit a few inviting shops. On our way into this lovely university town, we see an unusual sight: A young black man is walking down the street stark naked, escorted by two police officers. "It's a university tradition," Mohammed explains. "This poor bloke got caught!"

We visit one more extremely impressive vineyard – started by a French countess a few years ago when she was 83 – and are given a tour before tasting. The four-story establishment is amazing for its process, its setting, and the collections of glass and artwork that Madam collects and exhibits. We buy a bottle of Merlot and tired but happy, head home, where we nosh, pack, and set the alarm for 4:30 a.m.

Day Six

Our driver arrives at 5.20 a.m. and off we go for our flight to Johannesburg, where we have a most extraordinary experience. In the airport, having left one suitcase at Left Luggage, we ask a tall, lean black man of about 40 if he can kindly direct us to the gate area for our ongoing flight to Hoedspruit Airport (Gateway to Kruger and private game parks.) He generously takes us down the elevator and points the way, instructing us in his golden voice.

"Are you by any chance a radio announcer?" I ask. He looks at me quizzically.

"It's just that you have such a wonderful voice. Do you sing?"

"No, I'm not on the radio," he laughs. "But I sing in church. I'm actually a pastor."

Somehow, we begin a conversation that leads us to Apartheid. He tells us he was born and raised in Soweto and that "people have no idea." We speak of the District Six museum we visited.

"You are old enough to remember 1976 in Soweto…"

"Oh, yes," he says. "I was there." He pauses. "I have a huge gash on my thigh from…." Suddenly his eyes fill with tears. He apologizes.

"Please, don't be embarrassed," I say. "It is like the Holocaust for my people. I can understand."

He tries again to tell us his story but he is overcome and tears spill. "Sorry! So sorry! The wounds are very deep," he says, shaking his head.

My husband grasps him in a firm hug, weeping himself as I am, then I too hug him farewell. We part and the extraordinary moment of connection, shared pain, and human contact is gone. It is a moment I will never forget, nor I suspect, will the pastor, who happened to point two Americans in the right direction one day in the Johannesburg Airport.

Two hours later we board the small plane for our one-hour flight to Hoedspruit and the Elandela Lodge where we will spend three nights in the bush.

Our host, Rocco, greets us at the tiny airport and a few minutes later we enter the private game park he owns with his wife Yvonne. The Lodge is small – only five rooms and three family guest houses; we are 16 guests. It is gorgeously situated and beautiful. A large lounge tastefully decorated African style is open on three sides and overlooks the small swimming pool and understated gardens. A watering hole plays host to a wide assortment of animals, including giraffe, zebras, bucks, baboons, and the occasional hippo. Rocky, a baby rhino rescued after poachers killed her mother, plays in the garden fronting guest rooms but she must be removed when she becomes overexcited. A caged parrot talks to himself while guinea fowl and other birds stroll or fly around.

Rhino poaching has increased dramatically in the last year because of the Chinese market for their horns, used for herbal medicines. More than 400 have been killed this year alone in Kruger, despite the government having the park heavily policed. Rocco says it will not stop because the horns are so lucrative. Like other private camp owners he cannot afford the level of security needed to catch the poachers and isn't sure what to do to protect the rhinos on his preserve.

After lunch we take the first of our several safaris in an open, covered Land Rover. Our guide is the extraordinarily knowledgeable Jacques, at 28 impressively experienced. We take a three-hour trip around the park, seeing copious zebra, giraffe, impala, water buffalo, warthogs, bucks, and more – but no leopards. We stop for sundowners while Jacques answers questions and points out flora and fauna. Then we continue in darkness, with a huge searchlight, trying to find the elusive leopard. Finally, we give up and head back to the Lodge for a four-course dinner, after which we fall into bed.

A word about our companions, who at first seem aloof but then warm up: Australian Jesse and her mum have just spent two weeks volunteering at the nearby Moholo Animal Refuge (feeding and cleaning up after hyena and other animals is not my idea of a holiday but what do I know?); Spanish Laura and her husband who were married in Sevilla the previous Saturday (they smoke constantly and seem morose for honeymooners); an Argentinean family who leave and are replaced by three Dutch women; and a German couple who arrive the day before we leave. There is an odd atmosphere that feels unfriendly when we first arrive but gradually we all warm to each other as we get the Elandela vibe. Even Rocco and Yvonne become friendlier as the days pass in this place of understated elegance and quiet charm. Still, the best people here are the ever-smiling African staff who can't do enough to be sure we are comfortable.

Day Seven

Up at 5:30 for a 6:00 Safari, we jump into clothes and forgo tea. We head for the white tigers Elandela is so proud of but alas, having had a fresh kill the night before, they are sleeping it off somewhere (Jacques knows this because of the tracks he sees and the vultures hanging around in the trees above). Nevermind. There is still tomorrow morning, and for now we are happy with all the other wildlife grazing nearby as we drive on.

Safari here in the bushveld is much different than in the vast savannahs of Kenya and Tanzania. There the vistas are broad and big and animals tend to cluster, often at some distance. Here, they graze in small numbers or alone in their bushy habitat, very close to us, natural and surprising. Some, like impala, sprint away as we approach. Others, like zebra and giraffe, continue grazing as if we are just another harmless species in the bush.

Back at the Lodge for breakfast at 9:00, we stoke up on eggs, pancakes, bacon, fruit and yoghurt. Then I join a group going on a canyon boat trip while Arnold naps. The canyon, third deepest in the world, is an hour's drive away, so the vastness of this land becomes even clearer. Once onboard the open flat boat, we cruise quietly beneath beautiful canyon walls, our guide, an aging bushy, narrating the geology of this cool and picturesque place.

Home for lunch, we decide to forgo the afternoon safari in favor of quiet pool time and hopefully a sunset menagerie by the pool, near the watering hole. We are not disappointed: all manner of wildlife grace our view, including giraffe, waterbucks, baboons, and more. When the others return they tell us they have seen the lions; we're disappointed but hope to see them tomorrow....

Day Eight

....and see them we do! The entire pride -- a mix of white and brown lions eight in total including three new cubs not more than three weeks old -- is lounging; they are spectacular (and very close). These white lions exhibit the recessive gene that blanches their coats. They are rare because their whiteness makes them easy prey. Since they can't readily hunt without being hunted they weaken and die out. Elandela has begun a preserve and that is where we find them, the babies frolicking, suckling, and annoying their irritable father while Mom patiently keeps watch.

We also see two hippos and an African wild cat on our three hour safari, along with the now ubiquitous giraffe, zebra and impalas. ("What was that?" "Oh, just another impala...") Our guide/driver, Coleman, the spitting image of Cuba Gooding with his winning grin, does his best to find a leopard but despite fresh tracks, the cat eludes us. We promise to lie to Jacques telling him that we saw one because he and Coleman have a running competition to find the sly, spotted beast. (Neither of them manages during our stay.)

After lunch, we head to Kruger National Park, the vast veld

that takes days to cover; we are only driving part of one road in hopes, mainly, of finding elephants. We encounter three herds, one with a newborn, along with myriad other animals and beautiful birds. We picnic at a rest site on impala burgers and apples, then get "up close and personal" with many other animals before heading back to Elandela for the famous South African braai (barbeque). We are greeted on our return to the Lodge by two hippos grazing at the waterhole; it really is extraordinary to see these large animals (and all of them that languish right in front of us) so nonchalantly close to the Lodge.

Freshened up, we eat braai buffet-style around a roaring fire outside Elandela's rondela (round hut). The meat includes impala sausages, some kind of "beef", and barbequed chicken, along with salad, coleslaw and assorted veggies grown at the Lodge. (Oh, those yummy sweet potatoes!) We wash it down with a bottle of South African Merlot purchased at the Kruger Park gift shop and once again, we are asleep by 9:30. Safari is oddly exhausting!

Days Nine & Ten

We arrive at our airport hotel in Johannesburg before 2:00 p.m. and quickly realize that our travel agent was right: There really is nothing to see in J'burg, which has an entirely different feel than Cape Town. This is a big, concrete city with nothing to commend it and there are constant warnings about safety. We opt to take the hotel driver (a metered cab would have been cheaper perhaps but less reliable) to the Apartheid Museum which is on the other side of downtown J'burg (about 24 km from our hotel). It is worth the trip, providing an awesome history of South Africa historically and politically. The big focus is on Nelson Mandela and other democracy leaders (many of whom embraced Communism in its purest form) and again, one sees what an extraordinary path Mandela followed, maturing into the country's leader. We return to the safety and comfort of the hotel for dinner and an early night before departure.

The next morning, we enjoy a buffet breakfast, catch up on Internet, and I get a manicure. The young woman who does my nails is white and as she talks about her family's experience, and what it is like living in J'burg, she provides food for thought in terms of black/white relations as she worries about what will happen next in this politically fragile country. "My family hates black people, especially my parents," she tells me. "My dad lost a business because it was mandated that white business owners had to have black partners. He was happy to have a man who worked for him for years become a partner, but the law said that the black partner had to own 75% and the white partner only 25% so my dad gave up the business. Now my mum has to work to make ends meet." She doesn't want to generalize and she "knows that not all blacks are bad," but she hates the crime, the lurking danger that "makes our houses like jails," the shacks that spring up everywhere…

Like many other white South Africans, she and her family are deeply worried about what will happen when Mandela dies. "He is holding it together," she says. But if the leader of the youth movement, vitriolic in his hatred of whites, becomes president, "this country will be like Zimbabwe," she worries. We have heard this from others as well. It is complex and troubling. What a loss it would be to the world if the democracy so hard-won in this vast country, and the dignity it brought to so many, were to crumble because of renewed moral and political corruption.

Edna's Camel Bell

A Doula in Somaliland

Rent-a-Wreck Airlines

I arrive in Dubai and having claimed my bag and raced through immigration (since Emirates never heard of Daallo Airlines or Hargeisa and wouldn't check my baggage through) I take a taxi from Terminal 3 to Terminal 1 – in a "Ladies Only" taxi. My driver looks like an airline stewardess in her pink outfit as she ferries me for $9 (1/4 mile) to the terminal. "Not like Saudi Arabia," I say. No, 'here womens can drive. Helps family. Is good."

My Daallo flight to Djibouti is bizarre: the Airbus says Sky Bosnia on the outside, the life jackets say Lufthansa, and the crew of the slightly seedy airplane are all Russian. My seatmate, an elderly gentleman who lives in London but visits family in Hargeisa regularly, says the owner of Daallo, which doesn't own any aircraft, is Russian and leases his Airbus. The stewardess, wordless and unsmiling, slaps a croissant and a four-ounce plastic glass of tea down in front of us. "I already put sugar in," she says to the man.

"But I don't want sugar," he says.

"You people always take sugar," she snarls. "Hargeisa people always lots of sugar."

"But not me," he says. Begrudgingly, she gives him another plastic glass. He raises his eyebrows at me as if to say, "What can you do?"

Two hours later, at Djibouti International Airport – a misnomer if ever there was one – I befriend Laila, born in Hargeisa and now a US citizen living in Atlanta who recently started a foundation to serve Somaliland children in need of surgery for cleft palate, hydrocephalus, and spina bifida. We bond immediately which is a good thing because when we board the plane for the 45-minute trip to Hargeisa I panic.

The airplane which has four propellers and holds 100 people is so old it looks like bits and pieces of metal will fall off any minute. The tires are virtually bald. The interior is shocking with broken seats, most of which have no seatbelts, filthy carpet no longer glued to the floor, no working lights or air vents. There is no cabin crew and the aisles quickly fill up with luggage. (I know we are overweight having seen what was checked in.) There is the smell of urine and sweat. An unkempt middle-aged man in a golf shirt, tired trousers, and flip flops pulls a ladder in, seals the door, and heads to the cockpit. He is our pilot. Laila tells me she has flown this airplane six times in the last three years and it will be alright. It is smooth, she says, don't worry. She is reassuring up to a point but since, unlike the locals, I do not do "Inshallah" I just hope to bloody Christ we make it. Laila talks me through and we land at Hargeisa where another drama ensues.

I can't find the driver sent to meet me. Edna has forgotten to get my visa. The immigration guy won't let me in. In a classic scene at developing country airports, people are shouting, shoving, snarling themselves up, barking orders that are ignored. Thankfully Laila sticks with me until I spot a man who must be looking for me. He is the driver and he calls Edna. She tells me to leave my passport there; she will sort out the visa and I will get it back tomorrow. Inshallah a million times. We drive to the hospital, my luggage having been offloaded last, and I realize how safe the airplane was compared to being in the car with this driver.

Edna, stunning at 74, impressive and clearly the *major domo*, is the founder of the Edna Adan Hospital. She is a British-trained midwife, a retired UN official, and the ex-wife of Hargeisa's former President. She greets me warmly. I am shown to my room – a small, basic but perfectly adequate single with private bath in a dorm for visitors. I shower, unpack, rest, then join the others for lunch. Edna sits at the head of the table. Along with her are Brigitte, a retired French physician who has come to do 'hands on' work after years in research medicine; Finnish Hilke, a nurse-midwife and former missionary who has worked in Ethiopia and Somalia for most of her long career; Karina, a German-born nurse now from New York City; BreAnn, the youngest among us and a newly graduated nurse from Massachusetts; Dirk, an OB-GYN from Germany; and Martha, an English nurse-midwife who is stunningly rude.

The hospital is smaller and less developed than I had thought but still the best hospital in Hargeisa. It is clean and equipped with one (rarely used) incubator, two (probably overused) ultrasound machines, and a decent delivery room and surgery. There is a lab, a library, Edna's Computer Room, Edna's Pharmacy, Edna's Supermarket, and an ambulance on the well-guarded compound situated on a busy road unofficially called Edna Street. The hospital has a maternity wing and a medical-surgical wing which includes a room for pediatrics. It accommodates about 60 patients.

On my first encounter with Martha I ask her how long she has been here. "Too long," she snarls, stone-faced. She then launches into a diatribe about all that is wrong with the hospital, the country, and the people who live here. She warns me never to leave the compound because "they hate you."

"Why?" I ask. "Why would they want to hurt me?"

"Because you're white." Then she tells me that she locks the door to the dorm at 9 p.m. – a warning that I should not harbor delusions of staying up late or partying, I suppose.

After lunch on my first day I'm given a tour of the hospital by Ifsa, a local midwife. The hospital includes a lab, Edna's Pharmacy, Edna's Supermarket, and an ambulance (Edna Adan's Ambulance, of course) on the well-guarded compound. There are no bed linens.

Many people mill about in the compound; most of them are

family members and visitors for patients, some are guards or workers. The women, all in hijab and many fully covered with only eyes showing, examine me curiously (perhaps suspiciously) when I walk around the grounds. They do not allow me to take their picture. But behind the hospital is a laundry (we leave our clothes on the floor outside our rooms to be washed) and the women who work there giggle and compete to have me snap their images. Several mosques surround the compound in this deeply Muslim country and we frequently hear the mullahs' calls to prayer (including at 5:30 a.m.).

A word about Hargeisa: The history and politics of this country are complex and "beyond the scope of this summary." Suffice to say that it is one of several colonized regions of Somalia that tried to unite for independence from France, Italy, and Britain in the 1960s but failed to coalesce effectively. So Somaliland declared itself free and independent several decades ago (as Djibouti, the former French colony did) and has been fighting for recognition as an independent nation since. The reasons it still struggles for that identity are political within the international community (e.g. UN) which continues to recognize Somalia only. Edna, an ardent nationalist, believes that it is in the interest of other nations to recognize Somaliland quickly, with such unstable countries as Yemen and Somalia so close.

Somaliland is a dry and mostly flat place with a pleasant climate at 1300 feet above sea level. It is one of the poorest countries I've ever seen, comparing in my experience to Sierra Leone and Sudan (and probably to Haiti). The canvas or wood business stalls, the goats in the road, the deeply pocked dirt roads, and the shockingly inadequate houses all provide a visual for the deep poverty here. Life expectancy for men is 47; the maternal and infant mortality rates are very high (but not clear given the lack of records and research here.) Women are married between age 15-25 and can expect to have between five and 12 children. Female Genital Mutilation (FGM) is universally practiced. It is a deeply religious culture with such events as a baby death being "God's will" or "Inshallah." It is also a deeply mysterious place to me, and I think of my friend Vicki's remark about her first trip to India: "I've never felt such cultural dissonance. I had no idea what was actually going on around me." This is partly because I can't understand a word that's being said, and because people outside the compound, especially if they are deeply traditional, resist communicating (unless it's to beg). I think this is because they have no idea why we are here and what we are like, not as Margaret says because they hate us. It could also be, in the case of men, that they are totally crazy because of the local narcotic weed they would sell their souls to chew.

The first night at the hospital I have my initial doula experience. The mom is probably about 18; it is her first child. She labors so well I think she must be about 5 (of 10) cm. dilated but she is on the delivery table (women here always deliver in lithotomy position and always in a delivery room) and Ifsa is doing things that tell me the baby is coming. Mom moans and clings to my hand; I stroke her arm and whisper that she is strong and can do this; her body is doing just what it is meant to do; soon her baby will be born. A student nurse translates what I am saying. Mom nods to me. I support her head while she pushes; she grasps my arm. And then her son is born, his wet little head emerging first, then his body sliding quickly out. "Good job! Look! Look at your little baby!" I say to Mom. "Thank you!" she says in English. "Thank you," squeezing my hand. I go to bed exhausted but happy that I've been able to help in this remote place where I've been told, people hate me.

On the morning of my second day I have my second birth. This is Mom's third child and she too labors well, choosing to stand through most of her labor. Hidu is the midwife and a more gentle, calming, competent soul I've never met. I encourage Mom, massage her hips and back, stroke her arm, talk to her in whispers. Even when she doesn't know what I'm saying I sense that she is comforted by my voice and my touch. As she leans on my shoulders she lays her against me as if she were a child. I stroke her head, reassuring her. At 9 cm. she climbs onto the delivery table. Hidu gently examines her, tells her when to push and when to stop. She is holding onto me for dear life. Three student nurses observe; I hope they are seeing the importance of emotional support during birth.

Mom's mom appears -- I cannot tell from her expression if she thinks I am usurping her position, but then she says to Hidu, "This woman is beautiful the way she is helping my daughter." A bigger reward I cannot imagine. Finally, a big, healthy boy is born. Mom thanks me profusely. I try to tell her I honor what she has done but burst into tears. She kisses my hand and thanks me again. I kiss her hand back and thank her. Hidu is not surprised by this exchange (once I explain my weeping at almost every birth I see) but the young nurses seem stunned at what they have just witnessed. I feel so deeply rewarded again.

After lunch I spend over two hours with Edna, ostensibly to interview her about her work. But first I tell her how pleased I was with the response to my two doula experiences. She is pleased too and excited at the possibility of me demonstrating what I do. She suggests I give a class to the nursing students about the doula concept and the importance of emotional support during labor. I am glad for this assignment. My first day here I wondered what I would actually do for 12 days since I am not a clinician and have come without a clear scope of work. BreAnn and Karina are teaching English to the nurses (without any ESL training) and Edna clearly doesn't have time to work on her memoir. So, I tell her that if I can leave any legacy inside of two weeks I hope it will be to model support for laboring moms and to underscore the importance of such comfort.

We talk of many things including her marriage to an early president of Somaliland and her two subsequent husbands; her early life and education, her career, during which she has been an MP and WHO Regional Director. I'm pleasantly surprised by how much she shares with me; we are two women of a similar age talking about our lives and work (although she does most of the talking). As we conclude she asks me if I'd like to accompany her to the Mansour Hotel later where she will meet with a group of women advocating for women's rights in Somaliland. I cannot attend the meeting but I could see the town, she says. It is a supremely complimentary invitation which I accept with pleasure. Edna and I are now friends.

On my third morning, I wake again with a few strange bites. I have neither heard nor seen mosquitoes. Apparently, that's because the pigeons just outside my screened window have fleas that can pass through the mesh! From now on I use bug repellant and keep my window closed (thankfully I've acquired a fan).

Only Dirk and I appear at breakfast. He tells me that he will be doing a C-section later on a woman with a hydrocephalic baby and I can observe. The C-section is just beginning when I enter the OR in my scrubs and mask. Mom is getting an epidural. When she is numb, Karina – who finds herself unexpectedly assisting Dirk – swabs her belly with antiseptic. She is draped. Dirk takes a scalpel and makes the first cut. Working quickly, he opens the uterus and pulls out a baby whose head appears normal in size. "It's what's inside," he says. "Very little brain." I see at once that the baby has a terrible hair lip and cleft palate. She does not breathe readily and is whisked off to be resuscitated. She also has swallowed meconium and must be put on antibiotics as well as oxygen. Meanwhile Dirk is suturing Mom. It has all happened in about half an hour. Hidu is the one to tell the family what has occurred. By night Edna says the baby will not live.

I spend the next morning first on rounds in Maternity where four babies have been born during the night and a woman with eclampsia is in trouble, then in the Outpatient Department where the doctor is doing pre-natal checkups. I'm invited to palpate mothers' tummies and to listen to the fetal heartbeat through a primitive wooden instrument.

Later, with Karina, BreAnn and Brigitte, I visit the local market. Crowded with stalls and not always easy for western women, we are in search of cloth from which traditional long dresses can be sewn. We quickly choose colorful cloth for $4 each and then find two women sitting at sewing machines who in no time stitch the material into full-length "moo-moo" like dresses. (Cost: $1). The women are friendly and try speaking to us as they sew on their antique machines. "Inshallah, I see you again!" one of them says when she is finished. "Inshallah," I reply.

The next morning, I wonder into the maternity ward. Four babies have been born during the night but no one is in labor. I visit baby Hodu, everyone's favorite – a pretty six-month old little girl who keeps getting a dreadful infection on her head and face that has caused loss of pigmentation and scabbing. No one knows why she has this condition or why it recurs after treatment. Hodu is gorgeous but developmentally delayed. She faces an uncertain future. She lies in a bed all day with her young aunt watching over her.

I help the mom with eclampsia who has had a C-section in the night because of her severe hypertension. Her baby boy is a fighter at 28 weeks and less than three pounds. He seems to have a sucking reflex and has a good chance of survival if he can start nursing. For now, Mom pumps and feeds him through a syringe. I position the baby between his mother's breasts, a technique known as Kangaroo Care which has shown good results for survival with premature babies. I wrap him in blankets and encourage the exhausted mom. Her mother is there along with a young aunt who speaks good English so we visit as I sit with them. Mom is expert at breastfeeding having had seven other children; she is able to squeeze out a few drops of colostrum and get them into the baby's tiny mouth.

On Monday morning I hurry to the labor room where an induction is due to begin. Hidu tells me the husband has not yet given permission; he will come at 9:00 a.m. There are two other women in labor, and another woman awaits her husband's signature for an induction. The chances are the men will not consent; they have likely consulted numerous family members. More likely, they will take their wives on a round of doctor visits until they find one who tells them what they want to hear.

I am beginning to see the dark side of this country and culture, where voiceless, disempowered women must have their husbands' permission to have a C-section or an induction for medical reasons. (If they need a hysterectomy their father must agree – her body belongs to him.) I watch as husbands come to sign (or not), ignoring their laboring wives who walk the halls. Imperious and authoritarian, they swagger in and out self-importantly.

The doctor says he has seen them deny their wife her life, even when she is crying to be rescued, because "Inshallah" it is God's will (and maybe he doesn't like this wife so much anymore.) He has seen babies die unnecessarily - "Inshallah". A woman here often holds less value than a camel; she has absolutely no personhood. Her function in life is to marry, bear many children and obey her husband. Her body is not her own. She has no genitals remaining; by the age of nine or 10 they have been cut off. A husband expects to have sexual intercourse with his wife every morning and every evening, unless she is bleeding. No wonder women have upwards of nine to 12 pregnancies; they are not even given time to rest from the last pregnancy before their husband demands his right to enter her again. God only knows what kind of domestic abuse occurs in shacks and shanties throughout this country of ritual, tradition and male supremacy.

Watching women give birth here is something to behold; it is a testament to their strength and courage in the face of such a life. "She's doing all the work and I'm doing all the sweating!" I tell Hidu as she delivers a woman's ninth child. She makes no sound, not even a mild moan (Hidu says Somali women don't do that) and suddenly her baby pops out. It is whisked away to be cleaned up and Mom seems little interested for the moment; she lies patiently waiting for the placenta to be delivered. Then, cleaned up, she gets off the delivery table as if nothing out of the ordinary has happened, and is taken to her room. I follow carrying the baby boy she has just delivered.

In Prenatal Clinic a variety of situations present: a woman is worried about her frequent miscarriages and infertility; another has back pain with her periods; several others are doing routine check-ups; a shy woman appears with her husband complaining of urinary retention post-C-Section. Dirk can hardly contain his rage at the father who took so long to give permission for the C-section that she has had complications.

There are two C-sections in rapid succession. I observe and take photos. I'm astounded at how fast they are; it is a relatively simple (but quite bloody) operative procedure requiring great skill nonetheless. The mothers are again stoic as they are catheterized, receive epidurals and lie exposed on the OR table. (There is an irony about the prevailing female modesty in this culture while at the same time women seem to disregard the lack of privacy surrounding their bodies in the hospital. Do they feel their bodies, which have been infantilized by the removal of sexual organs and pubic hair, are not their own?)

On Wednesday I head for the wards at 9:00 a.m. Last night I missed a twin birth, a breech birth, a D&C and a prolapsed cord. Today in Prenatal Clinic there are lots of giggles among the patients and the friends they have brought with them, while the doctor, a pixy of a nurse and I joke back and forth between patients. The longer I'm here the more I like the Somali women I meet; they have a good sense of humor, are generally warm and appear to welcome our help. At lunch we are joined by an American missionary surgeon and his wife; the doctor can hardly control himself as he whispers to me, "Can you imagine going to Wyoming and telling people to change their ways?"

Thursday I teach 26 first-year nursing students about emotional support during labor and delivery. Before class I check to see what is happening in the maternity wing and find three women in labor. I visit briefly with each of them and promise a young new mom that I will return after my class to help her. She squeezes my hand. When I come back after class the midwife asks me where I have been. "The woman, she is asking for you. She says she want that lady!" The mom I promised to help has delivered her baby, asking for me the entire time! I go see her, apologize, and tell her how beautiful her new daughter is. "Next time, Inshallah!" I tell her. "Mashalla!" her mother says.

At the start of class I make small-talk with the students. Then we get down to business. I write "Doula" on the board and tell them it is Greek for "woman helper." I explain what we do and why and then talk about the importance of emotional support for all patients. I tell them that in America we don't always live close to our families like they do so we need others to help us when we are in pain or afraid.

I talk about how caring is at the heart of good nursing. I tell them about birthing practices in the 1950s and 60s in America and how women got together to reclaim their childbirth experience (careful to use language they can understand). I demonstrate what doulas can say and do to make moms less afraid and more comfortable during labor. They seem rapt when I am speaking, mesmerized perhaps by this elderly white lady who talks of strange things, but when I ask them questions or want to know what their questions or thoughts are, they are silent. I say, "Allah gave you a voice! Women's voices are beautiful! You must not be afraid to use your voice!" but this falls on deaf ears – they have been long socialized into silence.

I break the class into groups so that can practice techniques to support laboring mothers; they think the role play is hilarious and do not take it seriously so I reconvene the class and try a single demonstration; this too is seen as - quite literally - too funny for words. So I decide I've done what I can for one class and ask, in closing, that each of them tell me one thing they've learned today. A few whisper rote answers: "Massage." "Breathing." "Talk." A few actually seem interested. To my amazement, one student says, "I learned that 'doula' means woman helper!" I am so excited I pretend to ululate; the others laugh and do the real thing. When a few other students say something audible and original I wave my hands in a Hallelujah gesture. I've gotten through to a few of them! I conclude with a pep talk about the difference good nurses make, the need to honor as well as support the hard and amazing work women do in having babies, the healing touch and so on. I invite questions but silence prevails.

And so it comes to an end, this African adventure of extremes, of wild animals and willful males, of voiceless women and vibrant girls, of outrageous poverty and obscene affluence, of deep blue seas and desert sands, of market stalls and mega-malls, of breakaway nations and tradition-bound kingdoms, of visionary women and violent men. So much to absorb and try to understand; so much more to be done; so many new friends; such amazing experiences! May there be other such times in which to contribute and learn. Mashallah!

Edna gave me the camel bell when we went one evening to visit her camel farm. It makes a lovely sound as the camels are shepherded back to their shelter from the fields at night. Some drank milk straight from a camel but I declined.

A Masai Warrior in Kenya

Kenya and Tanzania

There is something in the vastness of Kenya and Tanzania, something in its stillness and silence stretching beyond where you can see, that lets you know your place in the cosmos. To me it was oddly reassuring to feel so small and to realize how tiny a corner of the universe I occupied.

Gazing down upon the Great Rift Valley from Kenya's Ngong Hills, I was breathless with exhilaration. In the Serengeti, this sensation only grew deeper. Watching the evening sun retreat over the landscape to the other side of the world, I contemplated the animal kingdom surrounding the oasis of comfort into which we travelers had been deposited for the night. Its beauty, its fragility, its natural order filled me with awe.

We had begun our journey in Nairobi, crossing the border into Tanzania at Namanga. While our amiable guide, Elias, negotiated customs on our behalf, swarms of colorful Massai women and children wrapped in earth-red cloth, beaded earrings, and extravagant necklaces decorating their deep brown skin, thrust their colorful handicrafts and wooden carvings at us.

"Special price for you!"

"Twenty dollars! Handmade!"

"Look! Look! This one! You like this one?"

Once away from the border town the peacefulness of the African landscape, with its round, thatch-roofed *bomas* and careful quilts of farmland surrounded us. Slender Massai herders waved slowly as we passed, and small children, some with hand-carved wooden masks and mock musical instruments, jumped and fiddled while women in bright *kangas* moved along the roadside in oceanic rhythm. Lush green vegetation swayed in stark relief against the red-brown earth. An occasional cow or goat labored across the road in front of us.

We stopped for lunch in Arusha, and then with our guide made our way to Lake Manyara. It was early evening when we arrived at the hotel, a white windowed rectangle perched atop the eastern escarpment of the Great Rift Valley. A cool breeze wafted over the warmth of the fading sun, and a flock of graceful birds swooped up, down, around while I held a pair of binoculars to my eyes so that I could see the park below where a giraffe lingered.

In the morning, we made our way eagerly into the park where a menagerie of baboons and a wave of pink flamingos met us at the edge of the lake. The giraffe I'd watched the night before reappeared, and a lone elephant joined him. Herds of wildebeest, water buffalo, and zebra grazed and wandered. At the hippo pool, marabou stork gathered, taking no notice of the enormous animals whose stench and strange noises made us laugh.

Several hours later, exhilarated by our first outing, we lunched from a huge and inviting buffet at a coffee plantation reminiscent of Karen Blixen's idyllic Kenyan days. The gardens were a lush canvas, tropical and full of vibrant reds, yellows, purples, white, green, and blue.

At the Ngorongoro Crater, we marveled at the largest collapsed volcano in the world. In that gaping hole in the earth, tropical forests lined the walls and cast its floor into pink and lavender relief as the light of day receded. The next morning, we descended into the crater where some 30,000 animals live. There we saw a lioness stalking a herd of wildebeest while her gloriously tufted mate waited and watched from a far hillside. On the way to Magadi, the central salt lake, we saw zebras, Thompson's and Grant's gazelles, hyenas, abundant bird life, and several huge rhino. A lone tusker elephant crossed our path in extraordinary proximity.

Back at the lodge, we were having tea when an apparition appeared, striding barefoot across the manicured lawns. Tall and lean, the Massai warrior in mud-red robe, ears dripping beads, a long stick in his slender brown hand, made his way toward us. We learned that he was guide to a local Massai village, his village before missionaries frightened his mother into relinquishing him to Arusha, short pants, leather shoes, and a catechism. "School," they said, "or we call the police." We learned this when "Edward" took us to his village where we trekked over dirt floors and through the fly-covered huts of a culture we could never understand. The mothers and children smiled tentatively at us. When two warriors came across the hill, spears in hand, Edward cajoled them into letting us steal their souls with our camera lenses. Later, by a roaring fire in the midst of parched landscape, Edward drank a Pepsi with us, metamorphosed into a Western khaki-wearing, striped-shirt tour guide. "Part time," he said of his village walks. "I live here now." The hotel lights sparkled in relief against the black void beyond.

But for me, the Serengeti Plains, savannas, and grasslands -- home to the world's most spectacular gathering of wildlife – in all their panoramic vastness, invaded my heart and made it race with excitement and humility. This was the Africa I loved. There, millions of animals and birds reside among lakes, rivers, swamps, and endless terrain. There, usually in June when the rainy season ends, the astonishing migration led by two million wildebeest takes place. Before that culminating event, animals spread out horizon to horizon over the southern plains, moving slowly north and west in long weaving lines. At first slow and languid, this movement becomes a race north into the Massai Mara of Kenya where pastures sustain the animals during the Serengeti's dry season. In the spring, tens of thousands of wildebeest, zebras, gazelles, and antelopes migrate there. I felt oddly close to that land and its animals, as if I too were primitive and powerful and knew how to survive.

By the time our tour ended, we had seen the "big five" (lion, leopard, cheetah, hippo, rhino) as well as all manner of other animals, extraordinary bird life, the villages and marketplaces of the Massai and other tribes, the lush countryside and compounds of graceful and gentle people, the site of Mary Leakey's astounding 1959 discovery at Olduvai Gorge, and perhaps most impressive of all, the timeless peacefulness of the Serengeti Plains at evening time, when the pink reflections of the setting sun reminded us ordinary mortals of our tiny place in an endless but well-ordered natural world.

On safari in Kenya and Tanzania, we had a chance to see two sides of Edward, the Massai warrior and the tourist guide, and to learn more about his life. He was a very special young man and meeting him was a highlight of the trip.

Khartoum Nights

The thing about Khartoum is the heat. It makes you feel like gasping for air for lack of a shower and clean underwear.

That's why I noticed her. She seemed so cool, so unperturbed shuffling across the linoleum floor of the hotel. The sight of her made me sad. She wasn't transient like the rest of us who stayed at the run-down hotel, counting the days until we could leave. She lived there.

I'd gone down on assignment, glad it was a short stint. Some journalists and aid workers were trapped for months. Before long, everyone knew each other and in the evening, sitting in the sparse lobby, it was like coming home to family. The hotel was a veritable oasis from which, thankfully, we could escape.

But she couldn't leave. I became obsessed with knowing who she was and how she came to be there, wandering the lobby for what seemed eternity in her black polka-dot dress, felt slippers, nylons knotted at the knees, and tattered plastic purse, carried in knurled hands which retained the elegance of earlier days. Thin wisps of white hair held back in a drooping French twist by a few hairpins framed a face now lined, but hosting the remnants of classic beauty, especially around the gray-blue pools of her eyes.

Once I thought we'd made contact with our eyes. Embarrassed by her solitude, afraid somehow that her situation would keep me prisoner in that place of no air, I only smiled politely and averted my eyes. The conditions of her confinement were private, I thought. But then, gradually, we began to hold each other's gaze, in an odd sort of trust and friendship. I'd be clutching my Coke bottle, pressing it's coldness against my neck , talking with the Belgian journalist just back from Addas , and she would appear like an apparition, dignified and quiet.

One day, I asked what the Belgian knew of her. He said she lived in the hotel at the will of her son, a businessman, who came to visit once a year. No one seemed to know what she had been in life before entering limbo.

I looked forward to seeing her, knowing she had survived another night. We smiled and exchanged nods. In an odd way, she made me feel safe when the oppression of Khartoum nights panicked me. I imagined that soon we would sit together, quiet and conspiratorial, revealing ourselves in deep understanding across the abyss of age and circumstance. I savored the moment when we would finally sip tea together and share life secrets. But we continued instead to nod, smile and like each other with our eyes.

Once, when I was talking to a missionary mother my silent friend passed by, lingering for a moment as if beckoning me. I had a deep urge to rise from the plastic chair stuck to my back and to put my arm around her frail shoulder, and say, "Yes, let's sit and talk!" But I didn't do that. I only offered a half smile.

I'm not sure what kept me from reaching out to her. I think it had to do with not wishing to open her pain. Also, I was loathe to intrude upon her dignity, or to give her something (friendship, hope) which would disappear with me on an airplane. I didn't want to make her uncomfortable in any way. I was also timid because everyone thought her crazy and I didn't know what would be unleashed if I opened the floodgates. I am ashamed to confess that now.

At the end of my assignment I escaped aboard a Lufthansa flight to Cairo and never saw her again.

Two weeks later the hotel was bombed. I contacted the Belgian. He said that the missionaries were killed along with two waiters.

And my friend, I asked?

He said she hadn't been near the explosion and she was staying on at the hotel.

Somehow that didn't surprise me. Nor did the fact that Khartoum was 110 degrees that day with no relief in sight.

Khartoum is probably much more developed than when I was there in the 1980s, but it was impossible to photograph the confluence of the Niles, the only noteworthy site at the time. This story won a first prize for fiction but it is actually a work of creative nonfiction.

Moroccan Plate

The Medieval Magic of Morocco

For anyone who has ever watched Humphrey Bogart bid farewell to Ingrid Bergman in a fog-shrouded airport in Casablanca, a visit to Morocco is likely to be high on their travel bucket list. But of all the walled cities in Morocco, Fes is the most incredible. Dating back to 809 A.D., it is a place of artisans and craftspeople virtually unchanged from its earliest days, although electricity and running water are now present. Fes, the country's second largest city, is also Morocco's most important intellectual, cultural and religious center. It is home to the oldest university in the world, some of the finest handcrafts made anywhere, and monuments second to none.

And then there is the world-famous Palais Jamai Hotel. Situated within the ramparts of old Fes, the hotel's view of the medina (walled city) is incomparable, and there is nothing like the sunrise sound of "Allah Akbar!" - the call to prayer echoing across the medina from Kairouyine Mosque by a chorus of muezzins.

Breakfast on a private terrace reveals a maze of rooftops bathed in periwinkle shades of daybreak, the sounds of an Arabic metropolis awakening, an amalgam of aromatic scents, and bird visitors to be shooed away as you enjoy yoghurt, fresh fruit, breads, and strong coffee or tea. The hotel, originally a "pleasure pavilion" for the landowning Jamai family, was built in 1879 and expanded in 1930. It takes pride in its pure Moorish architecture, a magnificent Andalusian garden, and a world class Moroccan restaurant with impeccable service.

A guide is a must for touring the medina if you want to emerge from the bustle at day's end. A good guide can also keep hawkers and vendors at bay. Ours, Mohib, was twenty-eight and had been educated abroad, returning to a promising teaching job that never materialized. He told us every neighborhood in Morocco has four things: a fountain for washing, a mosque for praying, a hammam (public bath), and a bakery where bread prepared at home can be brought to the communal ovens. That explained the children racing through the streets with round loaves under towels and the cries of "Batical!" (Out of the way) and "Balek! (Attention) as donkeys bearing goods and people were herded down the narrow streets.

The sights and sounds of Morocco's medinas are extraordinary. Winding every which way and tempting endless detours, narrow streets house vendors and stalls selling every conceivable item. There are traditional *babouche* (leather open-heeled slippers), leather bags and coats, perfume, bolts of fabric, spices, dates, and figs piled into pyramids. Tailors mend, women sell comb, barbers cut hair, rug and brass emporium hawkers compete for attention. While jewelry stalls reveal Berber handcrafted silver and gems and street foods attract people and flies in equal measure, it goes on and on, delighting the five senses.

But even more extraordinary than seeing the finished goods at market is watching how they are made. Fes is a city of artisans who have handed down their skills generation to generation, intentionally shunning technology that would alter what they do and how they do it. From the age of five, boys are at their fathers' sides, learning to etch brass, tan leather, carve or create mosaics. Young girls weave rugs so nimbly that their little fingers are gnarled, but they smile with pride and giggle as you look over their shoulders. We visited one worksite that was such a hum of activity it resembled a group of Santa's elves working in guilds to produce exquisite products that would make their way around the world.

The most astonishing site in all of Morocco, however, is the leather tannery in Fes, the only one in the world that operates virtually unchanged since medieval times. If you visit, wear sturdy shoes and old trousers and carry sprigs of mint to deflect the scent. You won't quite believe what awaits you as you climb to the top of the building surrounding the courtyard of stone vats, contiguous pools that swallow skins in various stages of leather-dying. Moving among them is an athletic feat nimbly handled by scantily clad men with saffron, poppy, and indigo-dyed arms and legs. Drying skins lie about on the walls of surrounding vats. The smell of animal skins, dye mixed with cow urine, and human perspiration surround you as you troop through narrow walkways to various vantage points. Lift your eyes long enough to notice the workers huddled in dark crevices and hollow spaces along the way, and imagine spending a lifetime working in such a place.

There is more to see in the medina, however, so your guide will urge you on. Among the many sites to behold is the Bou Inania Medrassa, an ancient lodging house for students who were strangers to Fes. This particular medrassa was built between 1350 and 1357 at a legendary cost by Sultan Abou Inan who, it is said, was competing with the Kairouyine Mosque. Like other medrassas, this one has a courtyard with a carved stucco façade, above which the majestic cedarwood arches support a frieze and porch. The building boasts some of the finest examples of cedarwood carving, stucco work, and Kufic script writing.

Fondouks are also worth noting. Created about the same time as madrassas (or medersas), these served as hotels for traders. One of the most well-known is the Fondouk Tsetaouyine, near the Kairouyine. Like most other fondouks, this one now serves as a carpet warehouse, but it was once known as a center of "loose living."

Just below the Souk Attarine, you enter a sacred area around the shrine of Moulay Idriss II. A wooden bar at donkey height, designed to keep donkeys, mules, Jews and Christians out, will tell you you've arrived. Here, beggars congregate, vendors sell sweets, candles and incense, and women come to lay wreaths at the the great tomb.

All roads in the medina will eventually lead to the Kairouyine Mosque, rivaled in size only by King Hassan's Casablanca mosque. Here, 20,000 people can pray at once, while in the Casablanca mosque 100,000 can. The Kairouyine Mosque is noted for its green tiled roofs, elegant courtyards and 16th century fountain. It was the first university in the western world and its reputation drew more than 8,000 students in the 14th century. The library, closed to the public, houses one of the most renowned collections of Islamic literature in the world.

Outside the media there is still more to see, including the Mellah, or Jewish Quarter, and the Merinid tombs. But those places, along with other nearby sights, are for another day when your senses can handle more of Morocco's medieval magic. Better now, after emerging from the darkening, cool medina to rest, dine on couscous or a flavorful *tangine,* and wait for the call of the muezzin at daybreak.

PUPPETS FROM THAILAND, INDONESIA, INDIA

Asia

"Asia is rich in people, rich in culture
and rich in resources. It is also rich in trouble."

HUBERT H. HUMPHREY

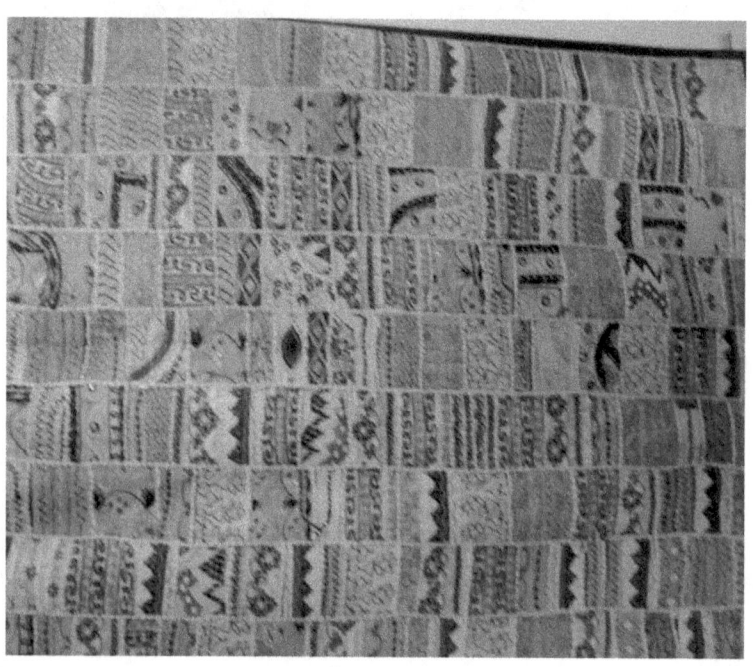
Indian Tapestry

A Cook, a Driver and a Train Station

India. A country of extraordinary extremes and strange juxtapositions. A place of overfed Brahmins and starving Untouchables. Home to Bangalore's high-speed call centers while in the rest of the country it's nearly impossible to find an Internet (and when you do the electricity is down.) Cell phones are ubiquitous; so are women still carrying water in brass jugs and loads of fire wood on their heads. Family planning billboards abound while the population tops a billion. Cows are sacred, women are expendable. A plethora of religions flourish. So does intolerance. Camels peer at passersby from gas stations. There are swastikas on top of six-pointed stars, both symbols of hope in this land of Hindus, Muslims, Sikhs, Christians, Jains, half-naked, dredlocked religious hermits, atheists. Men in dark business suits mingle with women in colorful flowing silk saris while starving children and beggars with missing limbs look on. Despite assassinations, multiple languages, sub-cultures, political parties, classes, topographies, an AIDS epidemic, grinding poverty, corruption and a billion people, democracy survives and life goes on. What better place to experience all that India has to offer than a train station in a town called Jhansi in the middle of the night?

The station, a miniature version of the one in Delhi, is filthy, its platform littered with sleeping bodies as if it were the London Underground during the war. Chaiwallahs and vendors hawk juice, snacks, toys, duffle bags and newspapers. Rats as big as rabbits race over the track in pursuit of garbage, competing with world-class roaches and other vermin. A clock gone mad spins its arms frantically in a race against time. A caravan of barefoot Gypsies, the women balancing battered suitcases on their heads while their children wipe sleep from tired eyes, marches past. A family huddles on a thin cotton cloth, the mother nursing her infant as she covers her sleeping daughter and the crazy clock plays with the minutes of their lives.

We have been escorted to the station by our driver and the cook from our Haveli, who twice prepared us delectable curried fish, dal and rice pudding. The driver is a quiet, silent man. But the cook is expansive, gracious, always smiling beneath his black moustache. He has hitched a ride to town with us but now will not leave until we are safely on our train back to Delhi. His smile never wavers when the announcement is made that our train is one, then two hours late. We insist that the driver take him home and then return to us, but he is having none of that. We are in his care now and he will do his duty to the fullest.

The heat is unbearable, even as our watches tick past one o'clock in the morning and the crazy clock dances wildly to a new day. We sit on a bench and watch humanity pass by. A nearly naked, seemingly well-fed, rotund religious zealot asks for rupies. Cook shoos him away. "He's a Brahmin," he whispers knowingly. "He shouldn't be doing that." A lecherous-looking man leers at us, then lights a cigarette and drifts away. A young man says in impeccable British English, "I hope you are not getting the wrong impression of India."

When they announce that our train is further delayed by four hours, all barriers between host and guest dissolve. Shirttails are now out, and there is none of the obsequious "Madam" or "Sir." Like athletes in a post-game locker room we are all sweating amiably together, no longer embarrassed by our sour-scented discomfort. Driver sits with his arm around my husband. I take pictures "to prove to your wife that you really did spend the night at the train station," I joke.

Driver suggests a visit to the station master's office to ask if we can board an earlier train. (The one preceding ours was 17 hours late and has just crawled away. We cannot afford to risk that kind of delay if we are to make our flight home.) Taking my husband by the hand, he leads him off while Cook watches over me. Time passes. When my husband and Driver return, the scene they describe in the station master's office is one of utter mayhem. "There were hordes of people!" Arnold exclaims. "They were waving and shouting and it was total pandemonium." Suddenly, he said, the crowds made way for him, parting like the Red Sea for Moses, and when he reached the station master, who a minute before had been flustered and flailing, the room became eerily silent. Offering Arnold a chair, Station Master said, "How may I help you, Sir?" My husband explained the situation and asked if there was any possibility of an earlier train. "Certainly," said Station Master. And that was how my husband came to have in his hand upon his return to Cook and me a signed permission allowing us to board the next train to Delhi.

A little after three o'clock in the morning, Driver and Cook loaded us onto the AP Express from Hyderabad, virtually tucking us into our upper and lower bunks in "2nd A/C". Compact but with clean sheets, water and a privacy curtain, we were grateful for the space in which to lie down. We bid farewell to our friends, Cook wrapping his arms around my husband in a bear hug while Driver looked on. The train pulled out as we collapsed onto cool sheets. The crazy clock seemed to go mad with relief.

This tapestry was purchased in Rajasthan on a day when the temperature hit 137 degrees Fahrenheit. I still perspire just looking at it.

The three Asian puppets are among my most treasured travel memorabilia. The Indian one was from a performer at a haveli where we stayed. We purchased the Indonesian one from a puppet maker in a village. The Thai puppet was another of my Night Market bargains.

Images of India

Women with brass jugs on their heads, brown babies on their hips,
Macho men who swagger, spit and urinate wherever they please.
Jeeps with forty people crammed inside,
Chaotic, cluttered marketplaces. Children seeking "pen?"
Cows and camels and silk-sari-ed women,
Swaying purposefully, everywhere.
Temples, forts, mosques, haveli, the Taj Mahal,
So breathtaking at daybreak it makes you weep.
Gandhi and Ganesh, Bollywood and Bangalore.
Vendors, tigers, pujas, pottery, kohl-eyed kids.
Strewn garbage, ubiquitous, as if the country itself were a landfill.
Buses barreling down potholed roads, horns blasting.
Macroman underwear ads painted on cement walls.
Swastikas and six-pointed stars, bizarre juxtapositions at every turn.
Pre-monsoon dust, barren landscapes, the heat of Hades.
Turbaned Sikhs, white-bearded Rajasthani elders,
Ganges and ghats, a pink city, an amber fort.
Kingfisher beer, black dal, white rice, yellow curry.
Fetid pools of water dotting the detritus of daily life.
A warren of streets in old Delhi, bazaars in Agra, a carpet vendor
in Mandawa, a rickshawwallah in Jaipur.
Street barbers, galubjamun, palaces and pallets, train porters.
Opulent weddings, cremation fires.
Overweight Brahmins, starving untouchables.

Camel caravans, water buffalo, goats, pigs, wild boar.
The timeless plowing of farmers in their fields.
Kids playing with paper balls, string, old bicycle tires,
Miniature merchants vending postcards,
Begging for rupies, baby brother in tow.
Women in bangled purdah. Women at the well.
Women plowing, planting, sewing, sweeping,
feeding, washing, shopping, brickmaking.
Women tethering goats, herding cows, wiping tears.
Nehru, Indira, Rajiv and Sonia, the Salt March.
Hindus, Muslims, Shikhs, Jains, Christians and a few Jews.
India: "A rich country full of poor people."
A kaleidoscope. An enigma. A place like no other.

A Twelve Mile Trek in Nepal

"Mountain clear! Mountain clear! sang out the steward at sunrise at the Fish Tail Lodge in Pokhara, Nepal. My husband and I jumped into our clothes for a closer look from the edge of Lake Phewa. Indeed, the sight of Fish Tail Mountain, part of the Annapurna Range, stretching beyond the lake to a misty morning pastel sky was something to behold.

On a clear day, Fish Tail is reflected in the lake, and the scene, including its fragrant and colorful wild flowers, is near to perfection. The stillness of the chilly morning, punctuated only by bird sounds and the silent rowing of a few early boaters, lent itself to an impressionist painting. It felt splendid to be standing in the middle of it.

We had come to be there by a stroke of good fortune. Work had brought me to Burma (Myanmar) at the same time that my husband had meetings in Nepal. It was the first time our dual careers in international development had given us the opportunity to rendezvous in one of the world's most exotic places.

Preparation had begun in Kathmandu a day earlier. Tickets on Royal Nepal Airways for the daily flight to Pokhara were easily obtained, but trekking permits took longer and required a last-minute dash to a photographer who could produce passport photos in record turnaround.

Fortunately, friends had provided us with backpacks replete with band-aids, toilet paper, flashlights, jackets and canteened fresh water. Even high-power binoculars were laid on. The only thing missing was solid walking shoes. But Kathmandu had been catering to trekkers for a long time so industrious entrepreneurs were on hand to sell used trekking gear ranging from anoraks to battered cooking utensils. In a medieval market we found an efficient, beautiful Tibetan woman refugee with a used shoe store who quickly produced clean socks and a wide array of walking shoes. In record time I had new Nikes and my husband's feet were snug in a worn pair of Swiss hiking boots. Our final chore was to purchase two handknit sweaters and we were ready for the trek.

On arrival at the airport we were told that the flight was full and we couldn't board. But after a melodious debate in Nepali between our drive and the airline official, we were permitted to board the 40-seat aircraft and soon found ourselves floating above rolling foothills and terraced farmland. Soon snow-capped Himalayas formed a spectacular backdrop, leading to unbounded enthusiasm among the camera-toting passengers whom I feared would tip the plane over as they rushed to one side for photo opps.

Once in Pokhara, we checked into the beautifully appointed small hotel made up of clusters of ethnic-style bungalows with clean, bright, *en suite* rooms. Situated on a lake, the lodge was reached by shuttle float and offered the warmth of a huge fireplace in the lounge. Dinner was followed by traditional dancers performed by glowing, graceful teens.

This restful environment meant we felt fit for anything when our Gurka guide appeared at 7.30 a.m. the next morning in the Land Rover that would take us to base camp to begin our trek. The Rover made its way quickly through the morning bustle of commercial enterprise. An important crossroad town 200 km. west of Kathmandu, Pokhara thrives on tourism and had grown rapidly. Even before its development it was known as a place of mystery and mysticism. It is still a unique place from which the great Himalayan peaks can be admired. Annapurna I, over 26,000 feet high, along with its sister peaks, is only 50 km. away. Fish Tail, known locally as Macchapuchhare, even closer, rises up without a single intervening ridge between it and Pokhara.

The ride to base camp was remarkable. We quickly found ourselves on a dirt path which the driver tackled with great skill. Passing a construction site, several small villages, and various pedestrians, we emerged in a glorious valley surrounded by verdant hills spotted with small, neat villages. Following the dry river bed, we continued for some time, the driver turning left and right for no apparent reason. Occasionally we crossed a stream, jostled severely and hanging onto the Rover's safety bar as our nails bit into the palms of our hands. Finally, as we approached base camp, we saw thatched lean-to huts where local people seemed barely able to survive. We wondered at their cheerfulness given the solitary and insecure life they led.

Base camp consisted of a few stone structures sporting hacienda-style verandas on which locals, drivers, and trekkers partook of thick, sweet tea or Coke. We joined them, and then energized by all the sugar, we began our twelve-mile roundtrip trek to the Lumli Agricultural Center, where my husband was expected.

We began our journey by ascending a steep, rocky path, the angle and terrain of which suggested the challenge that lay ahead. As the path continued ever steeper and rock ridden, I peeled of my jacket and then my sweater. "Is it all like this?" I asked the guide. We had been on our way all of fifteen minutes.

He smiled knowingly. "No, not all. Some parts hard, some easy."

But the sun was glorious, the sky brilliantly blue, and the emerging scenery awesome. Descending trekkers, who had spent the night on the mountain, offered encouragement. "Enjoy your walk! It gets better," they said.

"I'm sure you just have to get acclimatized," I told my husband reassuringly as a barefoot woman, weighing all of ninety pounds if that, passed us with a huge pile of cabbage greens on her head.

When the path leveled off somewhat we paused for our first glimpse of snow-peaked Annapurna. Between the mountain and us lay beautiful, lush, deep green hills, some covered with terraced cultivation, others rolling freely. The vastness of clear, uncluttered silence was truly awesome and I began to understand why people consider trekking in Nepal an essential travel experience.

The scenery continued to unfold, animated by human activity, as we made way ever higher. The path traveled, we soon realized, was the main thoroughfare, connecting villages to each other and to Pokhara, where goods and information could be found. Along this route merchants traveled taking goods to market while caravans of donkeys laden with food and raw materials followed families on the way to visit friends and family.

Taking goods to market could be a journey of several days and going to school, if one were so lucky, meant a walk of several hours each way. Yet each village stirred with the activities of daily life. Women chatted with each other as they filled jugs with well water or washed clothes at a communal spout. Babies in woven straw cradles hung from wooden beams and older children played ball with bits of paper and rolled string. In a few more prosperous villages, stalls offered trekkers cold drinks and jewelry vendors bargained over stone and silver necklaces. In the distance, women and men worked the fields to ensure a crop large enough to feed their families during the wet season.

As we passed from one village to another, the rocky road continued to ascend, providing ever more thrilling vistas of the magnificent land called "the top of the world." Our rest stops became, of necessity, longer and more frequent, affording us more amazing vistas. On one ridge overlooking a dip into the valley, a memorable stop occurred, for on the other side of the distance between us, Fish Tail Mountain suddenly appeared. Rising up like the huge tail of Moby Dick, the mountain commanded our full attention because of its striking strength and posture. The mountain reaches nearly 23,000 feet and because it is sacred, no one has ever climbed it. Perhaps its solitude in this solitary place is why the mountain is called the "abode of the Gods."

Just before reaching Lumli, I was so tired I thought I might actually die. My legs and back simply could no longer sustain the assault. But once a trek is started there is only thing to do and that is to go on, so with the thought of lunch and a beer awaiting us, I managed to scale the final rock path and weakly greet our hosts. Then I collapsed into the comfort of an easy chair where I promptly dozed off to the amusement of the agricultural center's residents.

The center was an extraordinary place. Perched on top of a mountain in the middle of nowhere, a group of expatriates and Nepalis had created an agricultural demonstration project of awesome proportions. What really fascinated me was the fact that such an incredible microcosm akin to an English village could exist at this remote height. How, I wondered, had they gotten supplies up the mountain to build this place? Had donkey caravans carried every single piece of furniture, crockery, fabric, utensil and appliance it took to live in such comfort? How often were essential supplies, food and drink delivered? Was their trash hauled down the mountain? A delicious and plentiful lunch of curried meat, rice, fresh vegetables and salad interrupted my ruminations.

We set off again after lunch restored by good food and gracious hospitality as we faced the daunting prospect of retracing our steps. In the cooling air of late afternoon, we recognized several previous milestones. As the early signs of approaching evening cast a different palette on the scenic vistas and village activities, we greeted people as we passed by. "Namaste," we said. "Namaste," they smiled back.

Men in scattered groups played a game that looked like checkers with hand-carved pieces that scooted across a board sprinkled with powder. Babies nursed contentedly while children frolicked with friends. Peacefulness rolled over the mountain communities, valleys, and terraced fields like a sweet-smelling blanket offering comfort as night approached.

Midway down the mountain my knees and ankles began to

rebel, feeling brittle and incapable of bearing my weight. I felt ridiculous when I saw a man carrying a burro on his back. Then I wished a porter would carry me down the mountain that way.

We plodded on. Our patient, watchful Sherpa guide offered me his hand as we made our way along the most difficult bits. The last hour proved most troublesome. Like a child on a long car journey, I asked repeatedly, "Are we nearly there?" How much longer?" Slowly, tediously, we continued, no longer able to see the mountains in the evening haze.

Finally, enormously relieved, we spotted the tops of base camp dwellings. Then the Land Rover came into view. The thought of the early morning jostling now seemed a relief as we made our bumpy way back to the lodge in the encroaching darkness, Pokhara still heavy with commerce. When we reached the shuttle float to Fish Tail Lodge, our driver and guide took leave of us, laughing heartily, no doubt at our depleted condition. Limping onto the float, my husband muttered, "Drinks!" like a dying soldier. "Shower first," I stuttered.

Half an hour later, as we sat bathed, drinks in hand, our aching feet propped up before a blazing fire, we reflected on the day's experience. "I wouldn't have missed it for the world!" my husband said smugly. "No one at home would believe what we did!"

Even now, looking back on it, we remember our twelve-mile trek as one of the most outstanding experiences of our traveling life. In the breadth and beauty of its majestic scenery, and in the warmth of its people, we had shared a magic day in the spirit of Annapurna, goddess of plenty, for whom the mountain range is aptly named.

Emerald Buddha

This is Thailand, Silly!
The Reality of Living in a Land you Love, Frustrations and All

There's an expression among *farang* (westerners) living in Thailand: "This is Thailand, Silly!" We use it to remind each other of Thai reality when things are hilarious or frustrating. They're often both.

* * * * *

With our Thai friends Lena and Dui we drive from Chiang Mai to Bangkok, a nine-hour journey. Early next morning, we head for the beach resort of Pattaya. No sooner have I navigated onto an eight-lane highway when suddenly our rental car belches grinding noises and slows to a near-halt. A burning odor is ominous. I inch left (Thais drive on the left side), cross eight lanes, and coast to a stop on the narrow shoulder.

Lena, epitomizing the Thai concept of *jai yen* – cool heart – pulls out her cell phone. She calls the Tourist Police and the Police Department's Road Services Division. Both promise to send help. Then she calls Avis Rental Car at Don Muang Airport, a few kilometers behind us. The agent offers a promotion. I get on the line to book it.

"What is your fax, please?" the agent asks.

"I'm in the middle of an eight-lane highway in a broken down car!"

"Oh, sorry. You have email address?"

By now my *jai* is not so *yen*. I hand the phone back to Lena. "I call you later," she says.

My husband, meanwhile, is on his cell to Khun Tan from whom we have rented the car. He explains the situation, then says, "I'm in the middle of Bangkok's busiest highway. I can't check the transmission fluid!"

An hour later we are still awaiting help. Lena suggests she and I grab a taxi and head for the airport to rent a car. Effortlessly, she flags a cab and we're off to Don Muang, leaving husbands to mind the Rent-a-Wreck. Hertz says they have a special "but only good for shift." I say I can drive manual. "Sorry," he says. "*Mai mee*" (don't have).

My cell rings. It's my husband. "I need a *hong nam* (toilet). Can you hurry?" Dui, meanwhile, has spotted a Mitsubishi dealer across the road from where they are stranded. He calls on his cell and tells the repair shop he has a dead car on the highway and a *farang* with a full bladder.

"Is it Mitsubishi?" the repairman asks.

Dui confirms so the guy says my husband can use the restroom. The Tourist Policeman arrives, stops eight lanes of traffic in the opposite direction, and leads my husband to the Mitsubishi *hong nam*. Simultaneously Lena and I arrive at the dealership in our new rental car. We head for the beach, only five hours behind schedule.

· · · · ·

It's 9:00 p.m. when our landlords knock on the door. We have recently informed them we would leave Chiang Mai sooner than expected because my work is finished. They demand the rent. We explain that since they are holding two months security, we have already paid for our last month. Mrs. Landlord, an atypically aggressive Thai woman, says we must forfeit our security deposit and pay another month's rent or she will change the locks. We invite her to return with a copy of the contract the next night.

At 5:00 p.m. everyone assembles, including a lawyer we have engaged and Lena, who is our real estate agent. We serve soft drinks and go through the expected amenities. Then the fireworks begin. We point to Clause Nine of the contract which states that we are entitled to a full refund of our deposit because we have given 30 days notice. Mrs. Landlord threatens to call the police. I say that's a good idea. Mr. Landlord impugns Lena's integrity. I threaten to evict him. Then I offer to take them to court to settle the matter. The lawyer waits for the shouting match to end before quietly informing Mr. and Mrs. Landlord that it's against Thai law to forcefully evict tenants. He suggests they accept our deposit as payment in full. Mr. Landlord weakens. Mrs. Landlord continues to rant. In the end, we agree to this solution and The Landlords depart, all smiles and *Kapunkas* (Thank you). I usher them out, *wai-ing* (bowing) only to the lawyer.

* * * * *

Our friends arrive from the States. After several days touring Chiang Mai, we head for the Golden Triangle. Our first stop is Mae Salong where, our travel book advises, we must not miss the Mae Salong Resort. As evening approaches, we snake our way up a mountain in foggy rain, anticipating "the best views of terraced hills" and outstanding Yunnanese food. (This village was founded by Chinese escaping Mao's Cultural Revolution).

The term "resort" is used loosely in Thailand, but what a misnomer for the hotel we find ourselves in! Without checking the rooms we plunk down 420 baht per couple – a supposed 40 percent discount on the usual rate, but after seeing the accommodation we upgrade to "VIP rooms." These are large, dirty digs adjacent to staff quarters. Our view is drying laundry, wood piles and motorbikes. The rooms are dank and dirty. Water runs brown from the taps; the waste baskets are fuzzy; the sheets and towels appear used, the odor is Eau de Mold.

We passed a luxurious place a mile back but would they have room and would driving in wet darkness be sensible? We accept our fate for the night – a Buddhist, but ultimately bad decision.

We visit the restaurant for the promised Chinese fare but find a motley crew of servers, stained tablecloths and a limited menu. We order several dishes. One plate of chicken appears with boiled rice and two plates of what look like weeds cooked in mud.

"Chinese eggplant! Very good – you try!" the waitress says.

We return hungry to our cobwebbed VIP lounge to drown our sorrows, agreeing to abscond in the morning without paying the difference owed on our rooms. None of us is able to sleep in the damp beds; no one dreams of showering. Our friends find a huge cockroach in their bed.

In the morning we head downhill to the beautifully gardened luxury hotel for breakfast and discover we could have stayed for 650 baht. Later the "resort" calls to ask for their 1500 baht. We say we are calling the Ministries of Health and Tourism. (Most accommodations and restaurants in Thailand are good to splendid but it's best to look before you book.)

Thailand is a wonderful country full of smiling people, colorful sights, delicious food, and glorious crafts. I'd live there again in a heartbeat. But having done so, I'd know that life can be frustrating, and very funny. Sometimes you just have to shrug and say, "This is Thailand, Silly!"

There is no shortage of Buddhas to see in Thailand. This one is called the Emerald Buddha and can be found in the Royal Palace in Bangkok.

Handcrafted dish made of eggshells

Vietnam

From Hanoi to Saigon: Visions of Vietnam

Vietnam is one of those places I'd wanted to visit but never thought I'd see.

Like most Americans, I suppose, I was intrigued with the ancient, long, narrow country bordered by Thailand, Cambodia, Laos and the China Sea ever since the Vietnam War ended. The opportunity to go there finally arose when I was teaching in Chiang Mai, a mere one-hour flight, via Bangkok, from Hanoi or Saigon (now Ho Chi Minh City). Here are six major impressions.

1. It's a hoot driving in Vietnam. Literally. Millions of motorbikes crowd the road and there are no rules, no lights, no cops. Right-of-way doesn't exist. Neither does taking turns. It's everyone for themselves in a free-for-all that exceeds the chaos of Athens, Boston and Chiang Mai combined. Crossing the street is one of the world's great challenges. "Don't look and keep moving!" one native advised. He was right. Just keep going and they will move around you, adept and in an odd way, courteous. You must see it to believe it. Just don't linger to have a long look!

2. All of Vietnam is a marketplace. There are the public markets of Asia, vast emporia of narrow aisles, copious goods ranging from silk to nuts, and eager vendors. And there are simply the eager vendors. They crowd around you like flies on sugar no matter where you are. The streets of Hanoi, Saigon and other cities are full of them. Descend from a boat or bus and they are in your face "Where you from?" "You just looking!" "Madame, I have sick baby!" "My shop just open!" "My husband is artist!" "What you pay? How many you want?" After a few days I wanted to hang a sign around my neck: "No dong, no dollar!" Instead I opted for the ubiquitous copout. "Later, later."

3. While the northern part of the country is beautiful in its own way, central and southern Vietnam are bucolic, fertile, peaceful and gorgeous. Green and mountainous, rice paddies are punctuated with water buffalo, farmers in conical hats bending over their crops, and women - stooped, squatting, solitary - working the fields. Occasional towns punctuate the landscape, their temples, narrow tube houses, palm trees, fish farms, and children animating the scene.

4. Vietnam is a country of young people. When school is out at 11:00 a.m. for the midday break it seems like thousands of them converge on the road. The little ones, skipping their way home, wear white shirts and navy-blue shorts or skirts. The high school girls are like brides on bicycles. They wear the traditional *ao dai* - white silk pants with high-necked, long sleeved, dramatically slit overdresses. They ride their bikes home, some in conical straw hats, some in sophisticated cloche, a few in baseball caps. They form a gorgeous brigade, a sea of white silk clouds trailing long, dark ponytails as they cycle by.

5. From the Cham towers of the ancient, indigenous Vietnamese to the old pagodas of the Chinese and the tombs of its kings, Vietnam is rich with history and iconic venues. In Hanoi's Haan Kiem Lake there is the Tortoise Tower. There is the Ambassador's Pagoda, the Hai Ba Trung Temple, and of course, "Uncle Ho's" house and mausoleum. The Temple of Literature, site of learning nearly a thousand years ago, is stunning with its gold painted red pillars, ornate gates and graceful buildings. Further north lies Halong Bay with its 3,000 islands spreading their way to China. In the central city of Hue, the Imperial Palace and its Purple

Forbidden City beckon, while the majestic tombs of Minh Mang, Thieu Tri and Emperor Gia Long provide a glimpse of former royal glory. At My Son are the ancient monuments of the Cham people. High in the mountains, in the former French hill station of Da Lat, is the home of Vietnam's last emperor, Bao Dai, who reigned from 1925 to 1945. Perhaps best of all, the city of Hoi An, now a World Heritage Site, is like walking through an Asian magic kingdom with its old assembly halls, temples and pagodas, and shophouses. At Nha Trang golden beaches and the warm waters of the China Sea provide respite from the tropical heat.

6. In Ho Chi Minh City, formerly Saigon, the pleasures of sophisticated urban life are abundant. There, too, one can visit Reunification Hall, site of the end of the Vietnam War, and the chilling War Remnants Museum, where photos, posters, planes and propaganda drive home the full horror of the war. It's all around you, the terrible things that happened here during "the American war." It's in the silent stone walls of the infamous Hanoi Hilton-Hoa Lo prison - where Vietnamese and American prisoners were incarcerated and tortured. It's in the stories of the guides, who insist "the war is past we are all good friends now." There is Thao, whose father was executed while working for the CIA when her mother was pregnant; Giap, whose father has been bedridden ever since shrapnel embedded itself in his brain; Van, whose brother suffers the disabling effects of dioxin; beggars with Agent Orange deformities too gross to look upon. It's in the pockmarked bronze statues and urns on display at temples, and in the My Lai monument, the extraordinary Cu Chi Tunnels of the guerilla fighters, and the cafes with names like "Good Morning Vietnam!" On every road and in every rice paddy I wonder what happened there. Where did the execution captured by a LIFE photographer take place? Was this the road where the little girl ran naked, burned by napalm? One day, I saw a woman whose child had just been killed in a roadside accident. I knew then the face of grief on Vietnam's mothers. We lost 57,000 of our young in that awful war; they lost 3 million people. It is unbearable to contemplate.

There are a few things not to like in Vietnam: the hawk-and-spit of men on the street and their propensity to point-and-blow (their noses); the squat and squirt toilets, the ubiquitous and often annoying vendors, the maniacal driving, coffee strong enough to grow hair on asphalt. But there is also much to love about the country: the waving and shouting "Hello!" The ubiquitous Chinese symbol for long life, green rice paddies, blue-green waters of the China Sea, beaches, mountain scenery, conical straw hats, wizened faces of women squatting on streets cooking, women bearing loads balanced on bars on their shoulders, baskets at either end, scenes of daily life, jumbo prawns, baguettes, water puppets, silk, embroidery and inlaid mother-of-pearl, bridal shops in every village, the town of Hoi An. All of it conspires to make Mekong magic. I wouldn't have missed it for the world.

Handcrafted tapestry

Laos Lite
Three Days in Luang Prabang

The bad news is we have only one weekend to visit Laos. The good news? Luang Prabang, named a UNESCO World Heritage site in 1995, is our destination. It's a magical place, small enough to explore in a short time.

My daughter and I board Lao Airlines' 72-seat prop plane in Chiang Mai midday and touch down an hour later at the miniature airport in Laos. Our descent is promising: Coconut palms, oversized green banana leaves, and sharply slanted orange rooftops along the muddy confluence of the Mekong and Khan Rivers suggest a picturesque respite.

After securing visas we climb into a *tuk tuk* for the five-minute drive into town where we have booked a room at one of the copious guest houses that have sprung up since Luang Prabang became the darling of Southeast Asia's visiting *farang* (foreigners). We deposit our backpacks in a basic but cheerful air-conditioned room with private bath for $10 a night, and head for lunch at a cafe on the river a block away.

The pleasures of Luang Prabang are simple. We wander the unpaved streets enjoying French provincial architecture and friendly, smiling people. We stop at a textile shop, a silversmith's, a woodcarver's. We sit in a cafe and indulge in cafe latte and a sweet pastry. We stroll the night market and marvel at the sea of vibrant colors and geometric designs gracing the world-famous textiles being sold by beautiful women with babies strapped on their backs. We bargain and laugh with a vendor when we strike a deal.

We rent bikes and ride over to one of the local noodle shops.

We joke with French jewelry designer Fabrice Munio at his inviting shop, Naga Creations, on the town's main street, Th Sisavangvong. I find this young man so charming I jokingly offer him 200,000 kip and two cows to marry my daughter. He laughs and says it's not a bad offer.

We stuff ourselves at the all-you-can-eat-for fifty-cents open-air food stalls at the foot of the night market. We explore wats and chat with monks. We rise at daybreak to offer them alms in the early, misty morning as they quietly proceed down the street, orange-robed, bowls in hand. We take a packed longtail boat up the Mekong to visit Pak Ou Caves, crammed with Buddha images. On the way there, we visit the village of Ban Xang Hai, known as Whiskey Village for its homebrew. Sadly, we do not have time to take in the waterfall at Tat Kuang Si.

We visit the Royal Palace Museum and its adjacent theater, where traditional music and dance is performed on Saturday nights. The Palace Museum is small and the story of the monarchs intriguing. Built in 1904 for King Sisavang Vong and his family the charm of the palace is its simplicity. The dining room looks like an oversized room in which any well-heeled family of the 1940s might have dined. Similarly. the bedrooms of the king and queen are untouched since the communist Pathet Lao takeover in 1975.

Of all the temples in Luang Prabang, the one that really wows us is Wat Xieng Thong. Built in 1560, it is one of only two wats that escaped demolition when the city was sacked in 1887, and a good thing too. It is a magnificent example of classic Luang Prabang temple architecture, its roofs sloping gracefully toward the ground and its Tree of Life mosaic shining in the sun. Equally impressive is our next visit to the temples on Phu Si, the hill that rises above the main thoroughfare and affords a wonderful view of the town.

The wats, the monks, the palace, the night market, the eateries and shops, the longboats that ply the river all form a vivid collage when I think now about Luang Prabang. So does Lei, who served us noodles and told us about her sister in California, and the baby

I visited every day in the textile shop opposite our guesthouse with its friendly proprietor who loaned my daughter a jacket for the chilly nights and mornings.

I remember a gorgeous hilltribe woman laughing with us over our bargaining skill, rice cakes drying in the sun, and golden temples glistening in the waning light of day as vendors plied their trinkets, T-shirts and fresh-squeezed orange juice. I remember the calm of evening, sipping hot coffee in the morning at Couleur's, a woman weaving in the shade of her porch, and an endless procession of monks seeking alms. Now I worry that Luang Prabang is no longer what it was when I was there. Still I tell my friends not to miss it. It is definitely at the top of places not to miss in that part of the world.

Angkor Wat

Cambodia
Beyond Angkor Wat, Sadness In Cambodia

It's the woman with the infant in her arms. I can't take my eyes off her. More than the other pictures of frightened children, of men with missing ears, their eyes swollen shut, or the faces reflecting sheer terror or numb acceptance, it is her face that mesmerizes me. Maybe it's that she doesn't seem to know about the torture. Perhaps she was still thinking they didn't kill women, or their babies. But she died here, in this school turned prison, along with 14,000 other people during the Khmer Rouge nightmare in the time of The Killing Fields. When it was over in 1979, half of Cambodia's population - three million people - were gone. Only seven prisoners were found alive in this hideous dungeon when it was liberated. One was an artist who, without bitterness, captured on canvas what happened at S 21, the notorious Toul Sleng Prison.

On the streets of Phnom Penh, it's the multitudes of limbless that make me want to stare and look away at the same time. Mostly men, they are legless, or have no arms, or are blind because of landmines. Children lead them as they beg. Everywhere you go there is begging. Naked little children beg. Women with babies hold out their palms and plead. "Yum, yum," they beseech, a hand on their mouth. Disfigured men and young boys try their best to flog postcards, shoe shines, sunglasses. What you don't see are old men. They are gone now, gone to Choeung Ek and the other fields of slaughter.

There is also the other Phnom Penh - a city of riverside cafes frequented by tourists, family picnics on the quay as the stifling day draws to a close, hustling tuk-tuk drivers and aggressive vendors, a stifling and claustrophobic central market, smiling people who seem genuinely happy to welcome you to their poor country. There is commerce and tourism flourishes as foreigners come to see the Royal Palace and its Silver Pagoda, to light incense at Wat Phnom, or to watch the sunset from a longboat on the mighty Mekong River.

Siem Reap, the rapidly growing and anachronistic base camp town for Angkor Wat, again reveals the abject poverty of Cambodia. Barefoot children, some following older siblings, drift about. Women sell fruit and other goods at roadside stands and small markets. Men languish in hammocks, prostrate from the heat. And yet, amidst its dirt roads and street commerce, a bizarre assortment of glitzy four and five-star hotels proliferate along the main drag. Strange and disturbing: Disneyland Meets Las Vegas. While Cambodians struggle for subsistence survival, tourists feast on Bacchanalian buffets, shop in upscale craft outlets, and enjoy chauffeured air-conditioned cars.

Behind this eerie facade lies reality. Here is what our guide shared with us. He is self-taught, speaks three languages, and supports his twice-widowed mother on the $10 he earns daily, when he has "clients." His father, sister and brother died during the Khmer Rouge genocide. Corruption is rife in Vietnam-controlled Cambodia. No one cares, he says. Everyone exploits everyone else. Health care is virtually non-existent if you can't bribe someone to take care of you, and most kids are lucky to make it through eighth grade. Listening to him I feel ashamed and embarrassed by my affluence.

Less than a mile from the glitzy hotels there is a state-of-the-art children's hospital founded by a Swiss physician, an iconoclast whom many believe violates agreed-upon international protocols for primary health care in impoverished countries. They think this because he uses western diagnostic tools like CT scans, an outrageous expenditure some say, in countries where people don't even know enough to wash their hands. But this doctor, for all his possible eccentricities, maintains the extraordinary belief that even poor children deserve to live, and saving their fragile lives often requires the same technology that rich kids can access. He is a thorn in the side of the Ministry of Health and, he claims, esteemed organizations like UNICEF and the World Health Organization, because he treats babies with non-contagious TB when the resources needed to do that could save a lot of kids with infectious disease. It's not cost-effective, his critics argue. These kids deserve to live too, he tells the critics, experts who stay in the fancy hotels when they come to Siem Reap to advise or evaluate him. I'd like to have met the Swiss doctor.

Something is amiss in the awesome land of Angkor Wat, one of the manmade wonders of the world. These amazing and prolific Buddhist and Hindu temples, scattered over nearly 200 miles and dating back to the 12th century, are exquisite, mysterious, and revealing. It is a privilege and a pleasure to see them, for no amount of research or documentary footage can capture their grandeur.

But why, I wonder, given today's technology and the advanced civilization we in the west take such pride in, can there not be other manmade wonders - an end to poverty, for example? An end to childhood mortality from preventable causes? An end to genocide?

Angkor Wat has much to teach us. So do Phnom Penh and Siem Reap. The Cambodian people, gentle and generous, deserve much more than gaping tourists snapping their pictures and bargaining for their souvenirs while they try, yet again, to live. May the awesome monuments of this struggling country never rise above the awful reality of its suffering. It has continued, unabated, for far too long now.

Tiennanmen Square

This is sacred space. Do you feel it sitting here,
on a balmy Sunday eve, watching dragon kites flap
tentatively as they ascend, then dip toward unseen tethers,
finally snapping their necks up, up and up, trying to be free?

This is sacred space. Do you see it sitting here,
in the eyes of the father teaching his daughter --
one and only girl child -- to ride a two-wheeler,
playing games and laughing with her, trying to be free?

This is sacred space. Do you sense it sitting here,
gazing across the wide expanse to Forbidden City,
where eunuchs and concubines served their masters silently,
never even trying to be free?

This is sacred space. Do you know it sitting here,
wondering what students slept on these very slates,
and whether a tank, red flags waving,
ran them down while they were trying to be free?

This is sacred space. Vast and barren though it is
beneath Mao's tomb, stark and solitary in the shadow
of the Great Hall of the People, cold and carefully watched.
This is sacred space, because memory resides here
where people gather to hope, maybe even to pray.
Do you feel it sitting here?
Sacred space.

I wrote this poem while at the 4th World Conference on Women, Beijing, China, 1995.

Caribbean, Central and South America

"Am I Latin? Am I American? What the hell am I?
I love my culture and I'm very proud of my culture."

AMERICA FERRERA

Dominican Whimsy

Dominican Republic

I. La Plaza, Ciudad Viejo

For five hundred years, we've sat,
people like me, *gringos*,
watching this Latino world pass by.
From the time of Christo Colon
and *las damas* until now,
we have resisted the hawkers and vendors,
pitied the one-legged man selling straw hats,
marveled at *muchachas* with swaying hips
oggled by *los hombres machismo*,
drifted into church of a Sunday
to listen to children's voices
glorify the *Spirito Sancto*,
bought a piece of larimar, or amber,
eaten *arroz con fritatas*, and drunk dark rum.
Now, at a café near the cathedral,
– the first in the Americas, –
I join the procession,
and in time-honored tradition,
ever *la turista*,
I lift my glass
and toast *la vida buena*.

II. Ballad for Barahona

In the tiniest of villages by the sea,
Live a group of friends, in poverty.
They don't have much, and their needs are many,
But their hearts are full and their gifts plenty.

In the tiniest of houses in this pueblo,
Live four people, and that may grow.
But Israel, Avia, and their children know,
There is much to savor when life is slow.

I helped them build a house one day,
Stopping only to eat, and play.
Lifting cinderblocks and earth and clay,
Their smiles and love were sufficient pay.

They gave to me their souls and hearts,
And 'though we live light-years apart,
We both knew friendship's early start,
And spoke with two tongues, but one heart.

So years from now, when I recall,
The tiniest house of them all,
In that tiny village by the sea,
I'll remember what they gave to me –

Hands and hearts full of grace,
Smiles of hope in their face,
And a lesson or two of love and care:
The simplest of gifts one can share.

And this little thing above the rest,
The lesson that we should all love best,
Know that from the tiniest hearths,
Often come the grandest hearts.

I wrote this poem while doing a Habitat for Humanity build.

III. House in Haina

Meringue music, laughter and light,
And the smell of *cosida* cooking.
Children running in and out,
While *El Presidente* is handed 'round
to cool the humid night.
Street sounds and friends calling "Mi Amor!"
A manicure, and more.
Meringue music, laughter and light,
And a smiling *mujer,* robust and round,
abuela to us all.

IV. Cemetario at Cabarete

Buried in the pouring rain,
Dust to dust are you again,
Years hence when skies weep with pain,
Who will even know your name?

Tended 'neath the crying sky,
Who in slumber next you doth lie?
Here comes a man with garland wreath,
What abiding love you did bequeath!

In this tiny place of Milady Perez,
And the long-gone Familia Martinez,
Stories are silenced, memories saved,
Sanctified beneath the grave.

Duerme bien, mi amigos,
Y por la vida, Gracias Dios.

V. Waves on A White Beach

Not this wave, nor that nor that,
Will crash again upon this shore.
What's more,
unnamed, and required,
They will relinquish power,
In the merest fraction of an hour.

Yet, though brief their froth and fury,
How absolute their gleaming glory!
With rolling, roiling glances,
Like high-stepping girls at dances,
Do they not convey – in their own white-crested way –
That spirited living may be worth the briefest day?

We visited the Dominican Republic several times to visit our friend and family caregiver, Violeta, who came to us for a year and stayed for twenty. No one could make a ros con pollo like she could. I found this pencil cup in a shop in Santo Domingo.

The Panama Canal

Panama

The only thing I will say about Panama is this:
　It is the hottest and most humid place I've ever been (outside of Chiang Mai, Thailand.) Your clothes sweat without you and it is impossible to have fabric furnishings in your house unless it is perpetually air-conditioned to the max.
　It is full of men who look like Sidney Greenstreet in a 1940s film noir. Everyone else is a happy mélange of color and complexion.
　The ceviche is wonderful.
　The Panama Canal is interesting to see – once.

I visited Panama on my honeymoon because my husband had business there. Every day a diplomatic wife took me on the canal tour. By the end of our visit I could give the tour myself.

Guatemala Revisited

Twenty-seven years had passed since I'd first gone to Guatemala. In 1972, on my honeymoon, I'd gazed upon Lake Attitlan, Antigua, and Chichicastenango, in "the Land of Eternal Spring." In Antigua, we'd met the artist Norman Rockwell and his wife Molly, and shared drinks with them at the hotel lounge. It was as though he'd stepped out of one of his paintings, his white wavy hair and cravat exactly as he appeared in his pictures. "He misses his studio," Molly whispered to me. We're leaving early." A few years later, he was dead.

On this second visit I was not with my husband, but with my filmmaker daughter. We had come back to Attilan, "the world's most beautiful lake," together, to learn and record the stories of Mayan women, keepers of the culture in both traditional and modern ways. In the intervening years, everything and nothing had changed.

Rachel had arrived two weeks before me. By the time her smiling face greeted me at the airport in Guatemala City, she was fluent in Spanish (in the present tense, at least) and fully familiar with the culture. On the three-hour drive to Panajachel, our base, she filled me in.

The "gringa" who'd arranged her liaison with a Mayan counterpart - a young woman trying to establish a Mayan communication center - was one of the many dissipated Americans who hide their past in the tropical paradise of the lake. But Emiliana, the Mayan woman with whom Rachel had been paired to make a documentary video, was extraordinary. Her family had worked with Rigoberta Menchu to organize *campesinos* during the civil war. They had lost a son, a daughter, and an uncle to the liberation movement. Panajachel was a tourist enclave but Solola, where they worked was the real thing. Our host family, headed by Don Pedro, was wonderful. All of this news was evident upon our arrival.

Don Pedro, proud owner of the new *Casa Suena Real,* greeted us with *"Hola!"* and a bashful smile. Then he carried my bags up to our room, a sparse but clean and pleasant whitewashed space with two beds, a dresser and a chair. Atop the dresser on a red woven tapestry were two bottles of spring water, two glasses, and an alarm clock. In the bathroom, shampoo sachets and small soaps rested on clean towels. I unpacked and returned downstairs to pay my respects to Dona Caterina and the children.

"Hola, Raquel, que tal?" they smiled shyly to Rachel.

"Hola, Raquel!" the parrot squawked.

"Hola, Pedro, Myra, Caterina!" Rachel replied.

Dona Caterina held plump, somber Juan in her arms. The *abuela,* Don Pedro's mother, smiled from the kitchen sink. Caterina offered us tea, and we sat at the kitchen table getting acquainted. My high school Spanish returned while Rachel filled in the blanks. They were a lovely family with whom we spent many happy moments in the calm of their mornings and evenings.

On my first morning, we took the "chicken bus," one of the reconstituted school buses that ferry people from town to town around the lake, to Solola. Rachel assured me that the buses were safe but I had my doubts as ours lumbered up the switchback mountain road. In Solola, we made our way through the crowded *mercado* taking place in the plaza, arriving at the office in time to greet Rachel's gringa and her "landlord," Juan, an ecologist who single-handedly worked to save Lake Attitlan from disastrous pollution. Juan was an extraordinary young man: By the age of 12 he had climbed every volcano in Guatemala. At 19 he narrowly escaped a massacre by fleeing over the mountains.

When I finally met Emiliana and her sister Elena, I could see at once why Rachel was so fond of them. Funny, bright, energetic, political, they were women trying to make a difference through modern technology. Emiliana had founded Centro IXIM de Communicacion Maya, an indigenous organization for the production of videos. (Ixim is the K'iche word for corn, source of life.) Her goal was to open up communication opportunities for the indigenous peoples to tell their own stories. "For too long," Emiliana said, "we have been treated as objects, but never as the subjects of our own stories."

The three generations of Mayan women weavers we met and filmed in Santa Caterina were women preserving their culture in traditional ways. Martina was the *abuela*. She wove in natural colors only, remembering her own mother. "When I weave in the natural colors we used when I was growing up, I remember my mama, who taught me how to weave," she said. Petrona, her daughter, was teaching her own two children to carry on the tradition through which Mayan culture lives, for the life stories of each village are embedded in the textiles the women weave.

Mayan culture teaches that to change the clothes is to change the person, thus Mayan women are fiercely dedicated to preserving their traditional dress (although few men maintain their clothing traditions). One can look at a skirt, a blouse, a cloth and know at once that it comes from Santa Caterina, for example, because of its rich blue tones, inspired by Lake Attitlan.

While the costume of all women is similar - blouse, skirt, apron, head dress - each design tells a different, rich tale, including that the culture of this land was subjected to a brutal civil war which ended only a short time ago. More than 100,000 people were killed in the years of unabated violence, and over 40,000 were still "missing." A million refugees were forced from their homes. Only at the time we were there, slowly was life returning to "normal," although it would never be the same as it was before the days of Western intervention.

Still, there was hope and high spirit in the land of the Mayans, those remarkable people who were experts in agriculture, art, and astronomy. People like Juan, Emiliana and Elena, Martina, Pedrona and her daughters were each carving out a future for Guatemala just as they strove to preserve its past. All those years ago, on my first visit, I saw the lake and the land of Guatemala and knew then that it was beautiful.

This time I met some of its people, and I knew that their country would survive.

Peruvian Weaving

A South American Journey

Departure

Oh, the trials – and occasional serendipitous surprises – of modern-day air travel. Having tried to get a UAL phone rep to correct an error on my ticket to no avail (I am Ms., not Mr., and my passport shows my middle initial G), I find I cannot board our flight from Miami to Houston due to the discrepancy. Jewel, a jewel of a Continental supervisor, escorts me to UAL to ensure a correction, and then gets us through security in time to board our flight to Continental's hub, from where we will take our flight to Rio. There, as I'm squatting on the floor outside Contintental's Presidential Club trying to pick up their WiFi signal (no obvious log-on sites in Houston airport!), a nice young man takes pity on us.

"How long is your layover?" he asks.

"Three hours."

"Would you like to be my guest in the lounge?"

"No scam?" says I, ever the jaded traveler.

"No scam," he says. "I can take in two guests and I just offer this to people who seem right," he says. It turns out he works for Continental and is simply a regular nice guy, so we get to spend three hours having free drinks and snacks while online in comfy chairs. Too bad there wasn't enough time for showers!

Rio

We arrive after a smooth overnight flight and taxi to the apartment we've rented in Copacabana. It is basic but convenient, if not as clean as we would like. Then we're off to lunch in an outdoor, seaside café followed by a stroll alongside the beach. Within minutes, a kid on a bike rips off the small gold chain around my neck bearing my mother's diamond, which I assumed was too small to notice under my shirt. He also gets my favorite "gold" earrings from Thailand. How he does all this simultaneously while riding a bike amazes me but I am pissed.

"Oh my God, he got my purse!" I scream, because I felt choked by his yank and thought he'd got my backpack handbag with all our important documents and money in it.

"My diamond! He got my diamond!" I screech when I realize what has taken place, unaware that you shouldn't scream or the miscreant might knife you. It is an effective strategy; he drops the goods and an amazingly sympathetic *abuela* (grandma) finds all three of my crown jewels. *Abrigado Dios*! (Thank God!)

Crime (and the tropical heat) are two big deterrents in Rio. The people generally couldn't be nicer or more helpful, but the *favela* (barrio) kids are a menace. And one feels sorry for them because they live in such terrible conditions of poverty. Stories abound of street kids, periodically rounded up and often murdered by the police or traffickers in human organs. Still, when they accost you, it is hard to feel sympathetic. What's even more irritating is the gaggle of tourist police who hang out in front of four and five-star hotels to give the impression of watching out for you, but when you tell them you've been ripped off, they shrug and lackadaisically tell you *"Cuidado"* - be careful. Anyway I got the goods back, hugged my angel abuela, and that was that.

Having recovered, we pick up some groceries and head for Arcos de Lapa, a 17th C. viaduct downtown under which the annual Easter Passion Play is being enacted. This narrated event, dramatized by 100 professional actors on Good Friday, re-creates Christ making his way through the Stations of the Cross. It is so well done and so moving that this old Jew wept, along with many Catholics in the crowd, as Christ, Barabas and the other guy were actually "crucified"; Mary's anguish was palpable.

On this first day we have ridden Rio's maniac buses which careen all over town, offering a great way to see the local sites. We return "home" hot and exhausted but exhilarated, full of anticipation for the next day.

Impanema, more upscale than Copa, is our first stop today. Both beaches are gorgeous but somehow different than what we had imagined, although neither of us can recall what it was we had anticipated. We are surprised that Impanema has no waterfront cafes but we meander, stopping at a bank ATM to talk with a lawyer from New York's upper west side and his Israeli girlfriend. Later we have a beer in a sidewalk cafe with a splendid couple of Brits, both in their upper 80s, who are on the Queen Mary World Cruise. We lunch al fresco at a pleasant, upscale restaurant – the food in Rio is superb, and then take coffee and ice cream at the Caffeina Café, noted for its gorgeous pastries. We stop in a nice curio shop, where we talk with the owner who has lived on Marcos Island (Fla.), agreeing that crime is Rio's only drawback and that *mujeres viejas y gordas* – old, fat women - should not wear bikinis!

In the afternoon we head for Sugar Loaf Mt. where we take two sequential cable cars to the top of two rocks (morros) for amazing views of the city and waterway landscapes; Rio is superbly situated with iconic mountains, the sea and the bay forming exquisite vistas any way you look from on high. While waiting in line to board the cable cars (which hold 70 people) we meet a nice Brazilian family, two teenage girls and their young uncle, who has just had his first child, a girl called Elena. Talking to them is a wonderful way to pass the waiting time. The views from the morros are spectacular as day gives way to illuminated evening and the city below lights up like a window at Tiffany's. Later we dine al fresco at another beachfront restaurant on Copacabana, where the seafood and wine are superb and reasonably priced. (Rio prices just about equal those in the US).

The next day we head for Christo Regentor (Christ the

Redeemer), the famous statue of Christ that looms large over the city. Despite the fact that it is entirely scaffolded for repairs, it is a don't-miss destination because of the views, so we find our way, again by bus, to the old cog tram that climbs up through lush tropical vegetation to the giant statue with outstretched arms.

Next, we make our way to the Bonde, famed trolley that travels over the Arcos de Lapa to the hilltop Bohemian neighborhood of Santa Teresa, an artist enclave that we find a bit overrated, perhaps because the rain that will become the talk of the town, has started. We catch a Metro back to Copa, where we head for the same seafood restaurant in which we ate last night.

Next day, umbrellas in hand, we catch a metro for Centro and Cinlandia, Rio's bustling downtown area, which combines skyscrapers ala New York with some of Rio's most intriguing old Portuguese architecture. We follow the walking tour to such sites as the old Reading Room, stacked with so many old books in an 18th C. dark-wood library that it seems like Trompe l'Oile. The gorgeous municipal theatre is also scaffolded for repair so we stop at a splendid Belle Epoch coffee house for lunch before heading for the Arabic market area, Saara. But there are no bargains to be had and defeated by the rain we head home, making do with ham and cheese sandwiches for dinner, assuming that tomorrow the weather will be better.

Not! The incessant heavy rain has now become the stuff of legend. It is torrential and unending. By evening we begin to worry about getting out the next day and reports start coming in that it hasn't rained like this in Brazil for 10 years and that floods are now occurring in Rio and Sao Paulo. In the morning, ripe for departure, we first learn that neither of the two elevators in our building is working, so we walk down nine flights of stairs while the poor porter schleps our bags down. Then the concierge says that the airport may be closed and that the streets are too flooded to get there anyway. Panic! It is impossible to get a reliable report about conditions so we decide not to try it, and I head for the travel agent we have been lucky enough to befriend at his agency-cum-lavanderia around the corner. His assistant eventually manages to get us rebooked on Aerolineas Argentinas to Buenos Aires the next morning and to book us into a good hotel nearby at reasonable rates. We drag our bags down the wet, rainy street, re-ensconce, and decide that as it looks brighter, we will head back to Impanema. By the time we get there on the microbus (a kind of local jitney), the rain is a pelting wall of water. We duck under awnings, then into a café but there is no waiting it out, so we catch a micro back to Copa, and soaked to the bone, get into our PJs to wait it out. We venture out later to our local open air restaurant and hope for the best in the morning. We've already lost a day in Buenos Aires!

The next morning the sky is somewhat more promising and despite unsourced warnings that the domestic airport is closed and we may not make it to the international airport, we catch a cab who delivers us without problem; two hours later we are in the air headed for Argentina.

Our general impressions of Rio include these: The food and wine are excellent! People are very kind but the high crime rate does tend to put a pall on things as we are continually worried about our money and passports. It is hotter than hell with high humidity but this is apparently being exacerbated by the looming rains. There is enormous respect for elders – everyone offers us their seats on buses and asks if they can help us with directions. One thing I'm impressed by is that the dads carry the babies and generally seem to do a great deal of excellent parenting! Perhaps this is because Mamacita has all the responsibility at home? (Later Alex explains that the man always carries the heavy load!) And there is an enormous amount of graffiti art everywhere. Some of it is quite good and a pleasure to see but mostly it is random "signing" that detracts from the urban landscape. The traffic is not too alarming but the careening buses are a bit scary. And then there is all the amazing topography and the ubiquitous vistas of sea, bay, monolithic rocks, and tropical foliage. Altogether a city to be recommended but not one we feel compelled to repeat. And so, on to Buenos Aires!

B.A. and an Estancia

Having made it out on the morning flight, we arrive in B.A. in the early afternoon and are immediately taken by its clean cosmopolitan atmosphere, quiet energy, and sophisticated people. Young women dress with the casual flair of their Parisian counterparts and the *jubliados* (elderly), both women and men, are old-world stately, with their scarves and well-trimmed moustaches respectively. No wonder B.A. is called the Paris of South America!

Our apartment in the Recoleta section of this large city is a small gem. Well-equipped, clean, and with an 8th floor balcony view of our temporary neighborhood, it is ideal. Recoleta is a rather fashionable neighborhood full of cafes, restaurants, bakeries, shops, and all manner of pleasant urban life. We meet our landlord, Max, then head out for medialunas (teatime croissant sandwiches) and our breakfast groceries. Later we make for one of the city's best parillas (steak houses), Mirador, a true B.A. experience. The place is jam-packed with aficionados at 10 p.m. We order sirloin tip steaks (served with nothing else on the plate) and Malbec wine, both of which melt in our mouths like butter! No wonder Argentineans take such pride in their beef.

Our first day of sightseeing is packed as we walk our feet off seeing many of the main sights. We start with Cemetario Recoleta, a small city in itself, where everyone who is anyone in Argentine history, including Evita, has a monument, many of them quite spectacular. One of the most moving is of a young woman who was inadvertently buried alive! Evita's family tomb is quite unremarkable and would go unnoticed if not for the flowers laid daily by devotees. From there we head downtown to walk Florida Avenue, noted for many of its exquisite buildings as well as for shopping. One of the most notable buildings is the Burger King, originally a private mansion. It is sheer travesty to see the exquisite upper floors looking down upon Whoppers, fries and cokes! That takes us to Plaza de Mayo and Casa Rosa, the old presidential palace from where Evita made her famous speech in which she claimed to be (or represent) all the people of Argentina. Luckily it is Thursday so at 3:30 we see the Madres de Plaza de Mayo as they march in remembrance of their disappeared children and grandchildren during the years of "the dirty war." It is extremely moving to hear the names of all the disappeared read out as the women, many with white bandanas on their heads, march behind their banners. Afterwards we head to the 19th C. Café Tortoni, famous for its décor and tango lessons, and from there, crossing Ave. 9th de Julio – said to be the widest boulevard in the world – we make our way to Congresso, the seat of government inspired architecturally by the US capital, the Brandenburg Gates and more. Exhausted by our nearly six hours of walking, we crawl home for tea and pastry and then pick up lovely carry-out food for dinner.

The next day we visit the area called San Telmo – famous for its antique stores – where we have lunch at another 19th C. café, El Federal. This area, once home to the city's upper echelon until an 1870 outbreak of yellow fever, reminds us of Brooklyn. (Some say it reminds them of old Havana and we can see why). It is home to many artists and writers and while it is rapidly becoming gentrified it still has a wonderful quality of real life in B.A. (There are many Bohemian men here with long hair who bear a striking resemblance to Jesus!) As we make our way to the bus for La Boca, I am – unbelievably – relieved yet again of a piece of jewelry: A kid comes out of nowhere and rips off my favorite $8 bracelet, which I assumed was safe to wear here. *No lo credo*! I don't believe it. But once again, nothing valuable is lost, Gracias Dio.

La Boca is a must see for its colorful street and neighborhood called Caminato, comprised of gaily painted corregated slum houses near the old docks. (It would make a great set for Sesame

Street!) This area was originally a Little Italy as immigrants landed and settled in. Its bold primary colors are a visual treat but sadly, it is now overrun by schlocky souvenir shops, faux-tango dancers, pushy vendors, and a few good artists. We head home for tea and cookies, a rest and a shower before going to dinner and a tango performance – which is, in a word, fabulous! How the dancers don't fall or trip each other up is nothing short of miraculous. For a reasonable price, we enjoy a 3-course meal (steak, of course) with another splendid bottle of Malbec, then a terrific show in which four couples perform the amazingly sensual and difficult dance of Argentina, a sexy woman with long black hair sings mournful songs, and a guy who fancies himself the late Gardel (most noted of tango singers) serenades while strutting around the stage like a Spanish cockerel or a Mafioso enraptured by his own good voice. The eight musicians are a treat as well. Happy but tired, we return to the apartment and fall into bed. In the morning we are off to La Estancia Portena in San Antonio d'Areco.

La Estancia, which we reach via deluxe bus and a short taxi ride (2+ hours from B.A.) is pure Isabel Allende (even though she is Chilean). The hacienda of Argentine writer Ricardo Guiraldos (1888-1927) is set in the vast expanse of Las Palmas, a region known for its open plains, romantic gauchos (cowboys), and hospitable estancias (gentlemen's farms/ranches). This estancia is exactly what we hoped for; it is a real working farm without pretention in a gorgeous rural setting where the warmth of the owners is immediate. Catalina greets us with a broad smile and her adorable one-year old *chico* on her slender hip. Her husband is as charming, attractive and welcoming as she is and he shows us to our room in their home. It is large, white-washed, and tastefully furnished with dark-wood antiques. A brick fireplace faces the double bed; on the mantel are assorted antiques. The walls are decorated with paintings of horses. A large modernized bathroom is off to one side and large windows look upon a pasture in which horses graze peacefully. We have arrived just in time for lunch al fresco as gauchos cook the famous Argentine barbeque, asado. We sit at a large table with a delightful Argentine family, the Basques, comprised of a charming abuelo and abuela, three of their four daughters, one son-in-law, and four pre-teen grandchildren. They are worldly and welcoming and all speak impeccable English. The food is plentiful, comprised of many salads, bread, wine, and an assortment of barbequed meats ranging from beef and pork to sausages. This feast, enhanced enormously by the company of the Basques, is followed by ice cream, coffee, and a wonderful serenade by Francisco, a singing gaucho. Afterward there is only one thing to do: Siesta. Waking refreshed, we take tea and cake in the garden, then rest again till we are summoned to dinner in the dining room at 8:30.

We dine with the Basques (one daughter and granddaughter have returned to B.A.) who have become our new best friends. We are the only guests for the night so we are ten at the table and conversation is lively, ranging from opera to politics to travel tales. (One Basque sister works in Vietnam; another lives in Malaysia.) Our meal – a delicious first course of rolled bread filled with ingredients flavorful but challenging to identify, followed by steak and vegetables, is accompanied by the now regular Malbec. Dessert is special. I have written ahead to tell Catalina that we are celebrating our 38th anniversary and Arnold is having his 75th birthday. Unbeknown to me at the time, it is also Sra. Basques 73rd birthday. A large cake – the best I have ever eaten in my life because of the dulce de leche con chocolate that fills the center – is presented to Arnold among cheers and singing. He and the Senora blow out the candles together amidst much clapping by the entire staff. We take copious pictures and I give Sra. B the big candle I brought from the US that says "Ageless". Then champagne is served in honor of our anniversary. Arnold is absolutely surprised and delighted: "The best birthday ever!" It is indeed a memorable party.

The next morning we have breakfast with the Basques and exchange business cards before bidding them a fond goodbye.

Then, after visiting the grounds and the house where the famous author lived and wrote (which the Basques have been occupying) we set out with Francisco for an hour of horseback riding around the estancia. On our return, we buy a few gift items in the small gift shop, eat empanadas, shower and change, and say our goodbyes to our host family. A taxi takes us into the charming town of San Antonio, but it is closed for Sunday so we catch an earlier bus back to B.A. A memorable estancia adventure!

These tapestries were made in a small village in Peru – the only place, we were told, where these amazing three-dimensional designs are woven.

The photo of Pablo Neruda and Salvador Allende was given to me by Lallie, a friend I made in Chile.

Galapagos Waters

Old George, who lived well past 100.

Every evening we gather in the common room,
Our catamaran rocking gently on Pacific waters,
Waiting for our guide's now familiar question:
"What was your favorite experience today?"

"Swimming with the sea turtles!" someone says.
"The stingray in the mango groves!"
"The blue-footed booby mating dance!"
"The purple starfish! Definitely that!"

I tell bold-faced lies, citing boobies or baby sea lions,
When really, it is the emerald-blue water I love best,
Water so clear you can look to the bottom of the sea
And find lavish wonders there with the naked eye.

What I love best is looking out upon the water
From an island's edge or the peak of a cliff,
Wondering what lies beyond or beneath vast, cool swells
Lapping endlessly, timelessly, against the shore.

Shimmering, sun-dappled turquoise, like cracks in a
Calving glacier, call up aquamarine childhood memories,
Beckoning me now toward daydreams and adult wishes,
While at night, water-sounds soothe me to contented sleep.

Is it blasphemy to call a swelling, soothing sea
My favorite thing when all about this tropical paradise
Sea mammals, birds, and impossibly beautiful flora and fauna
Prevail? I think not when it offers all the rest nothing less than life.

Street music and dancing in Old Havana

Cuba

A Journey Back in Time and Toward the Future

We're off to a good start. At the airport in Ft. Lauderdale there are no visa issues and we are upgraded by Jet Blue to "Extra Leg Room" for the one-hour flight to Santa Clara.

Upon arrival, we take a taxi to our first Casa Particulares, Cuba's version of Bed-n-Breakfast (marketed to the cognoscenti as Air B'n'B). It is an old, large house filled with "antiques" that are mostly collected junk – refrigerators, 1950s TVs, 1930s radios, family photos, dark paintings, ornate tables and tufted chairs, chandeliers, and glass-doored cabinets full of assorted chachkas. We're served a welcoming beer and shown to our room, which is straight out of an Isabelle Allende novel: Two big beds with iron bedframes covered with dark bedspreads, an old wooden chest of drawers, shuttered windows overlooking the densely gardened open-air dining area, dim lights, and a sink that doesn't work. In the bathroom, there is a toilet, a working sink, a shower and a drain from which something with large tentacles tries to escape while I am sitting on the john. I quickly slam the waste basket over the drain and hope the whatever sewer monster lies beneath it lacks the strength to push through.

On the recommendation of the casa manager we head to the Ay Mama café a block away, known for its black Cuban music tradition, for a lunch of "tapas" (tuna dip) and croquettes.

From there we go to the outdoor exhibit commemorating an important event in the Cuban Revolution. The *Monumento a la Toma del Tren Blindado* is where Che and a group of rebels, against all odds, successfully blew up an armored train carrying more than 400 of dictator Batista's soldiers in 1958. The bulldozer that tore up the tracks to stop the train is on view but the most impressive thing about the site are the large monolithic pieces of concrete sculpted to shoot upward from the wreck, representing the blast.

Next we take a horse-drawn carriage through the city to the Place de la Revolution where a larger than life, impressive statue of Che reaches majestically up to the sky. (When the clouds move it looks like Che himself is moving forward.) Inscribed on the base of the stature are the words *"Hasta La Victoria Siempre,"* (Ever onward to victory). We will see those words all over Cuba in the weeks to come.

We return to the casa where we have Cuba Libres on the roof of the house across the street that is also owned by our host and which is the better house in which to stay, we realize, having been updated, freed of clutter, redecorated, and freshly painted. Then we have dinner in our gardened restaurant where Arnold's lobster in red sauce is quite inviting while my meat stew marinated in red wine is underwhelming. Nevermind, the flan is great and so is the live Spanish music. After dinner, we walk to the Central Plaza alive with crowds, music, and strolling lovers and families. Its statues are impressive, especially the one of Jose Marti, Cuba's original liberator, and the curious Boy with the Boot.

The next day after breakfast we take a taxi to the bus station. Arnold has a reserved seat for the morning "luxury" bus to Havana; I am on the late afternoon bus, but we hope I can board with him. The bus is two hours late (at least), the large crowds are restless, and there is no guarantee that we will both get on the bus. We decide to take a private group taxi (a van) to Havana (illegal but popular), losing the price of our bus seats, and we join three Chinese students who have made the same decision. Along the way to Havana, the road is virtually free of other vehicles. The landscape is uninteresting. Occasionally men selling strings of garlic and large chunks of cheese dot the road. (Later, our driver

Santana tells us this is illegal. When they see police, he says, they throw the garlic and cheese into the woods. Once the police are gone, they retrieve their wares, wipe off the cheese, and hit the road again.)

Reaching Havana, we are dropped off at Park Centrale where we take a cab to our Casa on Ave. de la Presidentes in the Vedado (modern, quieter) section of the city. On the 5th floor of an apartment building, we are greeted by Marta, an OB/GYN who no longer practices because she makes a lot more money owning a popular casa, and by Daniel and Fabio, two delightful young men who manage the elegant property. Our room is lovely, as is the common sitting area; we feel like we are with family in their well-appointed Cuban home. Marta also owns the 11th floor, where breakfast is served and a bar is open in the evenings. From the terrace, we have a wonderful view of the Malecon with breakfast, the best meal of the day throughout Cuba, always consisting of fresh tropical fruit, delicious eggs, the ubiquitous ham and cheese, delicious Cuban bread and strong coffee with milk (black tea for my British husband.)

We have dinner a block away at Ilio, a lovely small restaurant, and turn in early, tired from our long drive from Santa Clara in a not-so air-conditioned van. We are glad for the modern accommodation where we'll be staying for five nights, and the lovely people who run it.

In the morning, we take a 4-hour tour of *Havana Viejo* with Daniel. It's well worth the cost and time. Daniel is a treasure trove of information as we walk the streets of the old city that link the four main plazas. We start at the Floridita, Hemingway's favorite watering hole on Calle Obisbo, old town's main thoroughfare. A statute of the great writer who so loved Cuba sits on his seat in the left corner of the bar and of course tourists, including Arnold, line up to have their mug shot with him.

The four squares that are must-sees in Old Havana are Plaza de Armas, Plaza Vieja, Plaza de San Francisco de Asis, and Plaza de la Catedral, (although not necessarily in that order.) Each has their own unique character and visual delights. Cafes, restaurants, shops, galleries, bars, historic venues, and serendipitous treats abound, like the costumed rhumba dancers we saw in front of the Hotel Ambos Mundos, where Hemingway rented a room with a view and wrote some of his most famous works. (The room is now a docented museum and it's definitely worth a stop.)

Plaza de Armas is the city's oldest square, dating back to the early 1520s. It is the site of a daily secondhand book market reminiscent of Paris's left bank and it hosts a statue of Carlos Manuel de Cespedes who set Cuba on the road to independence in 1868. The 5-star Palacio/Hotel Santa Isabel, where Hollywood's finest like to stay, is also on this square.

Plaza Viejo, quite eclectic in its architecture began as, an open-air market and site of military exercises. Today it offers places to eat and imbibe, a nice fountain and some of Havana's prettiest stained glass windows.

The Plaza de San Francisco de Asis, which faces the harbor and is therefore near the old forts that protected the city, was restored in the late 1990s but its cobblestone streets remain as does its Fountain of the Lions. It also hosts a statue of El Caballero de Paris, a well-known street person who roamed Havana during the 1950s dispersing philosophical thoughts to anyone who would listen. Nearby the cruise terminals that line the harbor are a few seafood restaurants, and further on is the huge city craft market, where vendors urge you into the stalls selling identical cheap souvenirs.

Plaza de la Catedral (yes, spelled that way) showcases "architectural jewels from every era" as the Lonely Planet guidebook claims. It is a uniform square with lots of Cuban baroque architecture, Palacios, and of course the cathedral itself. The remains of Christopher Columbus rested her for some time until they were moved to Spain's Seville Cathedral in 1898. On the cathedral walls are copies of works by Murillo and Rubens and the fresco above the alter is said to be inspired by the work of Michelangelo.

Some of the other highlights of our walk through old Havana included visiting an old apothecary, a chocolate factory, a perfumery, and the Buena Vista Social Club, which milks tourists for lots of money given that none of the performers are original. (We declined the $30/pp charge which included 2 drinks.) We also enjoyed a spaghetti lunch in one of the plazas, Italian food being ubiquitous in Cuba.

That evening, tired from our excursions, we went to another very good restaurant a block away from our Casa, Mediteraneo, where we had one of only a few excellent meals while in Cuba and helped a family celebrate the birthday of their 14-year old son. (We revisited this restaurant twice more because they make the best pizza we've ever tasted!)

The next day we took a Cooperativo – one of Havana's vintage 1950s cars used as communal taxis – to Park Centrale, where we shared a wonderful Cuban sandwich for breakfast at the 4-star Grand Hotel. (A little history of the Cuban sandwich, according to our 2nd week's driver, Santana: Allegedly a guy used to collect the scraps of ham, cheese and pork left on people's plates in a pre-revolution Cuban restaurant. He put them between two slices of good Cuban bread, toasted them in the oven, and served them as a Cuban specialty!)

From there we visited the Hotel Inglaterra, Havana's oldest hotel, opened in 1856. The popular outdoor bar El Louvre is still inviting, as is the Moorish interior décor of the hotel. It was here that Jose Marti made his famous speech advocating Cuban independence in 1879. Later, US journalists covering the Spanish-Cuban-American War stayed here.

This hotel is where I began my ritual search for Internet cards, which provide necessary numerical codes to access the weak to non-existent Internet system in Cuba. Upscale hotels have them, and Internet access, but both are reserved for guests, unless you are lucky enough to ask for one when they have just been delivered each day. Once you've secured a card or two (they are good for an hour only) you are stuck having to go to a public park where Internet access is frustratingly weak and intermittent at best.

We walked the Paseo del Prado that afternoon, a European style boulevard and the first street outside of the old city walls built from 1770 and completed almost a hundred years later. Bronze lions that guard either end of the passage reminiscent of Barcelona's Las Ramblas were added in 1928. The street is lined with notable and quite beautiful buildings in various stages of repair or disrepair but the highlight for us was meeting a group of school girls on their lunch break. They were delighted to show off the English they were learning and I talked with them (in my primitive Spanish) about the importance of women having an education because it was the gateway to independence and freedom. They agreed vigorously and I told them that when they got older they would remember me and I would be like a fairy whispering in their ear. They liked that!

These budding feminists led us to the nearby Museum of the Revolution, where I wanted to say I give them *abrazos* (hugs) but accidentally said I wanted to give them *basura* (trash)! Thankfully I was able to correct myself before they were offended!

The *Museo de la Revolucion* is housed in the former Presidential Palace built in the early 20th century. It was once the Tiffany-decorated home of dictator Rafael Batista. The chronological exhibits are a bit disappointing and quite propagandistic but of course the museum is a must-see. Unfortunately, when we were there the Pavilion Granma that houses the boat that carried Castro and 81 other revolutionaries from Mexico to Cuba in 1956 was closed for renovation, but we caught a small glimpse of the yacht through the guarded glass enclosure where it resides.

After that we visited the Belles Artes des Cuba museum (adjacent to the Belles Art museum which houses art from all over the world.) The collection was interestingly dark, surrealist, and reflective of Latin America' famous magical thinking. The darkness of the paintings (in both mood and color tones) was likely due to Cuba's very turbulent history, as well as the influence of such painters as Picasso. "Great place to visit but I wouldn't want to live there" kind of art!

Our next stop for the day, back at Park Centrale, was the opulently beautiful National Theater, one of the most breathtaking buildings I've seen anywhere. Like some cathedrals and other stunning edifices, it seems to have been carved out of the earth rather than built upon it, like a giant white sand castle. We would have been thrilled just to see the interior, as there were no performances all week in preparation for a concert by Placido Domingo that Saturday (canceled due to Castro's death), and I nearly talked my way in as a journalist, but at the final door to which we'd been sent (everyone sends you to another authority, another place, another source of information in Cuba) we were sadly turned away and told to try again. A major disappointment!

We decided to sprint over to Hemingway's hotel to see his writing room (# 511) which closed at 5 p.m.. We arrived at 4.45 only to be told that it was already closed. (It was 5 p.m. somewhere in Cuba obviously) so again, we had to drown our sorrows, which we did with tea in the outdoor 5th floor café of the Ambos Mundos Hotel before riding the famous iron-work elevator back to the lobby.

Before leaving the Park and returning to our comfortable casa, I tried to find out how to get tickets to visit the famous Partagas Cigar Factory the next day. Another runaround! (In Cuba you must be very patient and keep a sense of humor. Luckily I trained for that, not altogether successfully, while living in Thailand.) A desk clerk in the Grand Hotel sent me upstairs, where I was sent downstairs, where I was sent to the Annex across the street, where I was told the Partagas was closed and had been for four years (not true) and where somehow I finally got the correct information, and tickets, from a tour agency in the hotel!

A challenging and tiring day, but talking with the drivers of the vintage Chevys parked ostentatiously on one side of the park that beckon foreigners with 1950s fantasies, made up for it. We made a promise we had no plan to honor that we'd be back the next day for a sunset ride along the Malecon, which we drove past at the end of every day in an ordinary taxi or Cooperativo! Back home, we joked with Daniel and Fabio, relaxed with a drink, and went to Mediterraneo for a pizza before crashing into the casa's crisp sheets.

Our next day began with a visit to the cigar factory, where 600 workers labor on three floors producing 150 cigars per person every day. At the end of each day 2000 labels have been placed on those cigars, ready for sale and shipping. The factory is an amazing kind of 19th century benevolent sweat shop. A dining hall provides meals on the second floor, and while we were there a raise in wages for 2017 was announced, which prompted the beating of many happy hands on wooden work stations. For the uneducated, it's a Cuban worker's dream, if not exactly paradise, and many workers and family members have labored there for years. They work for eight hours a day, five days a week, for a salary ranging from 30 to 70 dollars a month, depending on seniority. (That is the same salary a doctor can expect, which is why many of them drive cabs, work in tourism, or try to leave the country, at least temporarily.)

From there we took a bicycle rickshaw to the Plaza de Armas, a journey so arduous that it's a miracle our driver, who had to bicycle two adults up hills and across town, didn't expire in the process. After a delicious cappuccino at O'Reilly's Café (the original O'Reilly having been a plantation owner in the old days), we made another attempt to see Hemingway's writing room at the hotel and this time we were successful. It was worth a second try. There we learned that Hemingway refused to fly to Norway to receive his Nobel prize (because he had already survived two plane crashes in Africa), causing a Norwegian notary to fly to him. We also learned that he donated the gold medal to a church in Santiago (which we later visited) and the prize money to help lepers in Cuba.

After our visit, we enjoyed roaming the streets of old Havana once again, talking to everyone we encountered, taking pictures of small school children napping or clearing up from lunch, their school windows being street level and wide open. (We took lots of pictures of Cuban children and adults. They liked that. Cubans are universally, in our experience, extremely friendly, kind and eager to engage with Americans. They gave us many happy memories and helped us understand their culture and history in a way that books and government scripts can't.)

Our next venue was Hemingway's Cuban home, *Finca la Vigia* ("farm outlook"), located about nine miles out of Havana in a town called San Francisco de Paula. (By the way, photos of Hemingway are as prolific as those of Che and Castro in Havana; he was another favored son, respected for his simple lifestyle and great writing.) The six-toed cats were really here, not in Key West, and so were the dogs Hemingway loved. Four of his favorites' tombstones adorn the boathouse grounds near the swimming pool. The house itself, which Hemingway and his then-wife Martha Gelhorn, first rented in 1939 before buying it a year later, is classic Hemingway: masculine, lined with books, laden with the heads of animals he's shot in Africa peering down at everyone who worked, ate or slept in its rooms. His typewriter is there, as is his boat, Pilar, which is near the pool in which Ava Gardner allegedly swam nude. When Hemmingway left his beloved Cuba in 1960 to return to the US, he and his then-wife Mary left the house and its contents to "the Cuban people." The great writer left Cuba because had he not, he wouldn't have been allowed back in the US, ever. It is striking to me that only a year later, he killed himself.

On the way home from Finca la Vigia we stopped at the famous National Hotel and the old Havana Hilton, both in Vedado, and both having their own fascinating histories.

The National, built in 1930 as a replica of the Breakers Hotel in Palm Beach, Fla., has an exquisite garden bar, restaurant and grounds overlooking the Malecon. It's art deco décor and location make it one of Havana's architectural emblems. But it also is the setting for important historical events. In 1933, when Fulgencio Bastista toppled the Machado regime, 300 army officers took refuge here hoping to be protected by the US ambassador Sumner Wells, who lived there. He abandoned them and Batista's troops fired on the hotel killing and injuring several soldiers; the next day more were executed. In 1946 the National again made headlines when US mobsters Meyer Lansky and Lucky Luciano used it to host the largest ever meeting of North America's Mafia, under the guise of attending a Frank Sinatra concert!

The Hilton, now known as the Hotel Habana Libre, was commandeered by Castro's revolutionaries in 1959. Fidel ruled from there for a time in a luxury suite on the 24th floor. Today it's rather run-down but worth a visit to see the Venetian tile mural on the front of the edifice as well as the ceramic work of art on the second floor, *Carro de la Revolucion,* by artist Alfredo Sosa Bravo.

Our day ends with a walk back to the hotel, another great conversation with Fabio, Daniel and Marta, and dinner at a seafood restaurant on the Malecon (where we meet a lovely Norwegian couple and their baby son).

On the day before we are to leave Havana we visit the Dance Museum just near our casa. It is small and delightful and features only one dancer, Cuba's amazing Alicia Alonso, famous for her portrayals of leading roles in classical and Romantic ballet. Best known for her interpretation of the ballet Giselle and for her sensual, tragic Carmen, she began experiencing eye problems as a young woman that left her blind. She then choreographed in her head while continuing to dance, even into her 70s.

After the museum, we catch a cab to the *Plaza de Revolucion*, a Russian-looking vast square surrounded by dull government buildings most notable for their mural sculptures of Che (*Hasta la Victoria Siempre* emblazoned again) and another heroic guerilla,

Camilo Cienfuegos (often mistaken for Castro or Jose Marti.) Its words read *"Vas Bien Fidel"* (You're going well, Fidel.) There is also a monument to Jose Marti, Havana's tallest structure. Little do we know that a day after our departure Castro will lie in state at this very place. For lunch, we return to pizza, having tired of ham and cheese sandwiches, then check out the famous Coppelia ice cream venue where lines are ever present for the flavor of the day. (Tourists are directed to a special section; we decline).

The next morning, we awake to the news of Castro's death and watch from the 11th floor balcony as students from the nearby University of Havana march up the Ave. de la Presidentes chanting "F-I-D-E-L!" When Santana arrives, we bid fond farewell to Fabio, Daniel and Marta with copious abrazos, and head for our next stop, Cienfuegos.

Cienfuegos, a three-hour drive from Havana, is known as Cuba's *Perla del Sur* (Pearl of the South). Situated around a beautiful bay it is among the many places in Cuba that have been designated a UNESCO site. It has two distinct parts, the central zone with its inviting Parque Marti, and Punta Gorda, a slender piece of land extending into the bay. Our casa there was a small house situated on the water and host Gertrudis and her husband couldn't have been more welcoming. The small terrace at the back of the house overlooking the water served as a dining room and the dinner meal Gertrudis served us there – fresh red snapper with salad, vegetables, rice and flan – was one of the best we had in all of Cuba.

Upon our arrival in Cienfuegos, Santana, well-known and much loved by all the drivers in Cuba, manages to find a small store where we can buy a bottle of rum. This is important because there is a nine-day mourning period for the late Castro underway and it includes, along with no theater, music, dance or museum openings, no alcohol! (This situation compromised our second week in Cuba dramatically but on the other hand it was an amazing time to be there.)

At our Casa we meet an American woman who works in government in Washington, DC. She is so depressed by Trump's election she's fled to Cuba for five days. We also meet a lovely young French couple and their two-year old son Flavian. We dine that night with them in a nearby tourist restaurant noted for barbeque. The four-course fixed price meal was a nice, if pricey, change, but not what you'd expect barbeque to be (although the meat was cooked over a fire, it was dry and somewhat tasteless).

In the one full day we had in Cienfuegos, which joined the revolution when officers at the local navy base revolted in 1957, we went first to the Parque Jose Marti, a serene square with two nice cafes on its rim. We chose the larger one with its red-and-white striped awnings, to have our lunch – always a ham and cheese sandwich, unless you get lucky and there is pasta or pizza with ham, cheese or small shrimp – and a virgin Pina Colada. We visited the Teatro Tomas Terry, a grand reminder of similar buildings of the late 19th century, where in its heyday Enrico Caruso and Anna Pavlova performed. (Terry was a Venezuelan industrialist.) There was the cathedral, of course, which has French stained-glass windows and Chinese writing on its columns. As it happened to be Sunday, we were able to hear the choir singing, exempted from the music ban it seems. (A note on religion in Cuba: Castro forbid it and even banned Santa Claus – until Pope John Paul's visit in 1998. Now Catholics worship openly.) Sadly, the Provincial Museum and Palacio de Gobierno were closed. We did, however, visit a house where the national religious group known as Santeria resides in the outlying community of Palmira. Santeria is practiced by black Cubans whose heritage is the Yoruba tribe of Nigeria. It is a complex religion derived from Cuba's slave days and practiced by an estimated three million Cubans; it combines elements of Christianity and African Voo Doo and its new initiates are recognizable by their totally white garb during the first year of their conversion.

In the afternoon, we visited Lago Laguna, a lake famous for its flamingos and other birds. Rowed across the large lake surrounded by mangrove greenery by a big man in a small rowboat, we spotted herons, ibis, and other birdlife, and enjoyed three groups of flamingos, one of which took flight like a giant pink ribbon stretched across the sky.

Our next stop was Trinidad, a charming town known for the sound of clip-clopping horses on cobblestone streets. A former Spanish colonial settlement, it is little changed from its booming 19th century days and its small plaza is one of the nicest in the country.

Unfortunately, the Casa we'd booked was terrible so Santana, who seemed to know everyone everywhere, made a quick call to a friend who advised us of another, better Casa on the main street, making everything walkable. It had a pleasant enough room and bath with its own large terrace and became our home for two nights.

Trinidad's Plaza Mejor situated in the *casco historico* (old town), is also a UNESCO site. Its museums were closed to the public but we watched as long lines of people, including school children, waited patiently to enter the lobbies in order to sign condolences for Castro. It was sad not to be able to see the interior of some of the city's major sights, including the Museo Historica Municipal and other museums, but we consoled ourselves with lunch in a lovely outdoor café (near other restaurants and shops) which served a huge shrimp cocktail followed by spaghetti and camerones (small shrimp). It was such a big meal we had no supper that night.

One place that was open was the famed tower adjacent to the history museum, a building that began as a mansion. The view from the top of the tower is legendary so we went there after lunch. The tower requires a steep set of staircases, the final ones being narrow, winding and wooden. I couldn't make it all the way to the open balcony but Arnold did! En route to the top, each floor had a gift shop and my view from the open windows sufficed.

Back on the main street near our Casa, we stopped for tea at a pleasant café called Dulcinea. Then we discovered Cecelia's Juice Bar where we were able to buy fresh squeezed fruit juice to add to our dwindling stash of rum!

Six miles south of the city is Playa Ancon, the south coast's best beach. We spent our second day resting there on shaded chaise lounges, looking out at the beautiful long crescent of warm water and beige sand. (Lunch – yes, ham and cheese sandwiches and virgin Mojitos – brought to us by beach waiters.) Cuban Heaven!

Back at our Casa I notice that across the street there is a Maternity Home. These are places where pregnant women at risk (from malnutrition, complications, domestic violence) stay for weeks or months until the safe birth of their child. Because I am writing about birth practices in Cuba I am eager to talk to some of the young women sitting in rocking chairs in front of the large open window facing the main street. Santana asks the nurse if I may do that and she agrees so long as I don't take photos. With Santana translating, I chat with three young women who are within two or three weeks of birthing. They are each no more than nineteen years old and they each have partners. It's not clear to me why they are there, although one may require a C-section because her baby is in breech position. They anticipate their births with excitement. "It will be wonderful to have a baby to love!" But despite the fact that they've been taught about having to have a fully effaced cervix and to dilate to 10 cm., even to some degree what to expect during labor, I think they have no idea what's in store during the hard work of delivering a baby, let alone raising a child.

That night we have dinner at a good local restaurant where we are joined by two Belgian stewardesses. And that night, I throw up and begin to feel awful for 24-hours.

We abort our plan for the next night and drive toward Sancti Spiritus, where I hope we can stay in a decent hotel where the sheets fit the bed and the shower spouts warm water. I feel quite ill and am glad to have a large part of the day sitting in the car. The rural scenery is pleasant. Men plow their fields walking behind oxen, sugar cane fields abound, often with mountain backdrops, farm animals graze, caballeros ride past us on horseback, horse or donkey-drawn carts make their way lazily along the roadside, sparse tiny concrete houses dot the way.

In the lovely town square of Sancti Spiritus we check into the Plaza Hotel. All hotels in Cuba are government-owned (like everything else) and most can be quite dismal, but this one is more than inviting. Its lobby is pleasant, the room sparkling clean, and it has internet and CNN! I promptly fall into bed, sleep for several hours, and in the evening I am served a bowl of broth in our room (Cuban hotels usually don't do room service) while Arnold dines downstairs.

This stop turns out to be fortuitous. Castro's funeral cortege has now caught up with us and in the morning, the sound of people gathering around the plaza to watch his cortege pass begins at 5:00 a.m. The crowd swells to about 5,000 by 11:00 a.m. when the cortege rolls slowing into town. We have waited for several hours sipping tea and talking with a lovely Cuban family and their three small daughters on the hotel veranda, but we relocate to our hotel balcony to watch the procession. The music that has been playing all morning swells and the crowds are revved up by leaders who chant "Viva Fidel!" "Yo soy Fidel!" "Nos son Fidel!" It's an extraordinary sight and sound and we are swept up into it like everyone else. As the cortege crawls past buildings draped in flags around the plaza, we watch military vehicles with stiff, starched, uniformed men sitting stock still move at a snail's pace, people shouting and waving flags. Then, a vehicle appears, pulling a flowered flatbed platform bearing the glass-encased small casket of Castro's ashes. (We captured it all on video.) It circles the plaza, stopping for the national anthem. Then, as slowly as it entered the square, it makes its way out and on to the next town on its itinerary. Women weep. Men weep. Groups of friends gather for group hugs. Slowly, people disperse into the streets surrounding the plaza. The music continues blaring from a building where some people gather. Slowly, the day continues towards normalcy. We make our way out of town, heading for Camaguey.

Unfortunately, Castro's entourage has beat us to it. The roads are totally clogged. It takes us hours to get on the road where we end up waiting for hours more for traffic to move. Buses, tourist cars, general local traffic are at a total standstill, diesel fumes spewing from the vehicles until drivers shut down their engines. We grab a cheese sandwich from a roadside rest stop. We marvel at how this day demonstrates Cuban patience as nothing else could while ours wears thin. We will lose an entire day in Camaguey!

Finally, at about 8:00 p.m. we reach our Casa. Raphael, the owner, is not pleased. We did not confirm our reservation until this morning and he requires 48 hours so he has given our room away. But not to worry, he says, we can stay at his daughter's Casa next door. We ask about the meal we phoned ahead to request. "Yes," he says, "but you will not have it here." (Others are dining as we speak). "You will have it at my son's Casa across the street." Viva Cuba! Our room, which is ultra-modern, is in the back of Raphael's daughter's garage, but it is immaculately clean and she is extremely charming. Dinner in her brother's kitchen is cooked by an elderly family member and served by his *muy serioso* wife. My chicken and Arnold's fish meals are unremarkable but plentiful; unfortunately, I still cannot eat and must explain to the cook that it is not because of his food but due to my still being ill. (I manage to do this in Spanish).

After dinner, we take a brief walk in an attempt to catch the flavor of this city known for its winding medieval-like maze of streets. This is Cuba's third largest city, the bastion of the Catholic Church, and a sophisticated place. It is full of hidden plazas, baroque churches, galleries, restaurants, and shops and we have to miss it!

Santana has warned us that we must depart at 4.30 a.m. if we are to get ahead of the Castro cortege. Raphael's daughter kindly wakes us with tea at 4:00 a.m. Later, on the road, we stop at an inviting thatch-roofed café for an excellent breakfast, surrounded by copious begging kittens. (I feel like I'm eating at Hemingway's house.)

We make a brief stop in the town of Bayamo, capital of Granma Province, where we visit the Women's Federation de Cuba and the local chapter of the Writer's Union (where we discuss American politics.) We wander past a "health library" and visit a church, where an annoying woman explains its history, tells us Mother Teresa's sister is a nun in town, and thanks us "for your business." About to depart, we discover a flat tire on our car which Santana changes in record time. We are off to Santiago de Cuba, where Castro will also end his journey. So we must get into to town before it is sealed off until after his burial.

En route we see the Sierra Maestra mountains where Castro hid out for two years, pass a large copper mine and more of the agricultural landscape of rural Cuba. As we approach Santiago, we stop at the church of the yellow-robed patron saint of Cuba, the *Virgin de la Cobra*. It is here that Hemingway's Nobel Prize resides. More about this in a moment, but first it is important to say something about the province of Granma in which Santiago lies and in which Jose Marti died and is buried. (Castro is now laid to rest next to him.) It is also the place where Cespedes freed his slaves in 1868 and declared Cuban independence for the first time. The province is named for the yacht that Castro and his revolutionaries used to return to Cuba from Mexico in 1956. (It is now on display in Havana.) The province is revered for its revolutionary spirit, and for its street parties replete with hand-operated hand organs, all of which we missed due to Castro's demise.

Rising above the village of El Cobre, the *Basilica de Nuestra Senora del Cobre*, Cuba's most revered, recently renovated religious site is surrounded by green hills. Built in 1927 on the site of a 17th century sanctuary, it is a place of pilgrimage and home to Hemingway's Nobel Prize for Literature, which he gave to the Catholic Church in1954 "for the Cuban people" rather than let the Batista regime get ahold of it. (It was stolen briefly in the 80s and is now kept under lock and key, but photographs are on view.) It is the church to which Fidel and his brother Raul's mother came to pray for their safety, and where contemporary dissident Cuban blogger Yoani Sanchez left her journalist award for safekeeping. High above the alter a petite La Virgen can be seen in her yellow robe in a glass case.

From there we pass the Cemetario where Castro will join Marti as we head to our pleasant Casa, where proprietor Angel, a young, friendly gay man, efficiently runs things. Our room is pleasant and from the rooftop terrace we can enjoy a beer from our room's fridge while overlooking the old French quarter. In the air-conditioned sitting room, we can also watch endless replays of Castro's cortege week.

The heat and humidity in Santiago is truly unbearable and adds to my near hysteria in the face of no Folklorico, no music, no rum, no museums and no Internet. By this time, I have moved from feeling the people's pain over losing Castro to wanting to kill him myself. Relief comes at the "white house" in the plaza, the Grand Hotel, which Graham Green wrote about in <u>Our Man in Havana</u> and from where Castro proclaimed victory in 1959. Its terraced restaurants, one high above the square, provide some respite even though they've run out of ice cream and flan and only offer the usual ham, cheese, pizza, pasta and virgin beverages.

Walking to and from the hotel we witness the usual street scenes, including men of all shapes, sizes and ages playing some serious Dominoes. They slam their tiles on the table as if it were a grand challenge and an act of resistance. And happily, they liked that we want to photograph them.

Santiago has an interesting history. It was here that Spanish conqueror Diego Valazquez established a capital, and here that Fidel Castro came down from the mountains to launch his revolution and to proclaim its victory. Diego's house is the oldest one in Cuba still standing and it adds to the elegance of Santiago's main plaza. Bacardi's first rum factory is here too.

We manage to venture out into the heat and humidity to see the little house that Castro lived in as a student. It is near our Casa as well as a school attended by Frank Paris, one of three young students killed in the revolution. Santiago's airport bears his name, and a statue of him as a young boy near the Palace of Justice commemorates his death as a symbol of all youth lost to the revolution.

We also walk down Calle Heredia, where "the music never stops" (unless Castro dies). The picturesque old street hosts numerous writers and artists, and offers some fine architecture. Further on we come to the city's commercial walking street. Here we play the Pied Piper, handing out pens to kids who think the colorful pens are the best *regalo* (gift) ever. Eventually we come upon Plaza Dolores, where the Bacardi Museum is located, and of course closed. We also pass a large maternity hospital where it turns out Santana was born. By the time we reach Plaza Marti, we can barely slump onto a bench to gulp water. There we meet a jovial group of men from The Bahamas who frequently visit Cuba. Somewhat restored, we forge ahead to the Moncado Barracks.

The barracks are famous because in July 1953 more than a hundred revolutionaries led by Castro unsuccessfully stormed Batista's troops at this military garrison. Some of Castro's men were killed; he escaped into the mountains. After the revolution, like all other military barracks in Cuba, it was converted to a school. In 1967 it became a museum (also closed.) Interestingly, the Bastista regime had cemented over the original bullet holes from the attack but Castro's government remade them (without firing guns) as a reminder of what had happened there.

Nearby the Moncado barracks we also saw the Palace of Justice, taken by Castro's brother Raul during the Moncado attack, and the sculptured fountain honoring Frank Paris. Exhausted from this excursion (Santana couldn't believe we'd done it on foot!) we taxied back to Angel's cool Casa and gulped down beers on the roof with a nice Swiss-French couple. Then it was soup for supper at the Casa and to bed.

Because Jet Blue doesn't have the route between Florida and Santiago we had to drive to the town of Holguin for our departure from Cuba. Leaving Santiago, we had a special treat. Santana had stayed with his aunt who lives rurally on a very small farm. She had done our laundry without charge and packed us corn tamales for lunch. I asked Santana if we could stop to visit her so that I could thank her and give her a small gift. Thus we had a lovely visit with Santana's aunt, who served us Cuban coffee, thick and sweet, and her husband. "I've never brought any of my guests to my aunt's house," Santana said as we drove off. "But you are like family."

Holguin is a quiet city, the place where both Batista and Castro were reared. Christopher Columbus was the first European to visit it and to meet the indigenous Tainos. The areas surrounding the city became important for sugar growing at the end of the 19th century when most of the land was bought and cleared by the US-owned United Fruit Company. Today Holguin is rather run down. The plaza near our casa was surrounded by empty, decaying buildings for the most part and the concrete in the park was ruptured and crumbling. But in its colonial heyday it must have been quite lovely and no doubt restoration will take place. (One of the shops still open was an ice cream parlor which served the best ice cream in all of Cuba!) We didn't see much more of the city, having arrived in the afternoon.

Our Casa was a lovely old private home on a quiet street hosted by a gentle middle-aged woman and her architecture professor husband, and our bedroom was the best we'd had in a Casa outside of Havana. The bathroom had been newly remodeled to the highest European standards. At the back of the house an inviting courtyard with a small swimming pool beckoned. It contained a tiny towered apartment, inhabited by a Cuban chef and his Canadian wife of six years, who had been traveling from Montreal to Holguin for several years in an attempt to secure permanent residence in Canada for her husband. It was here that we bid farewell to our driver, companion and friend, Santana.

On our final night in Cuba we had dinner at an inviting restaurant a block from our Casa. To our delight they were actually serving wine, but alas, it was undrinkable so I switched to second-rate Sangria to accompany our grilled camerones served with the traditional black rice that derives it color from being cooked with no longer distinguishable black beans.

In the morning, we headed to the airport and soon found ourselves, without complication, back in Ft. Lauderdale. (The general visas we had qualified for were never an issue; no one either in Cuba or the US cared at all what we'd been doing there.) And so ended an amazing journey captured only briefly in this rather long account. I will, however, add a short postscript with a few thoughts.

First, Cuba is incredibly complex and difficult to understand for many reasons. The country's history, politics and economics are challenging to grasp and their interactions are intricate and confusing. Answers to questions are often scripted, cautious or qualified. Then there is the fact that no one seems to answer your questions in a consistent way; ask five people the same thing and you will get five different answers of varying quality and accuracy. There is also the fact that individual responses will likely reflect one's pre/post experience of the revolution, their age, the extent of their education, their economic status relevant to other Cubans, and more. But talk to enough people, especially those eager to speak openly, and you begin to get a picture of an island country that suffered 400 years of occupation and oppression, was liberated by a well-meaning revolutionary turned dictator, and is now a country that looks with hope and caution toward a wider world. (Who knows what will happen after Raul Castro, now 86, dies, coupled with a Trump presidency.)

The second thing I want to emphasize is that Cuban people, almost without exception, are among the nicest, friendliest, most gracious fiesta-and-music loving folks I've ever met anywhere. Despite continuing hardships, especially among rural Cubans, visible shortages, government control of absolutely everything, tropical heat, a new kind of tourist invasion (which of course does bring dollars/CUCs with it), they are always smiling, helpful and engaging. And we've never felt safer anywhere. We never used our room safe or our money belts, I never removed my one piece of valuable neck jewelry, and we never once felt threatened, day or night. (Vendors can get pushy but they quickly back off.)

My lasting impression of Cuba will be this: It is not the prettiest island in the Caribbean I've ever seen, although it has its high points. It is not a country I'd want to live in or necessarily revisit (except for Havana, the mountains and beaches). Despite its universal health care (with well-trained providers and a failing infrastructure with inadequate supplies and resources), its 99.9% literacy rate, it's gorgeous, happy children and truly lovely people, it is a developing country still, with a dubious future and a long way to go before its citizens realize individual freedom, liberty and security. I wish that for Cubans with all my heart, and hope that one day the shouts of "Viva Cuba!" will stand for 21st century gains that benefit all the people of this special place, and enhance visitors' experience even more.

Music is ubiquitous in Cuba. We saw these street entertainers quite serendipitously outside the Ambos Mundos Hotel. After Castro died, there was a nine-day period of mourning in which no theater, music, or liquor was permitted. We missed the music, in all its variations, most of the time we were there, but we did get to see great samples of street music.

TOWER BRIDGE, LONDON (NOT TO BE CONFUSED WITH "LONDON BRIDGE")

Europe

"I met a lot of people in Europe.
I even encountered myself."

JAMES BALDWIN

Turkish Delights
Two Weeks of Treasures and Topography

After spending a delightful, if somewhat frenetic, week in Istanbul our first stop on this long-awaited trip to Turkey is a small town where we discover a local café for a lunch of home-cooked eggplant mousaka with thick yoghurt, which quickly becomes one of my favorite Turkish meals. No one in the restaurant, or the town, speaks a word of English and we are something of a curiosity but we get along fine – until we try to buy a SIM card for my Thai cell phone. (Only after running out of minutes after three local calls do we realize that our calls are being routed via Thailand!) In the Turkcel office (Turkcel is the largest cell phone carrier in Turkey) our passports are perused with the utmost scrutiny, every visa entry a curiosity. Then I am asked the names of my mother and father. I try to explain that they are dead and therefore irrelevant for this transaction but they persist so I say "Rebecca" and "Jacob" and this satisfies. We have our SIM card, useless though it proves to be.

We stop for the night in Bergama (Pergamum), a lovely little town which was once a major power in the world both B.C. and A.D. It's most dramatic remains are at the Acropolis that sits atop an impressive hill reached by car or by gondola. There are temple and theater remnants and the ruins of a famous library which rivaled that of Alexandria, Egypt. When the Egyptians denied papyrus to Pergamum the locals developed parchment and were the first to bind books as we do today. In 41 B.C. Mark Anthony had the Pergamum library transported to Alexandria as a gift for Cleopatra and sadly, it was destroyed later by a fanatical ruler who thought the books un-Islamic.

We stay in a boutique hotel, Les Pergamon, a lovingly restored former school, and in the morning make for Kusadasi to visit my old friend, Tulin, who summers here overlooking the Aegean from her third floor apartment. We catch up on her patio and await the arrival of another old pal, Yavuz and his wife Aysen who arrive at their nearby hotel shortly after we do. There, after 47 years, we are reunited, Yavuz and I having first met in Europe while traveling in the summer of 1965 and then getting reconnected when he and Tulin were students at the University of Washington.

In the morning we pile into Yavuz's SUV and head for nearby Ephesus, one of the must-see sights in Turkey. "City of the Gods," it is a sight to behold. As Fodor's guide puts it, "With an ancient arena that dwarfs the one in Pompeii, and a lofty library that rivals any structure in the Roman Forum, Ephesus – once the most important Greco-Roman city of the Eastern Mediterranean – is among the best preserved ancient sites in the world." Here, shrines honor the goddess Nike. St. Paul and Alexander the Great wandered the streets, and, if the legend is true, the Virgin Mary lived her last days nearby. Filled with temples, theaters, shops and homes, a stadium and more, Ephesus also boasted what must have been its own mosaic-sidewalked Rodeo Drive, along with a brothel and western-style public toilets! Even for those of us who find ancient ruins a trial, it being impossible to wrap our brains around such antiquity, Ephesus is one Wow place.

After Ephesus, we make for the village of Sirince, becoming noted for its wine and fine handicrafts. We buy a beautiful ribbon-embroidered cloth for a ridiculous $12 and then lunch at the Arsipel Restaurant. The meal is stunningly good and the ambience on the terraced veranda is perfect. A wonderful end to a terrific few days with old friends who promise to let us reciprocate their hospitality next year in the U.S.

After overnighting in the beach town of Bodrum, we drive on to Pamukkale. The terrain is brown and dry, with low-lying and higher mountains surrounding vast landscapes of valley and plain. The vistas are impressively huge, and one gets a sense of how big a country Turkey is. The mountains are for the most part barren with only a few of them sprouting bursts of green shrub, so that it looks like an epidemic of alopecia has taken over the countryside. Happily the roads are good and we are able to drive five or six hours a day.

Sometimes we come upon one of Turkey's huge cities in the distance and their size, sprawl and density amaze me. Places like Izmir, Ankara, Bursa, Konya, and of course Istanbul creep up and down every hill and mountainside in breathtaking conquest. I am stunned by their size and very glad I don't live in one of them.

Approaching Pamukkale, we stop for a buffet lunch, then avoiding hawkers, look for a place to spend the night. We are delighted to find the Melrose House Hotel, a small family run place that offers the traditional Turkish hospitality we have come to enjoy. Checked into our comfortable room, we make for the famed crystallized terrines - turquoise pools of mineral-rich volcanic spring water formed over time by cascading over basins and natural terraces. Chalky white solidified cliffs look like white curtains flowing down into the town 330 feet below. There are 17 hot springs at Pamukkale; visitors come to cure a variety of ailments. I dip my feet; it is lovely and inviting.

En route to Cappadocia the next day, we stop for lunch at the lake town of Egirdir. First we visit the bustling local market where there are no signs of trinkets for tourists; this is a real market where people come to buy what they need. It's a treat meandering around the foods and spices on offer. Huge rounds of various cheeses line one stall, in another more varieties of olives than we've ever seen are on display. (The merchant gives us lots to taste.) There are women in *hijab* selling fruits and vegetables, meat and seafood, spices and sweets (including Turkish Delight), and more. There are baby chicks died blue, green, and red for sale, presumably to the delight of children. There are cloth and clothing stalls, kitchen wares, drug store items. It is, like all wonderful local markets, colorful, loud, crowded, and great fun.

At lunch the young waiter seems never to have talked to a foreigner; when we ask for *meze* (Turkish appetizers) he doesn't understand. We repeat the word in various iterations and finally he nods his head vigorously, but no meze appear. So we order fresh lake bass, delicately breaded and fried with lemon. Afterward, we ask for fruit, produce in Turkey being amazingly big, fresh, and tasty. "Do you have peaches?" I ask. A shake of the head in the negative. "Bananas?" The meze-grin reappears and a shake of the head is affirmative. Then out comes a plentiful plate of peaches, oranges and grapes, but alas, no bananas!

Driving on we reach the small, unattractive lake city of Beysehir, a regional capital, where we find the Ali Bilir Otel, a minimalist 3-star hotel with a friendly staff. Our room is clean and there is a roof restaurant with a good lake view where we have our dinner.

In the morning we continue, lunching at a pleasant roadside restaurant. The young waiter has recently been to Holland and having taken a liking to us, shares some of his treasured Dutch coffee. We chat and eventually end up playing the age game. I guess him right at 25. Then I ask how old he thinks I am. "Fifty, maybe 52," he says. When I say I will soon be 70 his jaw drops. Stunned he asks, "Are you *sure*?"

Cappadocian town

That evening we arrive in Cappadocia (Kapadokya) and easily find The Stone House Cave Hotel which we have booked online. It is sheer delight, and although we don't have a cave room, we are upgraded to a family suite by the charming staff, young men who are all related and wonderfully friendly and gracious. We book the touristy dinner show, mainly to see the Whirling Dervishes, and walk around the town.

Goreme is definitely the place to stay in Cappadocia. Smaller and more colloquial than the other "base" towns, it is quaint and inviting, despite all the catering for tourists, and sits in the heart of the Goreme Valley where all the best sights are to be found. There are interesting shops selling old rugs, jewelry, souvenirs, and antiques (we buy a big brass key that once opened the door of a cave dwelling and pay far too much for it because in my enthusiasm I forget to bargain.) There are good restaurants and numerous hotels, all of which have the word "cave" in them. At night, curtains of little lights glitter festively over a small gulley of flowing water that runs along the main thoroughfare. From our room we can hear the clip-clop of horse-drawn buggies.

Cappadocia is a triangle of land with one of the most unusual natural landscapes in the world. It was formed by three volcanoes that erupted more than 10 million years ago. Over time the detritus of these explosions cooled and compressed to form soft, porous rocks easily worn by erosion so that they are ever changing. Valleys and rock ridges were gradually formed, shaped yet again by wind into "pinnacles, pillars, cones and mounds." Some of the pillars have basalt rock formations on top that look like hats. Early Christians in the region dubbed these particular formations "fairy chimneys" because the found the place so magical they believed only fairies could have made it.

These early Christians followed many others who had lived in Cappadocia since 1800 B.C., including Romans. The Christians found the rock caves in the region a good place to hide from Arab persecution. The caves also provided a place to live and one of the most amazing sites to visit here is the Underground City (one of about 40 such cities but the only one open to visitors), reminiscent of the Cu Chi Tunnels of Vietnam. Here, thousands of people lived on multiple stories underground. Replete with all the elements necessary for daily life it is an unbelievable warren of passageways, living spaces, religious practice sites, animal shelters, tombs and more. Cappadocia is also home to copious Christian churches, mainly built into caves between the 10th and 12th centuries and decorated with now faded frescoes.

We take the Red Tour on the first day which takes us to a cave castle, and then to the Open Air Museum, a place of many Byzantine Orthodox churches carved into the rocks. We stop at various view points for spectacular photo opps, visit a pottery factory in the nearby town of Avanos, stop in Urgup to see the three iconic fairy chimneys that appear in all of Cappadocia's PR, and conclude with the requisite visit to a carpet factory. In the evening our genial host and hotel owner, a handsome man in his mid-30s, drives us to the top of a nearby hill to show us the night view of Goreme and the fairy land becomes a valley of sparkling lights and silhouetted pillars of rock. "I love this place!" our host exclaims, and the joy of it is written upon his face.

The next day we take the Green Tour and are treated (in addition to the Underground City) to a 2-mile hike in the Ihiara Valley, the largest, deepest and longest canyon in Cappadocia. (It's no Grand Canyon but it's pretty). Along the way we stop at a floating tea house, then upon emerging have lunch at a riverside restaurant in Belisima. We then continue to Selime where some parts of Star Wars were filmed. In Pigeon Valley we take yet more pictures, then conclude with a visit to an onyx factory.

Upon returning to our hotel we are introduced to new guests, two young couples, one Turkish, the other their American friends who are on their honeymoon. Our handsome hotel owner decides we should all return to the hilltop for a sunset view of Goreme, after which we visit a local winery for a tasting. Then we eat dinner with the two young couples at My Mother's Café. About the only thing we have not done here on the Must Experience list is ballooning over the landscape at five in the morning. It's expensive and for someone with touches of acrophobia and claustrophobia easily, if sadly, missed. But what a spectacular place Cappadocia is!

We leave Goreme reluctantly to drive back to Istanbul, stopping for lunch the first day at Turkey's answer to Howard Johnson's. Reaching the town of Duzce at dusk, we find a strange, dark but acceptable hotel where, it appears, the guys on the desk, who turn out to be brothers, have never seen a foreign passport before. They have no idea what they are supposed to be recording from it, and consult each other somberly. Neither of them understands a word of English (and why should they? My Turkish is limited to about five words.) So when we ask for glasses for the room it becomes a game of charades until I finally draw two cups on a piece of paper. "Chai?" they ask. "Coffee?" No, just the containers, *lutfen* (please)! This leads to us being invited into the restaurant cupboard where we are invited to help ourselves.

The next challenge comes when we try to use the phone card we have bought. One of the brothers calls a friend who arrives sweaty and panting having raced to the rescue. But he doesn't know how to use it either, so he calls another friend who "speak English." Soon we have a cadre of young dudes arriving to try and help – to no avail. There is a phone store adjacent to the hotel so we go there, but no one knows how to use the card there either. Eventually the gaggle of young, tech-hungry do-gooders arrives at a consensus: "Not possible call America from here!" So we give it up and in the nearby grocery store buy fruit, bread and cheese to go with the excellent wine we have fortuitously brought from Cappadocia. We go to our barren, dimly lit room for a picnic dinner, having raided the kitchen cupboard for dishes and cutlery.

The next day we check into the TAV Airport Hotel at Ataturk Airport having aborted thoughts of the Black Sea because of rain and traffic. The friendly desk clerk upgrades us to a deluxe room since we will be spending the better part of two days there (we've arrived early and our flight the next day leaves late). Lucky for us since the allergy cold I developed in Cappadocia has morphed into a full-blown head cold. I take to the comfy bed, TV clicker in hand (finally, BBC!) not to rise again till the following day. Luckily I sign on to Turkish Airlines in time to see that our flight is leaving almost two hours earlier than originally scheduled.

And so home, with visions of fairy castles dancing in our heads, and the hope that we will return one day to the magic, the music, the moussaka and more that Turkey has to offer. *Inshallah!*

There is a lot to see and experience in Turkey. The ruins at Ephesus are amazing! But if you make only one excursion out of Istanbul, see the magic of Cappadocia. It's quite extraordinary.

Photo of Lisbon Tiles

The Pleasures of Portugal

Our 3-hour flight from London to Lisbon is smooth and our host/landlord Paulo is there to greet us at the airport. A charming man, he gives me *abrazos* on each cheek as if we are old friends, partly because we've been emailing about his apartment, partly because it's a Portuguese tradition, and partly because he is a very warm, cheerful person. The apartment we are renting from him for three nights is lovely – modern, spotless and inviting, despite a two-flight climb. Paulo shows us around the quiet neighborhood and treats us to coffee and the famous Portuguese custard sweet called Pasteis de Nata. Yum!

We begin our Lisboa exploration by taking the historic Tram 28 which originates three blocks from the apartment, guaranteeing that we will get a seat. The tram winds its way through Lisbon hitting many of the city's main sights. We ride to the end then jump off at the *miradouros* (viewpoint) at St. Luz church. The view is spectacular. Whitewashed houses with rust-colored clay roofs cluster in a community that dips down to the Tagus river estuary. Here we make the mistake of asking a Kenyan man selling beaded jewelry and leather bracelets to take our picture. He is happy to oblige and tells us that he loves America because his friend lives in New Jersey. "I'm from New Jersey!" I exclaim, at which he insists on gifting me with a necklace and two bracelets. He refuses money but somehow 15 minutes later we're out 15 Euros when our exchange ends. Never mind; I actually like the necklace and the bracelet (and have learned my lesson).

We walk up to Sao Jorge castle which affords pleasant

overlooks, then eat a lunch of sardines and French fries in an outdoor cafe. Sardines are famous in Portugal and they aren't anything like the puny little fish you get from tins at home. There are four sizeable ones on our lunch plates, marinated in olive oil, and they are really delicious. So is the beer that washes them down.

After lunch we walk down to Alfama, Lisbon's old city and catch the 15 tram to Belem. Part of Portugal's 15th C. Golden Age, Belem's two major attractions are the Monastery of Jeronimo and the Tower of Belem. The monastery is large, long and impressive. Its vaulted arcades and richly carved cloister columns are, as our guidebook put it, exuberant. The Tower of Belem, built as a fortress, reveal on its exterior ropes carved in stone, open balconies, and Moorish-style watchtowers. There is a vaulted dungeon (used as a prison until the 19th C.) a chapel and a King's room. Nearby and often mistaken for the Tower is the new, impressive Monument of the Discoveries, built in 1960 to mark the 500th anniversary of the death of Henry the Navigator.

Exhausted but unwilling to admit defeat, we return on the tram to Praca do Comercio, the grand Commercial, or Palace, Square, a huge plaza that hosted the royal place for 400 years. Set alongside the Tagus River, the square now houses government offices and of course, a customary statue of King Jose I. Here we restore ourselves with a beer in front of an impressive arch beyond which is a walking street of shops called Rua Augusta, gateway to Baixa (pronounced Basha) and Alfama, or Lower/newer and Upper/older Lisbon.

But the *piece de'resistance* of the day is the small, friendly restaurant we discover serendipitously in Alfama where Fado music is superbly sung by three women, one of whom is said to be 81, and a young man who seems to have stepped off an El Greco canvas. His deep set, sad eyes, lacquered hair and goatee are all jet black like the velvet jacket he wears and his elongated fingers punctuate the music as he serenades, eyes closed. The gray-haired

81-year old woman flirts with him in playful, sexy, tasteful ways that make the audience laugh. Then she smiles at the Norwegian man and his wife sharing our table, curling his hair around her finger. Fado music, accompanied by guitar and viola, is one of the things that define Lisbon. It's expressions of longing, sadness and lost love tear your heart out when sung well, so much so that some Lisboa natives don't like to hear it!

The next day we take a bus to Reststauradores Square, most noted for its Art Deco remnants, its requisite monument, the Palacio Foz and copious cafes. Adjacent to it is Rossio Square where the National Theater displays a banner reading " J'suis Paris." (It is only a few days since the Paris attacks.) The train station, where we are headed for the train to Sintra, is something to see with its double Moorish-style horseshoe arches.

Sintra, a 45 minute ride from Lisbon by train, is a UNESCO-protected town that most visitors to Lisbon visit, mainly to see the crazy castle there that recalls the madness of St. Simeon. (It is also reached by a somewhat hair-raising bus ride!) The Palacio de Pena stands on the highest peak of the Serra de Sintra Mountains. It's "an eclectic medley of architecture" to say the least, built in the 19th C. by Queen Maria II's husband. Visitors can tour the castle and capture the views its many terraces offer. On a uphill walk to reach the castle sculptured art paves the way. The town and its surroundings are inviting too. In summer it would probably be lovely to spend a night, exploring the shops, restaurants, walking paths, and the Sunday Market.

We lunch in a small restaurant where I enjoy sea bass and Arnold tries cod in cream sauce, all washed down with lovely white Portuguese wine at a ridiculously low cost. Before returning to the train station, we purchased a few small tiles in the atelier of the woman who designs and hand paints them, then we had our daily tea and pastry. Back in Lisboa, we go to see the famous Elevador de Santa Justa, a Neo-Gothic lift built at the turn of the 20th C. by a French architect who had apprenticed with Eiffel. It is strange and eccentric with its iron filigree and two old wooden passenger cars. At the top of the tower, and along a walkway linking the elevator to the Largo do Carmo in the Bairro Alto, there are spectacular views but we were there at night so we headed home to cook a pasta dinner before falling into bed.

In less than three days we fell in love with Lisbon. It's a capital city of manageable size with Parisian undertones in its architecture, boulevards, and ambience. The pace of life is just right, public transport is excellent, there are cafes everywhere and people are wonderfully friendly. There are beautiful squares, plazas, parks (in which old men play cards and checkers) and charming neighborhoods dotted by spectacular vistas. On top of that, the beer, wine and food are excellent, and not expensive by American standards!

Leaving the city we head south to the Algarve, driving 3 hours to one of its main towns, Faro. We check into the excellent 3-star Hotel Sol Algarve, exhausted from our unrelenting exploration of Lisbon, check out the orange-treed old square and have lunch before indulging in a long nap.

Our first excursion takes us to the town of Olhao, a fishing venue since the Middle Ages and still one of the largest fishing ports in the country. At the back of the church, Nossa Senhora do Rasario, a special chapel can be found where women come to pray for their men's safe return. From Olhao we drive to Tavira, a pretty town full of historic churches and fine mansions with filigree balconies on either side of the Gilao River, linked by a Roman bridge. We also stop at Cacela Velha, a hamlet perched on a cliff overlooking the sea and noted for its whitewashed fishermen's houses trimmed in various shades of blue.

Next we visit Albufeira, a city overbuilt with condos for the multitudes of tourists who converge there in summer because of its excellent, long, wide crescent beach of soft brown sand. We enjoy coffee overlooking the Mediterranean Sea in the old part of town, then head for the real fishing village of Pena where colorful *barcas* (boats) and copious fishing nets decorate the waterfront while deeply tanned fishermen busy themselves after a day's work on the water. We have a sandwich lunch on the beach, glad for the sunny 78-degree temperature that sees many people still sunbathing or swimming in November! Later we make our way to the Spartan but pleasant Alvor Guest House well-situated in the small town of Alvor, which is a happening place during the summer months but is blissfully quiet now. Our first night there we eat at a restaurant full of British tourists and make friends with the chirpy waitress but soon we see that the harbor is lined with seafood restaurants so it's fresh seafood tomorrow night!

The next day we discover Luz, another small town with a beautiful crescent beach on our way to Sagres, noted for its castle and nearby lighthouse. Henry the Navigator built a fortress on this windswept promontory but there is little to see here except for the wide expanse of the Atlantic Ocean and the suburb beaches it touches in the area. You can also see in the distance the Cabo de Sao Vicente lighthouse, said to be the most powerful in all of Europe with its 60 mile range. We drive to the lighthouse before having tea at the Pousada there as the sun sets, then return to Alvor to feast on fresh bream and potatoes (which accompany every meal along with overcooked green beans and carrots, washed down of course with excellent white wine.)

On our way inland and north to the UNESCO town of Evora the next day we enter the Alentejo region but first we stop at Peixa de la Rochas (Beach of Rocks), a stunning expanse bookended by huge rocks joined by a long boardwalk for walking and biking. We enjoy coffee with our last look at the green-blue sea and the extraordinary beaches that make the Algarve so popular and then make way to Silves, once renowned as a cultural center in the Moorish "Al-Gharb" until the town was overtaken in 1242.

As evening approaches, we arrive in the tiny town of Portal and find our "hacienda" for the next two nights, the "rural tourism" guest house called Hertad do Rio Torto. It's a lovely place situated in the bucolic fields outside Portal and we are its only guests. We are greeted by the young woman manager, have tea in our room, and after a rest make our way into town for dinner. This turns out to be an extraordinary experience. Portal is small and the one good restaurant is closed for the season. The two cafes we see are filled with men, not a woman in sight. They are watching soccer in bawdy groups. We bite the bullet and go into one of them. Every table is full of men in various stages of inebriation whose average age is somewhere around 70. Most of them have caps or hats on in about the same state of disrepair as the work clothes they wear and they look at us as if two zebras had just sauntered in. Cheers and jeers go up as the game on the large TV screen proceeds. Pretty soon the regulars lose interest in us and a cheery young waiter takes our orders for lamb stew and pork strips (with potatoes) - working men's fare -accompanied by beer. The food is salty but good and the evening is a hoot as we hang with the locals who wave to us when we leave.

The walled city of Evora proves to be an interesting town. It rose to prominence under the Romans and flourished throughout the Middle Ages. Once home to a Jesuit university, it now draws visitors year-round. The shopping street, Rua 5 de Outubro, is fun to browse and Praca do Giraldo, the main square, is lovely. On the day we are there the square provides the rowdy finish line for Evora's first-ever marathon in which we are told 5,000 people have run. It's a festive atmosphere with music blaring and awards being handed out but we move on to another fabulous old town called Monsaraz. En route we feast on filet mignon steak, the best spinach we've ever had; the owner says milk and flour along with olive oil, garlic, salt and pepper are the secret. He also makes his own red wine, the best we've had in Portugal. And all at a restaurant we happened upon as we entered the town of Reguengos do Monsaraz.

Monsaraz is a fabulous medieval walled town! It sits perched above the River Guadiana on the border with Spain and offers expansive views of lakes, vineyards and valleys. Access to the town is through the Porta da Vila. The main cobblestoned street leads up to the castle built in the 13th C. and along the way there are craft shops, a few small places of accommodation and restaurants – another lovely place to spend a summer night.

Alentejo is a wonderful part of Portugal. Filled with vineyards, olive groves, large herds of cattle, green fields, blooming flowers and occasional orange trees, its contrast to the coast of the Algarve region provides us with an entirely different sense of the country with lovely Lisbon as its capital. We have loved each region and every minute. From Lisbon to Luz to Monsaraz, it's been a sensory treat in a beautiful land. We leave for Lisbon airport replete with the pleasure of this very special place.

We fell in love with Lisbon, a beautiful and very manageable city, and indeed, the entire country. Just avoid the Algarve in summer. We bought this unique photograph, which captures the colors of the country, from a Liston street vendor.

Museum Treasure

Stockholm:
City of Surprises on the Sea

We have, it seems, arrived a week too late. The Strindberg Festival has ended. The UNESCO World Heritage Site for all things Viking closed the day we got here. The canal boats are no longer running. It's mid-September and Stockholm's tourist season is officially over. Not to worry. A warm sun beats gently on the city's domes and spires. The museums are queue-free. The ubiquitous waters glisten as bobbing boats and island ferries make their way to and from the quays. Copious outdoor cafes beckon.

We have rented a studio apartment for our short pre-Norway visit which turns out to be conveniently located in a pleasant neighborhood just four metro stops from the city "centrum." We pick up a few groceries, catch a quick nap to recover from our overnight travel via Iceland, then head for the Old Town. What a treat it is with its narrow winding medieval streets, Royal Palace, 17th century church, government buildings, antique shops, and restaurants. Too tired to eat a proper meal, we enjoy a pizza in one of the Italian restaurants that abound and sample Falcon beer, which now ranks among my favorite.

In the morning we metro to town and catch a boat to the Vasa Museum, home of a humongous, intricately carved, ridiculously top-heavy, once colorful, over-cannoned 17th century warship notorious for sinking within twenty minutes of its inaugural sailing. Raised in the 1960s, 333 years after its demise, the maritime work of art is now housed in the most visited site in Stockholm and definitely worth the visit.

We lunch al fresco on braised lamb and creamy mashed

potatoes at an indoor/outdoor restaurant called Mister French overlooking the harbor which hosts several large cruise ships. Then we board the Red Bus ("hop on/hop off") for a 2-hour city tour. Stockholm, comprised of several small islands connected by boat and bridge and more compact than you might think at first glance, is a beautiful city well known for its architecture. Church spires dot the landscape, government buildings – mostly from a former age – stand strong and proud, theaters and museums are grand. The city's various neighborhoods are perhaps less well touted but they are an inviting amalgam of Europe's best cities, replete with fine parks, inviting cafes and eateries, and shops offering everything from gorgeous jewelry to the modernity for which Scandinavia is known. At the Royal Palace stop we catch an impressive goose-stepping parade of blue-uniformed military, no doubt part of the Changing of the Guard.

But it is the Old Town and its proximity to the water that draws us back, over and over again. On our third day we return to sip café lattes and eat Swedish cinnamon rolls on the picturesque square that hosts the Nobel Prize Museum, a finely presented history of its prestigious recipients and founder, chemist Alfred Nobel. Soon to move to a large ultra-contemporary building near the city center, the museum will expand but perhaps lose the charm of its present setting among grand old Scandinavian buildings that now serve as restaurants, cafes and shops.

Stockholm boasts many inviting museums but we have meandered so long we miss the Nordic and National Museums, high on our list in the absence of a chance to go canal cruising or on a Viking expedition. So we head instead to the Ice Bar. Located a block from Central Station in the Nordic C Hotel, it is a bar made entirely of ice, including the walls, counters, and disposable glasses from which you can enjoy a vodka drink of choice, included in the admission fee. Upon buying tickets a cozy hooded parka and gloves are provided but about 15 minutes is sufficient, even though the vodka (compliments of Absolut) is briefly warming. A similar

Ice Bar can now be found in London, and of course at the Ice Hotel in northern Sweden.

Stockholm, in short, is rich with surprises. While silken-haired Nordic blondes are few and far between, an abundance of dark-haired young people, many of them Roma, beg endlessly in the streets and Metro stations. A gnome or two are also in evidence: One wizened old man who spoke no English seemed to pop up, smiling and pointing, whenever we needed directions. We were charmed by many people who helped us find our way, and surprised that the surly young staff employed by the Tourist Information offices were so ill-informed and unfriendly. (Later we learned that hospitality gestures are not customary in Scandinavian countries. Bus drivers and train conductors never help with baggage or boarding and one Norwegian whom we befriended said that she would never smile at or speak to strangers. "It's not in our culture," she explained.) Food and drink were excellent, prices hair-raising. Public transportation was more than impressive. And we loved how many dads were taking care of the kids.

In short, Stockholm is a city to be savored, even if all you can spare is three days. But if you have the time and can go "in season," six days would be decidedly better and allow for excursions further afield. The city is, after all, the jewel in a well-laden Scandinavian crown. It sparkles with assorted gems well worth an extended visit.

Stockholm has so many things to see, including the 17th C. warship at the Vasa Museum! The best way to approach the city is by sea so that you can see all the islands, a treat we missed even though we could have sailed from Helsinki on a former trip.

Oslo's Opera House

Norway
A Tale of Two Cities, and a Ship

Arriving from Stockholm after a six-hour train journey, we were happy to see our friends Gerd Inger and Ulf smiling at us when we arrived at Oslo's train station, tired and hungry. They whisked us off to their home, fed us scrambled eggs, bread and cheese washed down with good red wine, and tucked us into bed after mutual updates.

The next morning, rested and refreshed, we headed for a city tour and our first view of Oslo's impressive Opera House, new since we'd last been to the city. Situated on the waterfront, the 2008 architectural marvel suggests a large ship arriving through a fjord, or perhaps through snow-covered mountains. An abstract glass-sculpted sailboat, jarring at first, tilts and seems to sail into the harbor, depending on your vantage point while contemplating its place in the plan. Intrusive at first, its appeal grows as the perspective changes. The interior of the grand theater in which drama, ballet and music are offered is majestic. High glass walls, rounded wooden balconies, steel, marble and concrete all come together to create a liberating sense of space and light and the café is a perfect place to sip coffee while contemplating the marvelous edifice.

To see the most charming parts of Oslo a walk down Karl Johanns Gate is necessary. Not much had changed since our prior visit years earlier. Here on the main boulevard sat the grand *fin de'siecle* hotel we remembered, the National Theater with its statue of Ibsen keeping watch, the Parliament, the university, and at the far end, the modestly imposing yellow Royal Palace. Close by sits the two-towered red brick City Hall, and the old railway station, now site of the Nobel Peace Prize Center. Nearby, the site of the 2011 bombing of a government building that killed six people is a chilling reminder that violence can occur anywhere.

Among Oslo's most important museums, Vikingskipshuset, or the Viking Museum, is not to be missed and we were glad to see it again. Housing three of the world's best preserved 9th century Viking ships discovered on farmland that once served as burial grounds, they are among Norway's most outstanding cultural treasures. The ships were used to transport high-ranking members of society to their final resting place. One of the boats held two women, possibly mother and daughter or noble and servant; another revealed an older man, three small boats, and 64 shields. All three inhabitants remain a mystery. Other seagoing vessels of note in Oslo are the Kon-Tiki raft on which Thor Heyerdahl and his crew of five sailed across the Pacific in 1947, and the Fram, used by Roald Amundsen in 1911 when he planted a flag on the South Pole.

Another must-see in Oslo is the Munch Museum, soon to be moved to newer, modern quarters downtown. Munch, best known for his chilling painting "The Scream" - which was stolen in 2004 and found two years later - was a prolific artist whose work reveals the darker side of human nature. Obsessed with the relationship between life and death, much of his work draws on the human capacity for love, longing and fear.

Our all-too-short visit with friends ended as we boarded the train for the first leg of "Norway in a Nutshell," a day trip that delivered us to Bergen in the evening. The train passed idyllic waters, bucolic farms, villages and greenery, reaching Myrdal after four hours. At the small station we grabbed a hot dog before boarding the narrow-gage Flam Railway which climbs almost 2,000 feet in about twelve miles, famously revealing towering mountains and abundant waterfalls descending from impressive heights.

In Flam we boarded a boat for a two-hour cruise through the beautiful Aurlandsfjord, then arriving in Gudvangen, we transfered to a bus for a one-hour drive to Stalheim, a journey that took us on a winding road of twists and turns down thirteen hairpin curves into the majestic, verdant Maeroydalen Valley.

From there we boarded another train for the final leg of our "long day's journey into night," reaching the old port city of Bergen in time to check in to our centrally located hotel and enjoy a good meal in the popular restaurant, Dickens, where the fish was excellent and the bill "hilariously expensive," as Gerd Inger would say.

Bergen: Historic City by the Sea

Bergen, once the largest town in the country and capital of a region that included Iceland, Greenland and parts of Scotland, feels like a small town although it remains a vital center of trade and commerce. The area around the harbor, Bryggen, is its most compelling venue. Here a street lined with colorful old and new buildings paints a picture of what the city must have been like in its heyday when it was a major shipping center. Several small alleys with crooked, overhanging wood buildings now housing cafes and inviting shops reveal a long-ago time when this UNESCO World Heritage City reigned as the Hanseatic capital.

Another popular tourist attraction is the funicular that carries people to the top of Floyen Mountain, one of seven peaks in Bergen, named for the weathervane that sits atop the summit. Here are wonderful panoramic views of the city and its waterways as well as lovely walking paths. Sadly, defeated by rain and wind, we gave this treat a miss and drowned our sorrows in a bowl of extraordinary fish stew at the locally famous Sostrene Hagelin. Opened by two sisters ("sostrene") almost a century ago, the little corner fish restaurant was originally meant as a venue for the city's women. When the Hagelin family closed it, the city went into a collective depression until three friends took over, maintaining the sisters' recipes for their famous stew and fish cakes.

Other places of note in Bergen, in addition to its notable museums, include the shopping area near Ole Bull, a short boulevard named for the city's 19th century violinist (and ladies' man) who founded the Norwegian National Theater. Den Nationale Scene, which replaced the original theater bombed in WWII, sits at the end of Ole Bull, an imposing landmark. The aquarium, fish market and cathedral are also sights worth a visit. And for those who are staying longer than a day or two in order to board the Hurtigruten cruise north as we were, there are wonderful sites just outside of town. Gamle Bergen, three miles north of the city, is an open-air museum that recreates 18th and 19th century life and south of Bergen lies Gamlehaugen, the King's official Bergen residence. Nearby is Stave church, originally built of wood in 1150. It was destroyed by fire in 1992 but was rebuilt in its original form in 1995.

Hurtigruten: A Voyage to the Arctic Circle

After a wet two days in Bergen we boarded the MS Trollfjord, one of Hurtigruten's "millennial ships," built after 2000. The main, two-storied salon was tastefully decorated in sea blues with star-lit ceilings and large wrap-around viewing windows. Several smaller lounges provided stunning vantage points and the glass elevator and large windows in the dining room (and in the restrooms) ensured that no scenic view was missed. Our cabin was equally inviting. One twin bed converted to a sofa during the day and there were ample closets and a very adequate bathroom. Two portholes meant we could search for Northern Lights at night (which never appeared on our trip).

We boarded the ship at 4:00 p.m., settled in and learned the ship's nine story layout. At 8:00 p.m. an open seating, drool-inducing, plentiful and varied smorgasbord was served, replete with assorted fish, meat (including reindeer), vegetables and always present potatoes, salads, cheeses, breads, and sweets. Having bought the "wine plan" which included a bottle of fine wine and two bottles of water daily, we enjoyed a splendid Spanish red, the perfect accompaniment.

On our first full day aboard, we passed through beautiful landscapes, including the narrow Hjorundfjord, with its majestic mountains spawning long-flowing white waterfalls. Although the summer's rich green had given way to autumn hues that might have been more stunning without clouds casting broad gray shadows, the landscape helped us understand why this journey has been called "the world's most beautiful voyage."

That night, dinner - a three-course meal that set the standard for subsequent evenings -included a smoked trout starter, luscious lamb, and the ubiquitous potatoes, all locally grown, and a baked apple which we forfeited for a cheese plate to compliment an excellent Spanish Rioja.

On Day Three we stopped in Trondheim where we had three hours to visit the city and its famous Nidarosdomen Cathedral. Our only hindrance was a fierce wind that drove the rain slant. "It's the season," one resigned ship steward shrugged, which is why cruising in September is cheaper and less crowded than during the summer.

Trondheim is Norway's third largest city. Founded in 997 by the Viking King Olav Trygvason, it was once Norway's capital. Like many other Norwegian cities, it has been devastated by fires and war but today Trondheim is a peaceful, pretty place surrounded by river and fjord. It boasts several sights of interest including the Archbishop's palace, the Trondheim Museum of Art, the Royal residence, and the 12th century church, Var Frue Kirke. But for a short stop, there is pleasure in simply walking the Bryggen, where warehouses and wharves at the mouth of the Nidelva River have been the focus of commerce for years. Their colorful red and yellow facades, reflected in the water, are best seen from the red double-arched walking bridge called the Gamle

Bybrua ("old town bridge"), a symbol of the city built in 1861 and once the only way into the town center.

The most visited site in Trondheim is Nidarosdomen, the cathedral built over the grave of Olav the Holy, dating back to 1320. The cathedral is the largest building in Norway from the Middle Ages and incorporates Norman, Romanesque and Gothic styles. Also victim to several fires, restoration began in 1869 and an awesome Gothic reconstruction is what visitors see now. The stained glass rose window and two impressive organs along with flying buttresses and high vaulted ceilings are not to be missed. The Norwegian Crown Jewels are also on display in an adjacent building.

Upon departure from Trondheim we sailed past Monk Island, a former prison and fort, and the notable lighthouse, Kjeungskjaer Fyr. However, the weather thwarted our passage through the narrow Stokksundet sound which has such a sharp bend that ships must sound their horns to warn oncoming traffic.

Sometime between 6.30 and 8:00 a.m. on Day Four we crossed the Arctic Circle, an occasion that called some passengers to rise and sip Champagne at a hefty $14 a glass. We settled for the certificate passengers to verify the event. Later we stopped in Bodo, capital of Nordland County, and Samsund, then made our way to Svolvaer, the center of the Lofoten Islands, the mountains coming into view like a wall of high silhouettes in the distance.

On departing Svolvaer, one of 34 ports on the northbound journey, we passed through "the beautiful and narrow strait of Rafsundet" but given the season, darkness had set in. Some passengers were comforted by sipping Trollfjordsoup or the hot drink Trollfjordknert on the uppermost deck as the ship sailed on.

The next day we reached the picturesque town of Finnesnes. En route we passed snow-covered mountains, small homesteads nestled in still-deeply green inlets, and lesser mountains draped in autumn gold. The skies were briefly clear as a struggling sun tried to expose blue patches, suggesting that the afternoon would bring a bright, dry visit to Tromso.

Tromso is northern Norway's largest town with 70,000 inhabitants. Called the Capital of the Arctic and "the Paris of the North" its best known site is the Arctic Ocean Cathedral, or Ishavskatedralen, consecrated in 1965. Built of concrete, the triangular shape of the roof is said to symbolize the way in which the Northern Lights brighten the city's dark winter nights. One side of the church, a 75-foot triangle, is made of stained glass, its 86 panels depicting the Second Coming of Christ. On the southbound journey, a midnight concert takes place here.

Located 186 miles inside the Arctic Circle, Tromso is base camp for polar explorers, including Amundsen. It boasts the world's northernmost university, and Polaria, a marvelous museum of sea life where aquaria reveal astounding examples of underwater creatures, seals can be observed feeding and playing, and a film about the Arctic landscape takes viewers on an amazing helicopter journey over a part of the earth only few have seen.

On our last day aboard the ship we stopped in the small town of Honnignsvag, "gateway to the wonders of the spectacular North Cape." An optional excursion – one of many offered daily – takes passengers to the huge promontory rising high above the sea. Those who go can boast of having stood about 1200 miles from the Geographical North Pole.

We opted to take the evening excursion to learn about the Sami, Scandinavia's indigenous people, famous for reindeer herding. That evening we shared a grand time with new friends from Oslo and Abu Dhabi, vowing to keep in touch, before packing for our departure in the morning.

At 8:00 a.m. we disembarked and boarded a bus to the Kirkenes airport. Twenty-six hours and three flights later, we climbed into our own bed, exhausted and happy, for we had taken "the world's most beautiful voyage," and even though it wasn't summer when sunshine is likely and the seas are calmer, we felt blessed. We had, after all, been to the Arctic Circle on a working boat that wove its way through Norway's spectacular landscape! Who could ask for more than that?

Oslo's Opera House is a stunning contemporary addition to the city's traditional landscape.

Norway is quite expensive so my only souvenir was the ubiquitous windbreaker and a pair of woolen socks! It was lovely to be shown around by dear friends. In the end, it's always the people who make a place special.

The Turkish Street in Pidgeon Square

A Balkan Reprise

It's been (dare I admit it) five decades since I visited the former Yugoslavia, never thinking that I'd be back, but here I am in Sarajevo, Bosnia-Hercegovina on the start of a ten-day trip in the Balkans!

I arrive at the airport from Thessaloniki, Greece via Istanbul and wait one hour for my free hotel pick-up ("Sorry, afternoon prayers went on so long today!" my Muslim driver apologizes). After sussing out the apartment in the heart of the old city that we have rented for three days from the Garni Konak Hotel - a lovely place with a view of a minaret and the orange-roofed houses clinging to a hillside just as I remember them - I take a walk to explore. Starting from Pigeon Square (Sarajevo's San Marco Square) I check out the shops, cafes, historic Turkish shopping street (a UNESCO site), town clock, old mosques, people in various dress (this is a predominantly Muslim country).

Then I have a cappuccino in one of the ubiquitous cafes, and a delicious chocolate ice cream (gelato) cone from one of the many street vendors.

My husband is supposed to take a cab to the hotel since his flight is scheduled to arrive in the evening and there's only one free pickup, but I decide it would be nice to surprise him as he exits and one of the three sweet guys who manage the hotel that I've befriended offers to take me. He says it will take about 20 minutes to the airport and swears that leaving at 8 p.m. for an 8.15 arrival is sufficient. I'm pretty sure it's not having done the trip once already, but off we go at 8. But no one knew, it seems, that a marathon race was being run that evening in town and all the main roads would be closed so we crawl our way to the airport only to find that the flight arrived 10 minutes early and there is no sign of my spouse or anyone else. Hopefully he's in a cab since he didn't know I was coming. I am distraught since I'm paying to do the pickup and also don't know for sure that Arnold is actually in a cab so Adnan, the driver, says he will not charge me. Then he calls the hotel – no sign of hubby yet – with the result that we are getting a 10% discount per day for the trouble! It takes us nearly 1.5 hours to get back to the hotel during which we keep calling to see if my husband has arrived – not. But when we finally get there, he is sitting in the lobby – having paid US$ 40 to get there instead of 40 BK (local currency)! Typical Clift travel story. Never mind, he says, and off we go with Adnan to eat pizza and drink beer before collapsing into bed.

The next morning Adnan, who is off duty, drives us into the hills above the city where the views are absolutely stunning. (Sarajevo sits in a valley surrounded by lush green mountains.) We see the city's old wall ruins and gates and overlook the Military Cemetery where those who lost their lives in the 1990s Balkan war are buried, while Adnan tells us about Bosnian history and stories of the war that took thousands of lives, 1600 children among them.

One of the stories is about the first two victims of the Serbian attack in which two women, one Muslim and one Christian, met in the middle of a bridge as a gesture for peace and were gunned down by Serbian troops. The other is the Romeo and Juliet story of Sarajevo: A young couple, one Muslim, one Christian, fleeing the city, were also killed on the same bridge. The woman died first and he crawled to her to hold her in his arms before he died. The bodies lay there for seven days because no one had the courage to remove them.

The stories of the war here are truly heartbreaking and it still seems impossible that this could have happened in Europe, again, at the end of the 20th century. Indiscriminate bombing, shelling, shooting and fires set aimed solely at "driving them crazy" as the Serbs put it. No heat, no water, no electricity, no food in the longest siege of a city in modern warfare. People hanging from balconies as their apartments burned. Children coming out of their basement hiding places to see daylight being shot. The national library and all its books being burnt to the ground. And of course, the concentration camps. It is absolutely amazing how the people of Sarejevo not only survived this hell for years but kept up their lives and their acts of resistance, which we learn more about at the Tunnel Museum.

With Sarejevo surrounded on all sides by hostile Serbian forces and UN forces at the airport, the only way in or out for supplies (including weapons) was the 800-meter tunnel, dug under the airport (unbeknown to the Serbs or the UN till close to the war's end). The Museum includes part of that tunnel (you can enter it and walk a portion), assorted displays and videos. Some of the guides who go there talk about their own experiences traipsing through the tunnel.

After this sobering experience, we head back to Pigeon Square and eat a typical Bosnian lunch of seasoned mini-sausages tucked into a large pita bread with onions on the side, then meet "Arnold" (his hotel name), another of the hotel lads who takes us on a walking tour of the old city. "Arnold" is a combination of Mr. Bean and the wedding planner played hilariously by Martin Short! When asked a question he lets loose a barrage of staccato rapid fire "Yeah, yeah, yeah, yeahs," or "No, no, no, nos" and when he thinks we say something funny he nearly collapses into hysterical laughter! But he is terribly sweet and amazed at our ages, he refuses to be paid for the tour because, he says, we are fun to be with despite our age. He hugs us a lot and when, while having coffee, I tell him he should not smoke and he should listen to his Jewish mother, he almost expires with glee and kisses the top of my head! Oh, he cries, "I like you. You are like family!"

Our walking tour takes us through winding streets and includes places like the library that was burnt down, now City Hall, a variety of mosques and churches, and the Latin Bridge over the River Mil Jacka. We also stand on the corner where Ferdinand and his wife Sophia were assassinated, launching WWI. We visit a covered bazaar/shopping market where I buy a lovely cotton scarf for $4 and end our walk with Bosnian coffee and baklava in a secluded café that includes a colorful Asian market selling crafts, carpets, clothes and more.

After a rest, we make our way to the famous Sarajevo brewery for a dinner of lamb shank with vegetables and excellent beer and wine. The place is historic and huge and includes a museum but we give that a miss.

The next day we awake to heavy gray clouds, fog in the mountains, and rain, which lets up a bit as we make our way by tram to the National Museum to see the original Sarajevo Haggadah. As we approach, Arnold says, jokingly, "I bet it's not open." Bingo. The museum is open but the Haggadah is not on display – it was on view yesterday for the Museum's free day, but normally you must book in advance and it is expensive. So we decide to see the replica at the Jewish Museum, formerly a Shephardic synagogue, the oldest in Europe. But it has closed at 1:00 p.m.. So we eat lunch – a Bosnia Pot – meat, potato, cabbage in a salty gravy in a restaurant near our apartment. There we chat with a young Korean woman traveling solo, a man from Columbus, OH, and a Polish guy who tell us about the Children's Wartime Museum.

It's a new museum with a fascinating story and a moving exhibit comprised of 50 annotated artifacts from people who were children during the war. The museum came to be because a man asked people to send him short statements or remembrances from the war, which he published in a book. He then decided to talk to some of the people and they started sending him memorabilia. Word got around and he received thousands of things, they are still coming in. So he decided to create the museum, which is expanding to rotating exhibits soon, the first of which will capture artifacts and reflections from Syrian children. It was one of the most moving exhibitions I've ever seen, and we would have missed it without the tip because our guidebook was too old to list it, nor did the maps of the city designed for tourists!

Home for a nap and a news catchup (caught Trump's boring speech in Saudi Arabia) and then to a supper of soup at the same restaurant as lunch as we're told their soups are very good.

When we return to the hotel Arnold is met with a "special delivery," Kerim says, handing him a bag with two bottles of IPA beer in it for which he will not accept payment. (They have been talking beer.) Our three "Bosnia Boys" from the hotel just couldn't be sweeter to us. They are all so different from each other but so special.

In the morning, we leave the apartment and return to the hotel lobby where Adnan has just returned from taking tourists to Dubrovnik the day before. Bear hugs all around! (Mr. Bean is there but not Kerim.) We dump our luggage and head to the Jewish Museum to see the replica of a page from the Sarajevo Haggadah. But there is much more in the old building, one of the oldest synagogues in Europe.

The Holocaust exhibit is deeply touching, focusing largely on the brave young resisters and their leaders, male and female, who before the war were professors, writers, doctors, poets, pharmacists. Twelve thousand Jews died from Bosnia under the Nazis. The museum gives them faces and life stories and a large book with all 12,000 names inscribed in it sways from the ceiling.

We return to the hotel to collect our things and bid our "boys" fond farewell. Adnan says he may visit Boston next year and we insist he come to stay with us. Mr. Bean hugs me hard and kissing the top of my head again says he loves me. The hotel owner waves goodbye and we jump into a cab and head to Europecar.

Our first stop on the way to Dubrovnik is Konjik, which we reach by driving through gorgeous, lush mountain scenery, mostly green and forested but with occasional rocky walls climbing to the sky. A long green river winds its way alongside us. Konjik is a small medieval village inhabited for at least 4,000 years. It is home to the Stara Cuprija, the best-preserved Ottoman-era bridge in Bosnia, although Mostar's Stari Most and village surroundings are better known because they are a UNESCO World Heritage Site.

We continue on to Mostar and find our way to the old city and its famous bridge but it is so crowded and crassly commercial we flee. What a difference from 50 years ago when I first stood on that bridge, bookmarked by two sides of a small rural village, and now full of cheap kiosk shops and ice cream vendors. (The original ancient bridge was bombed by the Serbs in the 1990s war and is now reconstructed. It's not nearly as impressive as the one in Konjik.)

We make two more stops en route to Dubrovnik. The first, just outside Mostar, is Pocitelj where the medieval Kula fortress is visible above the village from the road. Here Italian painter Vittorio Miele started an artist colony in the 1960s. But we now realize our drive to Dubrovnik is longer than we thought, and wanting to arrive in daylight, we press on to Blagaj, where a mausoleum and lodge built for Sufi dervishes sits atop a spring in a stunning setting of water, rocks, and caves. Nominated for UNESCO World Site recognition, it is still home to several Sufi religious.

We reach Dubrovnik at 8 p.m. and find our way to a parking lot just outside the famous walled city. Wisely, we leave our two suitcases in the car until we can find long term parking and the location of the studio apartment we have reserved, and a good thing too: There are mountains of steps to descend to enter the city (later we learn how to enter and exit the walled city without doing the challenging stone steps.) We find the registration office and after showing us to our digs they call a porter to help us bring our luggage once we have parked at a somewhat distant hotel for three days. Back at the apartment we tip the poor man who has schlepped us to our resting place only to realize that we have done the exchange rate wrong and have given him an insulting tip, which we rectify the next morning with a great 'mea culpa.'

The "apartment" is one room with bath and very mini-kitchen (sink, two burners, kettle and small fridge) but it's convenient and the beds are comfy. However, the one window overlooks a stone wall and a trash depot to which porters bring large, noisy rolling bins at night. The cats love it and break bottles well into the night. Then there is the proverbial elephant in the room – right above us. These are tourist apartments so God knows what the inhabitants up there do at night but it sounds like they are moving furniture from one end to the other and back again. At least it is quiet from midnight to about 6 a.m.

Exhausted by our long day and getting settled in, we go to the restaurant near us which is owned by the Amoret apartment complex we're staying in, 10% discount cards in hand. We order soup, starters and wine and when we get the bill we are gobsmacked: $70! Welcome to gorgeous, crowded, heinously expensive Dubrovnik. (2 cappuccinos - $18; laundry - $20 and that's just for someone to throw it in the washer and dryer and fold it!)

At first glance Dubrovnik's magnificent medieval walled city seems overwhelming to figure out, but we realize on our first day's venturing out that it is really quite small with only two parallel main streets (no cars allowed inside the walls) and many squares interspersed between them among its narrow side streets. The town is quite a bit like Italian medieval cities with churches, towers, a few museums, a palace (under renovation) and lovely old stone buildings. Of course, it has all the shops one would expect in such a venue and more cafes and restaurants than you can imagine. Even though it's only May the streets are jammed with tourists, some on tours, some from cruise ships, and some like us doing individual travel from every corner of the world.

Dubrovnik, like Mostar and of course Sarajevo, suffered bombing under the Serbian attack, with the loss of 500 lives. Pictures of the destruction are heartbreaking. But today there are no visible signs of the terror that filled the narrow streets of this unique place except for a small exhibit revealing the faces of those lost in the war, and photographs surrounding the home of a defiant artist whose resistance inspired many.

After a lazy morning and breakfast I go to the local market for bread, cereal, fruit and milk and find a farmer's market in the square where I add lovely strawberries. We stroll around in the hot sun, stopping for coffee at one of the copious cafes, finding a post office, visiting two churches, and generally getting the lay of the land. The highlight of the day is walking the mile-and-a-half around the wall that overlooks the old city and its orange tiled roofs as well as seeing the modern city on distant hills, and the gorgeous Adriatic Sea, dotted with islands and assorted boats. Along the wall there are a few cafes and we stop at one to cool off with beer and a view.

Then home to refresh before going to dinner – delicious Dory fish with risotto and notable Croatian white wine. Our evening entertainment is Croatian folk dance and music and what a treat. Luckily, we were here on one of the nights the young dancers and musicians perform.

Our second day here begins slowly again with an easy breakfast at home – we have asked for a toaster and a bread knife and can now jockey the electric tea kettle with the toaster. By now we are desperate for a laundry and hey presto! We walk out the door and see a guy with a big bundle of laundry on a trolley. "Is there a laundry near here?" I ask enthusiastically, having been led astray numerous times in search of one. Yes, he says. So we follow him and seeing the location race back to our digs to bring in our laundry so that it will be ready for pick up the next morning before we leave. Oh, the simple pleasures of a traveling life!

Back to the post office after that because in the old city there are no mail boxes, you must go to the P.O. to have the stamps you bought stamped by a clerk. (Remember no vehicles; I can't imagine how they deliver all the food and haul out all the trash each day!) Then a stroll along the port just outside the wall until a thunderstorm rolls in. We take cover at a café and order coffee. The rain falls harder so we join a British couple of similar age and enjoy a conversation with them till the rain lets up, whereupon we head to a small restaurant we've seen that serves seafood spaghetti at a reasonable price. The wine is good but strong so we retire for a nap. Tomorrow we will head up the hill, driving the hairpin road instead of taking the expensive cable car, for a panoramic view and then make our way to Split, also on the Adriatic coast.

We awake to rain so decide not to risk driving up the switch-backed road for the view and instead head straight out of town. For the next six hours, we wind our way along the exquisite Dalmatian coast, hugging a road that overlooks the sapphire and turquoise Adriatic Sea all the way. With its mountain backdrops, occasional vineyards neatly climbing over and sometimes up the hills, small islands in the sea, lovely villages along the way (two of which with their small harbors and tiny beaches I'd have loved to stay in for a few days), slopes covered in yellow broom and occasional rock croppings, and one massive view of a fertile valley below, it is truly stunning. So are the tunnels – some of which are miles long – and the viaduct bridges that are truly engineering feats! The rain having abated, we stop for coffee at a new marina (yacht club?) and later for a sunny seaside lunch in the town of Makarska where we have lovely sea bream, grilled veggies, and of course the requisite wine. Then it's off to find our way in Split.

Fifty years ago, Split (from where I took a boat to Italy) was a small town with a tiny harbor. Today it's Croatia's second largest city after Zagreb and finding our accommodation is challenging. But with my excellent navigator (I'm the driver) we make it. And while our place in Dubrovnik was really just a *sobe* (room) this *apartmeni* is a roomy two-bedroom place with a lovely living room, a full kitchen, a huge bath, and a washing machine – which would have saved us $20 for laundry! Situated right next to the old city, it's the perfect place and notably cheaper than the sobe. (However, food is still pricey).

We stroll to the ancient Roman city, stopping at a street market to buy fresh fruit and a hat for Sir Arnold-the-Navigator, then enter the world of Diocletian (AD 243 – 303), which starts with what is now an open-air museum, the highlight of which is the ruler's palace, one of the world's most imposing Roman ruins. The imperial residence that is the focal point for this UNESCO World Heritage Site includes a mausoleum and temples surrounded by a labyrinth of narrow winding streets that now house a multitude of restaurants, bars, and some private homes (with laundry hanging overhead.) It's really an amazing place.

We find a small family-run restaurant that we think is the one highly recommended by Lonely Planet and make a reservation for the next night (assuming we can find it again), then shop at the local market for provisions for supper.

The next day we day trip to Trogir and Salona. Trogir is small, beautiful and notable for its medieval walled city full of "knotted, mazed streets" as the guidebook puts it. It boasts a wide seaside promenade lined with restaurants and cafes and luxurious yachts, beating St. Tropez by a long shot. Unique among Dalmatian towns, it has "a profuse collection" of Romanesque and Renaissance architecture as well as a magnificent cathedral, making it a World Heritage site. The three-naved cathedral showcases nude statues of Adam and Eve at the entrance, the earliest example of the nude in Dalmatian sculpture.

Solona (as the Romans called it), is hard to find but worth the search (signage is not Croatia's strong suite). Here lie the ruins of the ancient city of Solin, dating back to the time of Caesar, and they are vast and amazing. To see them all you must walk a mile and a bit round-trip.

Exhausted from that excursion, we head back to our apartment in Split for a shower and a rest before going to our much-anticipated dinner. Of course, we can't find the restaurant again and multiple queries – having neglected to take down either the name of the place or its address - lead nowhere. Then, miraculously, we suddenly come upon the woman we made the reservation with standing in the street having a cigarette break. Voila! We settle in for a wonderful (if not cheap) meal starting with gorgeous sardines and anchovy starters and followed by a traditional meat dish, long marinated and covered in plum sauce for me, and beautiful scampi in a special sauce for the Navigator. We are served by Dunja, a lovely young woman who is part of the family that owns the restaurant. Her enthusiasm for food is remarkable and her warmth is contagious. A place for gourmet aficionados, we befriend the owners because of our own culinary enthusiasm. We also decide that Dunja is exactly the woman for Adnan. When I suggest introducing them to each other online she doesn't resist but says with a wide smile, "We'll be in touch" as she writes down her email for me. Hey, stranger things have happened and Sarejevo isn't all that far from Split!(We promise to come to the wedding.)

The next day is a long inland drive to Rovinj. We take the highway but still find ourselves winding through thickly-forested green mountains, occasional poppy and broom outbursts, and high, rocky, mountains in the distance. We stop in Zadar for lunch – an unremarkable seaside city with a strange combination of Roman ruins scattered about in the midst of Russian looking modern buildings. We reach Rovinj in the early evening.

Rovinj is a lovely small place by the sea and has a walled medieval old city that takes the prize for mazed narrow streets in which to get lost. It's is lined with cafes, of course, and offers a variety of boat excursions, including a day trip to Venice. (We are very close to Trieste.) After checking into our very pleasant apartment (which has a small balcony affording a glimpse of the sea) in a suburban part of the modern town we make for the old city where we enjoy a supper of spaghetti with scampi before retiring.

The next day we make excursions to the towns of Porec and

Pula. Porec's main attraction is its Basilica, another UNESCO site, with its amazing golden apse covered in mosaics, icons, and paintings.

Pula is a larger town and lacks a walled interior, but it is home to one of the most amazing and the sixth largest Roman amphitheaters in the world. It was created in the first century AD. Visitors can enter the grounds and even more importantly visit the subterranean chambers where animals and gladiatorial combat instruments were kept. These chambers now showcase amazing original vessels for transporting trade items like olive oil, and replica of huge olive presses and a wagon used to transport goods. Today the arena is the site of concerts, the Pula Film Festival and other events. We also see the Temple of Augustus and the Forum before moving on.

Moving on involves finding Gina's – a restaurant recommended by our Split restaurant friends – where we are told we will have a wonderful dining experience. When we do manage to find it up a hill away from the city it is "closed on Sundays." Disappointed and very hungry, we head back to Rovinj, where we find an elegant if empty restaurant on a quiet street which is bound to have the clean restrooms we desperately need and the likelihood of good food. The restrooms are terrific, the food is not. Fish soup is broth with some fish bits in it. My tuna is dry and tasteless but for the very salty bits it is covered in. The Navigator's scampi is unremarkable. Win some, lose some but this was an expensive disappointment! And so on to our final destination, Zagreb for a day-and-a-half before we depart for home.

Zagreb is a big city and not easy to navigate with its one-way streets and its tram-only routes. (The blue 3-car trams are wonderful and so efficient!) But somehow, we always manage to locate our digs, this time a room conveniently located near the city's main square, cathedral and upper town, which is the truly lovely part of the city. We check in and catch up on email before heading to the cathedral, which dominates a quiet small square. Its spires are impressive and the entire edifice is enhanced by its recent renovation. Then we return to the big central square for a drink in one of the ubiquitous cafes before having dinner.

On our last day in Zagreb, and Croatia, we take the short funicular ride up the hill to the old city where Parliament and the palace dominate but which also showcases quiet streets lined with lovely old homes with stately architecture and numerous museums of note. We visit one of them - an amazing sculpture museum by Croatia's late, world-renowned sculptor Ivan Mestrovic, whose work is powerful and moving in its strength yet calm. Then we stroll down the hill back to the main square before heading to the airport "pansion" where we will overnight for our early morning flights. It's a relief to return the car unscathed and to relax in the pleasant small hotel just a stone's throw from Zagreb's new airport. In the morning, we are up and out by 6 a.m. and after an easy check-in, the Navigator and I part ways for our separate flights home. We will meet in Boston this evening after this truly amazing and wonderful trip, armed with copious pictures and wonderful memories of gorgeous places and friendly people.

Croatia has the best gelato I've had anywhere, including Italy. It also has splendid wine but doesn't produce enough for export.

Dunja and Adnan emailed each other frequently after we introduced them and met briefly several months after we'd gone. They decided to be friends and as far as I know continue to email. Both of them have promised to visit us in the States.

Brigitte and our Polycastro Neighbors

A Greek Journal

Day One

I arrive after smooth flights and am greeted by the man from whom I am renting a car. He drops me at the Air BnB where I'm staying after an ATM stop. My landlord, Panos, who will turn out to be a lifesaver, meets me and shows me around the apartment which is clean, pleasant, well- equipped and in a quiet neighborhood. Then Panos takes me on a walkabout and drops me at a local market where I pick up some groceries and then proceed to get 'bigly' lost finding my way back to the apartment. Once there I go right instead of left and find myself trying to break into several apartments to the squawking consternation of the old ladies who live there. Shades of Zorba the Greek! One of them figures out my mistake and leads me to my digs on the other side of the building. I fall into bed. Tomorrow I will try to find my first pregnant lady. (I have come to Greece, joined by my friend Brigitte from Somaliland, to volunteer with pregnant refugees.)

Day Two

I wake at 3 a.m., worried about not having any juice in either phone or computer. Luckily, I had charged my phone sufficiently to text Panos when I woke up again. He came to the rescue and took me to a shop where I got the proper adapter. He's a gem.

He agreed to go with me to find the apartment of the first pregnant woman I was to visit and bring food. I never would have found it without him. Google maps here are a mess, all streets are written in Greek, and Thessaloniki has an overwhelming assortment of merging streets all of which are lined with apartment buildings and shops that all look alike.

We manage to find Yusra, a Syrian refugee, after I pick up food staples to take her. Sweet and seven months pregnant with her second child at age 19, her husband and father-in-law live in the apartment too. Hospitality gestures are big here so despite having no food on hand she manages to serve me a big bowl of delicious rice pudding. We communicate by the translation program on her phone. It's challenging getting consistent information but it seems she isn't getting much if any prenatal care so I am concerned when she reports headaches and fatigue - could be normal or signs of early pre-eclampsia (high blood pressure). If I can, with her permission, I will try to contact her doctor group as she doesn't seem to have an appointment with them for this month.

It strikes me as ridiculous that the organization that sent me here provided no addresses, no translator and no clear scope of work or other vital information. It's catch as catch can and What's App talk with many questions unanswered.

Still, having sorted out the adaptor and managed to see the woman I was meant to visit somewhat urgently today I felt hugely relieved. I took Panos out to lunch as he has been so generous with his time and so helpful. We ate al fresco by the sea (80 degrees, sunny, lovely breeze) - assorted fresh fish tapas - fabulous grilled octopus among them - washed down with Ouzo! Tomorrow being Sunday, I will play tourist.

Day Three

After cooking fried bread (no toaster in the apartment), egg, ham and tomato, which I enjoy on my terrace – but for sighting a rather large rat running around in the alley below – I head downtown on the bus as instructed by Panos. I disembarked at the Aristoteles stop, a lovely wide boulevard leading to the sea, buy some olive oil soap, and make my way along the port/harbor with its large tankers and small sailboats in the distance. The street is lined on the opposite side of the street with wall-to-wall cafes, all filled to the brim. A landmark 15th C. tower (former prison), called the White Tower because in 1890 a prisoner whitewashed it in exchange for his release, is at the symbolic heart of the city and houses a museum about Thessaloniki.

I decide to skip the tower museum and the half hour boat ride which simply circles the harbor and opt for the Red Hop On, Hop Off bus. No time to hop on/off but worth the trip just to see the view from the high hillside Old Town. I also get a quick glimpse of Orthodox churches, some ruins, and other places of note. Afterwards I have a café lunch of mediocre Moussaka washed down with Greek beer. To assuage my disappointment over the Moussaka (heavy on potatoes, almost no eggplant) I treat myself to a mocha gelato as I stroll back to the bus stop. After freshening up Panos picks me up to go to the airport to fetch Brigitte, who arrives from France on time to my great relief. We gab for a while after Panos delivers us home and try a local restaurant for a meal of lamb meatballs and salad with a carafe of red wine.

Day Four

We had two visits scheduled today – one with Aman and her family, another with Yusra. Aman and her husband, toddler, and six-month old baby share an apartment with her husband's sister-in-law her toddler (Dad is in Germany where they hope to resettle shortly), and her husband's parents. They are a lovely family who endured a boat crossing and 15 months in a refugee camp living in a tent during the cold winter. They were incredibly gracious, serving us coffee, then mocha frappes, and inviting us to lunch (which we declined). There is no obvious need in this close-knit family and it is apparent that they had the means to make the transition; it costs money to get this far. We leave with hugs and kisses amid promises to return after we return from Polycastro where the refugee camps are.

We return to Yusra, who has been having problems with a

painful vaginal infection. Brigitte checks her blood pressure (normal), does a urinalysis and listens to baby's heartbeat. All seems well. While there, an agent from the social service agency that is helping them arrives to take Yusra's husband to the social worker because their monthly UNHCR fund allocation has not arrived and their bank account is empty. We set about getting Yusra what she needs – a doctor's appointment next week; and medication for her infection. During this visit I learn that her relationship with her husband is good and loving, and that the social service agency has not done everything that was expected. Yusra is very happy to see us and to receive the donated baby clothes we brought. I think she has not had any visits as friendly as ours. (When I asked where my promised rice pudding from Saturday was she grinned and said her little boy had eaten it! We had a good laugh about that.) We left with huge hugs, cheek kisses and a promise to return.

I felt our work today was really worthwhile and good. We have brought not just goods and services but friendship, understanding and love to these people who I already feel deep affection for. Their feelings for us derive, I think, from their sense of being heard, believed, and helped.

Day Five

Rainy and cold this morning! Arrived Polycastro, less than an hour's drive from the city, in the afternoon and had coffee at the small, local Park Hotel while waiting for Veronica, our landlady, to lead us to our apartment. This is a small town with not much to commend it except for the British Military cemetery where almost 1500 English soldiers from WWI are buried, and the world-renown feta cheese factory. At the cemetery, it was stunning to see all the markers interspersed with red roses fully in bloom between each grave as the stretched up a hill to a central marker.

Our large, sparsely-furnished apartment here is part of Veronica's house. It is rented by Kayra, an airline stewardess who, when she isn't flying, works here pretty independently. She shares her second floor digs, a large open space with four beds (but no sofa), a kitchen and bath, with other volunteers for $12/night.

Brigitte and I suss out the town and enjoy a leisurely buffet lunch of chicken, rice and veggies with white wine for $4/pp including the complimentary ice cream dessert. Then we head home to call people we are supposed to meet with from the camp. We are here for a week (which seems long given the fact that we aren't allowed into the camp and don't have much specific to do). Tomorrow we meet two couples, one from Congo who will give us the names of other families to connect with.

Day Six

We meet Fanny and Arnold from the Congo at the camp gate. I immediately fall in love with them. They are a young couple expecting their first baby, well-educated and regal. Fanny studied Latin and philosophy and Arnold is in Information Technology. Over coffee at the Park Hotel they share their story with us and show us pictures of the appalling tent conditions they suffered through the winter on the island of Lesbos before being relocated here.

It is so hard on them living now in a big box, although it is an improvement, with A/C, small frig, 2-burner cooker, proper beds. But the communal toilets/showers are unclean and they feel huge despair as they try to cling to hope that they will get settled in a European country "where we can live properly, raise our family, and have a decent life." Fanny seems so sad and fatigued; she is probably not eating enough. And boredom is a big mental health issue here and in all camps. It is serious, and in my view could easily be called a potential "terminal disease."

After coffee and, I hope, reassurance, we take them to town and buy them groceries, then give them donated baby clothes and promise another visit. Their gratitude makes me want to weep.

Then it was off to meet Mike Henshaw and his wife Dari from

Nigeria. (Don't ask me how he got to be called Mike Henshaw, he is pure Nigerian!) They are expecting their first child in the fall and have decided to go to Thessaloniki and stay with friends because Dari especially cannot tolerate camp conditions. She is a teacher (he's a "retailer") and could be easily kept busy by reading to children or tutoring them in the camp but there is no skills assessment at intake with a view to meaningful "work" in the camp as an antidote to the unrelenting boredom. This drives me crazy! There is more to feed than the body; the soul needs nourishment too! How is it that Save the Children or other NGOs haven't realized this?

Day Seven

Today we met Irene and Stephen from Uganda and Ginette from Congo. Irene is four months pregnant and being monitored because she has miscarried once and is now spotting. They are a sweet couple, well-educated, gracious and deeply grateful for our attention.

Ginette's story is heartbreaking and it's not an uncommon one: She was promised rescue from Congo by a man who took her to Turkey where she was trafficked into violent prostitution that left her physically and emotionally scarred. She was sold from one trafficker to another, all of whom promised to save her from the last perpetrator, from one country to another. Finally, she escaped and got to Greece on her own. She now has a partner in the camp but no telling if he is "safe." She has left a 7-year old daughter behind in Congo. You would never expect any of this from such a composed, self-contained woman of 27.

Conditions in the camp, we learn, are appalling: All the NGOs have pulled out so the small nutritional supplements Save the Children were giving pregnant women, for example, and other assistance is now gone. It sickens me that NGOs come and go like this. How can they possibly justify such promise and follow it with abandonment? There is no medical personnel in the camp;

Red Cross literally does nothing more than hand out aspirin. Residents must walk miles to get food or to the bus that takes them for medical care. Why, I wonder, isn't UNHCR working with an NGO to provide van transport at least a couple of times a week? There are no activities, no productive use of skills refugees bring with them that could keep them busy and provide them dignity e.g., teachers could read to kids - if there were any books here, or they could tutor. They could even hold literacy classes for kids, none of whom are being schooled; they could be translators, carpenters, seamstresses.

Boredom is the primary mental health issue and yet it is not taken seriously or even into consideration. The latrines are filthy, and there are no lights in them at night so people defecate outside. There is no curfew for quiet time at night. There are no partnerships developed so that, for example, a local grocery chain could donate oranges and nuts once a month to the pregnant women. So much of this is relatively simple, inexpensive stuff that could be addressed if agencies cared and thought creatively. I have so much to say about such matters but who will listen? Act? The bureaucrats don't want to deal with these issues. But I am writing a report about all of this. It's the least I can do. Perhaps it will reach the right hands.

Meanwhile, these young couples (and particularly the women) touch me deeply. They are living indefinitely in terrible conditions, away from their families and countries/cultures, have no money, no work, very little privacy or hope, fight despair daily, and yet, yet – they are charming, grateful, affectionate, dignified. (I wish you could see Fanny, whose African twisted curls take 12 hours to arrange and make her look like a queen.) They smile, thank us profusely for a few bags of nuts, dates, and chocolate, hug us when we part. "Mama," they say. "God bless you!" I embrace them, promise that they will one day tell this story to their children, and hope that I am not lying to them.

Day Eight

No appointments today so we begin our day with a Ladies' Coffee Klatch with Veronica and her elderly neighbors. Veronica is a young mom with two kids and the neighbors are her adopted grannies. Our hostess is the 87-year old woman next door whose name translates as Little Gold One; we have dubbed her Goldy, and what a piece of work she is! Widowed over 20 years ago, mother, grandmother, great-grandmother, she has a wicked and wonderful sense of humor and an extraordinary spirit. When she drops a saucer in the kitchen while preparing our coffee she says, "Nevermind. There are plenty more and nothing lasts forever, not even me!" When she has trouble getting off the sofa, bent over nearly in half, she says, "I limp a little. Nevermind!" And when she shows us pictures of her huge family going back God knows how long, she says, "This one died." Then "this one died." By the fourth or fifth "This one's dead," she breaks into laughter and by the time we've seen the last of the dead relatives we are all laughing with her! She serves us delicious Greek coffee, cookies and crepes. They are so good, we're told, because she once ran a café out of her front room. When that became too much to handle she opened a small grocery shop. Now she does her own repairs and maintenance and keeps up her neighborly social life. Her other guests include her 63-year old son and two other elderly women. So we have a true taste of village life and hospitality.

After coffee, Brigitte and I decide to have a tourist day as no one has contacted us for new or reprised visits. We head for Lake Doirani which hosts an incredible bird sanctuary where we see heron, pelicans, cormorants, magpies, and more. Then we try crossing the border into Macedonia for lunch but are refused entry as the rental car is not insured internationally. So we head to the town of Kilkris where we have a lunch of assorted appetizers, meatballs, fried eggplant and the customary dessert, rich, thick chocolate mousse. Not our usual $4 but worth the change of venue.

From there we walk to the antiquities museum only to find it closed so we set out for a stop en route home to see the Women's Court – a 14th C. castle ruin high on a hill in an area that has been inhabited since 1100 B.C. It is said to be called that because it was so well fortified that "even women could defend it."

A word or two about the landscape and the economy: Here in the region surrounding Polycastro the land is green, hilly, and fragrant beyond belief from an assortment of flourishing flowers. There are roses as wonderful as those in Picardy, France in June, fields of brilliant red poppies, yellow bloom – the name of a wild flower – everywhere, along with petunias, chamomile, and more. Some fields are plowed for new crops, and wheat fields are abundant. All of this is set against a backdrop of mountains, some quite high over which clouds often hang like the famous Table Mountain of South Africa. The temperature is moderate – I actually wore a lightweight fleece last evening to take a walk – and the skies cloudy, but we're expecting a heat wave.

As for the economy, the situation is dreadful all over Greece. Virtually everyone is suffering with many families going hungry and, we are told, many suicides. This is a café culture and they are ubiquitous but either empty or inhabited by a few people, young and old, who sit together for long periods of time over a single coffee, out of work and with nothing to do. Here in Polycastro the only employment is farming or working in the large cheese factory that manufactures and exports Feta cheese. Veronica, who studied economics, says she will try to get a job there when her kids are in school. Her husband, an electrician, has some work but not like he used to. If things don't get better, she says, they will return to Russia because they speak the language (via family history). This story can be multiplied exponentially all over the country. So far people are not being evicted from their apartments or homes as it's against the law but there is fear of that to come. Shops are still open, except for the ones that are vacant. When we eat in local restaurants we are not the only ones, but there are only a few others. So while the crisis isn't totally obvious, it is real and it is everywhere. Somehow the Greek people we see seem to take it in stride, so far, but no one can envision a way out. This description mirrors the one we received in Thessaloniki too.

Day Nine

We go to the Farmers Market where we buy fruit and treat ourselves: a shirt for Brigitte and a crocheted sweater for me. We bump into Arnold and promise to take him and Fanny to church in the morning.

We are informed by Kayra – the messages fly fast and furious on What's App among everyone involved here – that a Syrian family who have been in the camp for over a year need to be moved to the Park Hotel so we arranged to pick them up. But when we get to the camp and wait for 20 minutes, to the annoyance of the military gatekeepers, they don't appear. So we go to the Park Hotel to see if they are there – not. We message Kayra who messages them; seems they were waiting for us to contact them at the gate, so back I go, message them, and take them to the hotel.

They are a lovely family, Mohamed, his wife Noor and their two sweet sons, ages 6 and 7. They are from Damascus and have been in refugee camps for over five years. Noor has lost two brothers and a sister to the Syrian war and they were nearly drowned crossing the sea to get to Greece. The two children were born in Turkey. The stories just continue to be heartbreaking and they put a human face on the suffering we see on the news or social media. Once again, I have fallen love with a couple we've met. Their dignity and warmth in the face of unimaginable tragedy and trauma amaze me and make me want to hug them close and carry them home with me to safe, sane lives.

After taking Noor grocery shopping we buy crayons and drawing pads for the two boys after which we stop in the crowded "plateia" (plaza) for a glass of wine. It is full of families enjoying their evening out – inter-generational, replete with beautiful babies and children, surprisingly high numbers of pregnant women, and folks who you would think hadn't a care in the world.

Day Ten

Arose today at 7:00 a.m. to take Arnold and Fanny to church but when we arrived at the camp gate, no Arnold or Fanny. After 15 minutes we message them. No reply. We call. The phone is answered by a sleepy Arnold. "Fanny is not feeling well. We are not going." How convenient pregnant wives can be! And how frustrating it has become that no one calls or messages when expected or has a change of plans, or is at the gate on time, yet we are assumed to be on call almost 24/7! Congo time, Syria time, but for two efficient elders it is wearing thin!

However, it gave us a chance to visit a small town about 10 miles from Polycastro known for its old narrow streets and fine wine. It is surrounded by vineyards and a magnificent, sprawling landscape of cultivated green fields, gorgeous mountains, and scenes of distant villages, some I think, in Macedonia. There we walk around and see remnants of old houses made of mud brick. We visit a newly restored Eastern Orthodox church, and have a magnificent al fresco lunch of roasted eggplant with melted cheese, zucchini fritters, delicious chicken in mushroom and red pepper sauce, and lovely white wine followed by yummy Greek coffee.

We return to the hotel to see if our Syrian family – who were supposed to message us about a pick up – are there. "No," said the proprietor. "They just left with some people in a yellow car." I go to message them again and find a note asking where we are. I tell them we are going to the camp to fetch some Congolese couples and will pick them up on the way back.

There are three Congolese men and a pregnant woman waiting for us at the gate when we arrive promptly at 4 p.m. as planned. "Where have you been?" they demand. "It's just 4 p.m. now," Brigitte tells them sharply in French, "as planned!" (Do they have any idea how much time we spend waiting for people who never show up and driving around in circles?) After much animated discussion in French, translated for me by the patient Brigitte, we get it: two of the wives (all pregnant) don't feel well but everyone wants to meet us tomorrow. Thereupon Rita and her partner climb into the car with us and off we go back to the Park Hotel for coffee.

Rita is four months pregnant and says little. But her partner is irritated at camp conditions, especially because "it's not good for pregnant woman." Usually gentle and demure, Brigitte says, "Well, then, you shouldn't have got her pregnant!" Brava Brigitte! This couple is alive, together, and have only been in camps for 4 months. We tell them that we've met a family with two small children who have spent more than 5 years in camps. Partner, who wants to be given a cell phone, also thinks not enough is being done for them, and is shocked to learn that people are starving in Greece because of their economic situation. Brigitte reminds him that Congo is not the only country where people are struggling under a dictatorship. He quiets down and we have a spirited but neutral discussion about world politics. I remind him that even Americans don't feel entirely safe now.

When we are ready to return them to camp, I message our Syrian family that we will be there in five minutes to pick them up and return them to the hotel. "Not now," he messages back. "Nour is cooking." I send him a clenched-teeth message: "Tell me when ready to be picked up."

Day Eleven

We have no appointments until late afternoon so we take Veronica's advice and head out to see Nickolemus Monastery, located high in the hills beyond the town of Goumenissa where we were yesterday.

The drive up the hillside is breathtaking – a 180-degree panorama of mountains, fertile green valleys, villages, and fluffy white clouds overhead. The monastery perched at the top of the hill we climb is amazing and almost seems like something out of Tibet. Built only 36 years ago, it is inhabited by about three dozen monks who raise goats, paint icons, chop wood, prepare herbs, make wine, receive guests for whom they serve coffee, and presumably pray a lot. We walk the grounds and visit a small side chapel before a quiet friendly monk invites us into the gift shop-cum-visitor lounge, serves us coffee and cookies, and converses with us (really with Brigitte who lives part time in Greece and speaks fluent Greek and who translates yet again for me) about theological history here and elsewhere with a bit of politics cautiously thrown in. It's so peaceful and beautiful in this place and there is such kind hospitality that I write in the guest book: "This place serves as a reminder that such harmony still exists."

After our visit we go in search of a vineyard we saw yesterday but we are thwarted trying to find it again, so we head back to Polycastro for lunch in our usual restaurant. At 3 p.m. we arrive at the camp gate and wait 15 minutes but none of our expected Congolese shows up, not even Arnold and Fanny, whom we trusted to be responsive to us, despite being stood up for church yesterday. We suspect that Rita and Partner have told the others not to bother meeting us as we are not giving out cell phones or being very sympathetic but it's damned annoying as we plan our day around these meetings with people to whom we have given time, attention, nutritional food, treated to coffee off-site, and taxied around! We message Arnold, then phone him, but receive no reply or return call. Brigitte tells me it's the same with Greek people and that she has grown used to this kind of thing but I can't help feeling extremely annoyed!

We return home, phone the woman who is supposed to be going to Athens but now may still be in Thessaloniki when we are there - and Amina, who lives in another town near here and with whom I've been trying to make contact since I arrived, still to no avail. Exhausted and frustrated I take a nap. Expect nothing, Brigitte says. I think she is right.

Day Twelve

We eat a breakfast of scrambled eggs – provided by Veronica's chickens – then pack up to bid farewell to Polycastro. On the way to town to pick up provisions and have lunch we visit our sweet Syrian family at the Park Hotel. Mohamad shows us pictures of the tent they lived in for over three years – with two babies, and through the freezing winter. The tents are collapsing, there is standing water everywhere, and there are snakes, he tells us. Then he shows us a picture of the snake at the Nea Kavala camp where they are now that had wrapped itself around Noor's waist! I ask him why Nour doesn't wear a wedding ring. "She must say she is widow," he explains. "I was policeman in Syria. Very dangerous. She lie to get out." He then tells me that he sold everything – all the jewelry she had, his own wedding ring, "everything, and borrow from friends, everyone." He has spent over $5,000 to get here and still no sight of moving on, although since Kayra has placed them in the hotel, perhaps an apartment soon?

We have lunch in our usual $4-a-meal restaurant, and the owner treats us to our daily piche of white wine.

And then we are off to Thessaloniki, where thanks to GPS and Brigitte's navigating skills we arrive at our new digs, another of Panos's Air BnBs in a different neighborhood. He meets us, shows us how to work the TV, which I manage to screw up (but we get it back on). Two days more and I will leave this adventure, having met Kayra, hopefully having seen Yusra again, and maybe met the elusive Raquida who may or may not be going to Athens. My Greek vocabulary is now up to +/- six words!

Day Thirteen

We phone Raquida to confirm our morning appointment and again get no answer, so we head to Yusra's apartment where we have a lovely visit with her and her clever, happy little son. Yusra is much better than when we left her. She has been to the doctor and tomorrow returns to get lab results and meds. Their monthly allowance has been received and she seems far more relaxed. She also tells us the baby is a girl! We converse via Google Translate and when the time comes to say goodbye I weep. I have become so fond of her and she has told me she will have no one with her during labor and delivery. I tell her "I will be with you in my heart. Remember that!" and she writes back, "I am happy with you."

Because of a bus strike the traffic downtown is terrible but we manage to find a parking space within walking distance of a market Brigitte wants to show me. After half an hour's walk, we arrive to find it vastly changed since her last visit. Most of the stalls are closed but a huge fish market nearby is functioning and we buy bananas, tomatoes, beautiful strawberries and an eggplant at a produce stand. We stop for lunch, a delicious treat of Turkish style beef in a tomato-based sauce with "smashed" eggplant and assorted roasted veggies followed by a totally decadent dessert of ice cream, cake, and chocolate sauce. Then we walk back to the car, stopping to see the Aga Sophia – a UNESCO church with both Muslim and Christian history but once again it is closed.

Then we head to the airport to meet Kayra. She describes a bleak situation that reinforces our own sense of frustration about people not showing up or responding, tells us how useless the Red Cross is, talks about her own efforts that go nowhere and says she is overwhelmed by the amount of help needed. She bemoans the lack of health care, the poor nutrition, the boredom issue and more. To her credit, Kayra is doing good work here. She has started an organization modeled somewhat on Save the Children or Kiva whereby she relates (online) the story of individual families she has helped move into apartments, fully supported for six months, while they await UN placement (we wonder what they do if that doesn't happen w/n six months). People can sponsor them via regular payments.

And yet, there is something of the martyr in how she describes how busy she is in Polycastro, how little sleep she gets, how her work is virtually the only true support the refugees she works with get. I understand where she is coming from and admire the work she is doing; at the same time, I notice that, as Brigitte says later, "she takes herself very seriously." I reflect on the fact that the groups we are working with have morphed into behaviors and attitudes they complain about with other programs. (Lack of coordination with each other, a who-does-it-better mentality, the hint of 'only we get it.') "It's deja vu all over again," I tell Brigitte, referring to my years working in international development.

Day Fourteen

We make our way to Raquida's apartment through the dense traffic and clogged streets. Her husband Said meets us on the street and leads us to their apartment. They both speak some English and we meet their sweet 1-year old daughter and their newborn son. When we ask what they need Raquida says, "clothes." We explain that we can't provide clothes but we can help with food. She says somewhat confusingly that she has money for food but she needs clothes. But when I ask what she has in the kitchen she says "nothing." I go with her to the kitchen to see what's in stock and she's right – the cupboards and fridge are empty but for a plate of rice pudding and some milk. I repeat that we can get her food. She asks again for clothes. "You are my friend, you can give me money, clothes," she says. At this I grow firm, explaining that we have spent a lot of money to come and help her and others, that we are volunteers, and that food comes first. In other words, we are not just cash cows! Ok, Ok, she says, and off we go to the market to buy fruit, vegetables, milk, eggs, rice, yogurt and diapers – which she insists must be Pampers and which we insist can be bought cheaper with the store brand.

Back at the apartment we phone Yusra so they can meet by phone; they are both 19 years old and have two babies – well, Yusra almost. Who knows if any kind of friendship will come of it. (I doubt it.) She tells us that Yusra is going to the doctor because she "is opening" and I worry that if she is indeed dilating at seven months she could have a premature baby. I send Kayra an email asking her to check on this and let me know. We then say our farewells.

That evening, our last in Thessaloniki, Panos and his cousin Mimi, with whom he manages the Air BnB apartments, come for a promised farewell drink. We walk to the pedestrian street lined with cafes in our neighborhood. Mimi, a former interior designer and now nursing student, is every bit as charming as Panos and speaks English well so we talk politics, babies, and birthing practices in Greece (not good). We have a lot of laughs. They are so sweet and we agree that we are family now, so much so that they are not charging Brigitte for her last night here!

And so I bid farewell to Greece after a memorable two week stay. It's been challenging, frustrating, rewarding, sad, deeply moving, and in its own way inspiring. It's been worth the investment of time, energy, money, effort. I will be forever grateful to Brigitte for being with me. I will remember Panos and Mimi, Yusra, the Syrian family, Fanny and Arnold, Ginette, Veronica and the Coffee klatch ladies. It has been an experience I will never forget, and one I will always feel deeply grateful to have had.

In 2017 I traveled to northern Greece to volunteer as a doula (birth coach) to work with pregnant refugees. It was an amazing experience and the strength and courage of the refugees will always be with me. Unlike other pieces in this book this is my unedited journal.

Icelandic Landscape

Iceland
Nice Place to Transit but Would You Want to Live There?

"I don't know what to do to celebrate your [70th] birthday!" my husband lamented. "I know you don't want a party or jewelry, but I can't decide what to do for you."

"I'm going to Scotland by way of Iceland!" my friend said exuberantly. "Why don't you come with me?"

So it was that I found myself on Icelandic Air to Reyjavik one balmy night in July with my friend Sloane, an artist and former helicopter pilot who had been there in the 1960s when the airline had one prop plane and a dicey landing field.

We arrived at Iceland's slightly less than bustling international airport in Keflavik, about half an hour from the capital city, at midnight. Exhausted and hungry (Icelandic Air didn't serve meals on the five hour flight from Boston), we were disappointed not to find our B'n'B greeters waiting for us as promised. When the two surly teenagers finally showed up their greeting was almost as chilly as the night air that took our breath away as we exited the airport. The trudge to the van was long and we were tired. "You are eighteen!" I finally seethed through shivering teeth. "My friend is nearly eighty-one. Take her bag!" They did, while I was left to drag my own, chalking it up with a certain amount of pleasure to not looking my age.

Iceland, it turns out, can seem like a hostile place sometimes. "It comes from our pioneering culture," my friend and former student, Anna, with whom I was staying in Reyjavik, explained apologetically. "We don't even have a word for 'please'. The literal translation of 'Please pass the butter is, can you be bothered to pass the butter?'"

That can-do-so-you-do-it-too spirit explained a lot as my visit progressed and I realized that a great many Icelandic people live in isolated farmhouses fending for themselves on an island often wet, windy, dark and cold. (There are actually more of Iceland's special horses than people.)

Still, the landscape is stunning in all manner of weather and a three or four day layover en route to Europe should not be discounted.

For people (like me) who have been to Scotland or New Zealand, done whale-watching, trekked across a glacier, and have no desire to swim in frigid waters or rappel off an ice mountain, four days in Iceland is plenty. On the other hand, if you're into hiking, biking or winter sports, the Scandinavian country that belonged to Denmark until WWII could be a destination unto itself.

Among the high points of a short visit is the famed Golden Circle, a 300 km. World Heritage Site encompassing much of Iceland's history and extraordinary topography. Looping from the capital city into central Iceland and back there are three main sites: Pingvellir, where Iceland's first parliament was situated, the Gullfoss Waterfall, often said to be more spectacular than Niagara although their drop is not as deep, and the geothermally active valley of Haukadalur, home to several geysers. But perhaps the most spectacular site on this route is the rocky, waterfall-dotted scenery showcasing the Continental Shift at its most visible on earth.

Another place to experience is the famous Blue Lagoon, Iceland's most famous attraction. Close to Reyjavik it boasts a pool of superheated neon blue water known for its restorative effects, although most of its annual 400,000 visitors probably go there because they've been told not to miss it. Unlike the naturally occurring hot spring pools that Iceland is known for, the hot water in the Blue Lagoon comes from a nearby geothermal power plant used to create electricity for the capital city. A full-service spa in a setting of lava rock and aqua water, the hotel, restaurant and bar all offer views of the Lagoon, making it a great overnight excursion, if you can afford the hefty tab.

Reyjavik itself is worth a day's wandering. Small for a capital city, it hosts several good to excellent restaurants (although one of its most enticing meals is a hot dog "all on" from the street vendor that anyone in town can direct you to), a few nice museums, a lot of shops for handmade woolens (at a price) on the walking street, a huge monolith of an arts center, a strangely phallic central church, and a five-star hotel where you can end up for happy hour when you've had enough hustle and bustle.

Any excursion into the island and its coastlines provides spectacular scenery. Anna and I drove to the Snaefellsnes peninsula for an overnight visit with her friend's family and despite the worst summer weather Iceland has experienced in fifteen years the landscape was amazing. From the random ribbons of water cascading down mountainsides to views of the glacier that marks that region to the huge white seal we saw basking on a beach, there was always something wonderful to see no matter which way the car pointed. And while the fishing village where we spent the night was not as pretty as I might have hoped, the local lamb we ate for dinner more than made up for it.

At the end of the week, leaving Sloane happily researching her ancestral home in Scotland, I boarded the flight back to Boston glad to have visited a country I'd never seen before, even if I did need woolies and a windbreaker the whole time I was there. Grateful for Anna's hospitality, and for the beauty of a northern island I'd flown over many times, always hoping that one day I'd see what I perceived as a mysterious place, I had to admit it was the best birthday present my husband had ever given me.

Italian Bowl

Tortura Pura

A Diary of Driving in Italy

Italian Drivers are mad!

Driving gets no easier and again we marvel at the lack of signage, and the insanity of Italians behind the wheel. Their tooting, shouting and gesturing begins to seriously grate on my nerves. Surely they can see we have a rented car (Europcar sticker on rear window) and a French license plate! I am increasingly driven mad by Italian drivers and am now shouting at them when they toot and holler at me!

In Pistoia we can't find the *citte vecchio* (old city) or the *centre historic* (historical center), although both cities have been recommended as not to be missed. It's frustrating but I quickly give up because driving in Italy is *tortura pura* (pure torture), especially in the larger, bustling towns where all Italians, it seems, are hot-tempered, impatient, rude, and always in a hurry. I have by now reached my limit. My own road rage has turned murderous; one more person honking and shouting at me and I'm going to commit a crime in which there will be at least one *Italiano morte*. (dead Italian) It's so awful that even my husband has taken to joining me in frequent flips of the finger and foul-mouthed shouting, both wonderfully cathartic. On one occasion, when I was backing into a parking space, he actually jumped out of the car to wave at my assailant, "just bloody wait" writ large upon his British face.

I, meanwhile, now have obsessive fantasies behind the wheel that go something like this: Some unlucky idiot has won the lottery. He's the one I've been waiting for, my patience and civility shot. "I'm getting out of the car," I say. "This one's had it." I slam on the brakes, punch on the flashers, open the car door, hitch up my pants, and head for the miscreant whose *insistanza* is driving me nuts. I approach his vehicle, lips clenched, hand raised like a stern traffic cop. *"Basta!"* I say. *"Basta!"* I've been practicing this scene in my mind almost every waking hour and now I accost him in my best fractured Italian. *"Sono una turista! No lo so la via. Sono una donne vecchia e sono molte stanco con tutti Italianos en machinas crawling up my ass blowing their horns a mio!* (I couldn't quite master that bit altogether in Italian but I assume he gets the picture.) *Patienza! Respecto! Cappice? Alora, aspetti, tu bambino di puta!"* Translation: Stop! Stop! I'm a tourist. I don't know the way. I am an older woman and I am fed up (very tired) with all the Italians in their cars crawling up my ass blowing their horns at me! Patience! Respect! Understand? Then wait, you son of a whore! Ah, now I feel better, at least in my fractured mind as I flip a finger in lieu of this oft-practiced tirade.

We reach Genoa on the autostrada without incident but there we enter our own version of Dante's Inferno. Suddenly we find ourselves exiting the highway without one sign indicating how to continue to France (or for that matter, Sanremo, a well-known seaside town in Italy)! Once again we are stymied by Italy's appalling lack of *directione*. We drive in circles, onto the autstrada, off the austrada, Husband in such a state of fury that he looks like he might have a stroke as he shouts and curses at the (lack of) system. Finally, realizing that we have now paid the same toll taker at least twice, we implode. "Directione Vermiglia" he says, indicating that we must turn around, which is totally impossible without driving into the city. Somehow (actually by making an illegal U-turn) we manage to get on the proper A-road, accosted all the while by irate Italians who have no business being behind the wheel of a car.

Fantasy #2: Having worked out that the best revenge lies in a "go slow" until the madman behind me is apoplectic, upon which I stop the car altogether, I take my time exiting my vehicle, saunter up to his open window, and point to the rear windowpane of our car with its Europcar sticker, and to the French license plate. "*Mira!*" I say, hoping the Italian word for "look" is the same as the Spanish one. Then I ask, "*Que dice tua mama? 'Ecco! Un uomo simpatico, con patienza e respecto! Questi e mi bambino!' Io no pienso. Io pienso tua mama dice, 'quella uomo non e mio!'"* Then I top it off with, "*Que dice si en America io non simpatico a tua quando no lo so la via? Piechere?*" Translation: "What would your mother say? 'Behold- a nice man, with patience and respect? This is my child!' I don't think so. I think your mother would say 'that guy is not mine.... What would you say if in America I was not nice to you when you don't know the way? Would you like it?"

Instead of acting out this relief fantasy, however, I resort to lobbing F-bombs out my window, and having now morphed into a flailing, sputtering lunatic, I actually stop the car in such a way that the driver has no option but to wait for me to move on, wave my arm in a back-off gesture, and shout "Shut up! Just wait, you SOB!" Far from feeling relieved, I beat the steering wheel, fight off tears, clutch the clutch, and lurch onward – to France, where sanity – mine and that of French drivers – seems to prevail. *Grazie Dio!*)

We purchased this beautiful bowl some years ago in the town of Ravello. The man who sold it to us was the son of the artist.

QE II

Culinary Crossings

The binge began an hour before boarding. While my husband and I contented ourselves with champagne and cashew nuts, the children stacked their cocktail plates with neatly cut sandwiches of roast beef, ham, and cheese garnished with pickles and accompanied by Scottish shortbread.

"Traveling on Concorde today, are you?" asked the First Class Lounge hostess somewhat condescendingly of my five-year old son as he decimated the treats provided to First Class and Concorde passengers.

"Um hmmm." He replied, stuffing a shortbread in his mouth.

"Ohhhhh," the hostess replied with a twinge of Oxford accent.

We were doing a Concorde/QE II trip to England courtesy of my husband's employer whose benefits included "home leave" for all of us to the UK bi-annually.

Once aboard the elegant if narrow airplane and settled into the plush leather seats, two abreast each side of the aisle, we examined the dinner menu to see what the ten-mile high offerings were. Concorde's reputation for food and drink had preceded our planning and we were curious to see if it held up. As we pondered, the best white wine I could every remember having was served in lieu of more champagne while my husband nursed a perfect martini.

"I'm going to start with lobster and smoked salmon, followed by the sirloin steak," he exclaimed gleefully.

"Me too," I smiled, wondering if that was a wise choice over stuffed quail.

The kids approached the situation pragmatically. "We're just having the hors d'oeuvres, the starter and the dessert," they agreed. "We don't want to waste anything."

By the time we'd reached Mach 2, reassuringly flashed on a screen at the front of the cabin along with our altitude, mph, and "miles to go," we were well into the petite pastry shells stuffed with caviar and the miniature pate with truffles.

"Amazing!" I declared.

"Yeah," said my husband. "Caviar! Truffles!"

"No, I mean that we're ten miles up and moving at the rate of 1350 miles per hour!"

"Oh, right. Pass me your pate if you're not going to finish it."

Nearly a third of the way across the Atlantic Ocean, the appetizer appeared. My son wondered what the smoked salmon was. "I'll trade you salmon for lobster," my husband cajoled.

By the time we reached the coast of Ireland, we had eaten our way through hefty portions of steak, gourmet veggies, a savory salad, and a raspberry parfait, along with a bottle of exquisite red wine. We were just over England when the last after-dinner mint was devoured.

I needed to stretch my legs but my husband promptly fell into a comatose sleep, wired to a headset playing raucous John Cleese British humor.

Once on terra firma, we vowed to be modest in our future intake. However, three weeks later, having sausaged, sconed, trifled, haggised, and pigged our way through England and Scotland, we boarded the QE II bound for home.

Everyone knows it's possible to eat your way across the Atlantic on a cruise ship. Breakfast is followed by morning snack, lunch is followed by high tea, and dinner is followed by a midnight buffet. Room services follows whatever you wish it to. We decided to splurge only at dinnertime.

Our waiters, Gary and Martin, were most accommodating. And then there was "Brunhilde," so-called by us for the Germanic efficiency with which she managed the dining room and its staff.

The fraulein's job was to "make sure you are getting whatever you want, yah?" It helped that we'd sailed on the QE II once before. This time we knew how to think like First Class passengers, no longer shy about ordering off menu. Within a day or two we had hit our stride, in collusion with Gary and Martin.

"We don't want to be any trouble," we'd tell them, "but do you think we could have Beef Wellington tomorrow night?"

"No problem, Madam," they chortled. "We quite like when guest order off menu. Means we don't have to queue in the kitchen. We go to the 'special orders' queue."

"Who eats the leftovers when we order something special?" I asked one night.

"We do, Madam. Do you think tomorrow night you might like a poached salmon?"

We actually became something of a 'cause celebre' in the dining room. Each evening our special order would arrive with great pomp and ceremony, occasionally cooked on the flambe trolley. Muffled sounds emanated from surrounding tables as others tried to guess what we'd ordered. One night, out of appreciation for our culinary flair, Brunhilde insisted that we have a special starter. "I know just the thing," she said. Then she presented us with rollmops of smoked salmon stuffed with caviar. I thought my husband would faint, but Brunhilde seemed deeply satisfied, as she did when she prepared a crepe suzette or carved a duck for us.

By our last night on board, we were all fast friends enjoying the dinner hour together. "It's a wonder people don't drop dead of high cholesterol," I said to Martin as my husband delved into the Baked Alaska.

"Oh, they do, Madam," Martin said. "We lose them like flies on the World Cruise. Had one at this very table last time. Fell right into his soup, he did. Everyone else just kept eating."

"It was actually very funny," Gary added. "Here came the doctor in his white dinner jacket. The nurses were runnin' after him, waving their newly manicured nails. When they got here they realized the resuscitation equipment had an English plug and the outlets were American! Lost him, poor chap." This may not sound like a funny story but it's hilarious when told with a Yorkshire accent.

Just for old times' sake, we went to the dining room for a full traditional English breakfast before disembarking the next day in New York. Martin, Gary and Brunhilde were all there to see us off (and to ensure a proper goodbye for them too.)

"We hope you come back," they said, shaking our hands and hugging the kids.

After boarding an Amtrak train for the journey home to Washington, DC, reality hit hard. Lunch was a pasty chicken salad with brown-edged lettuce on a plastic plate, and coffee in a paper cup. I smiled woefully at my husband. "Looks great," he said, attacking a stale roll like someone coming off a hunger strike. "I'm starving."

I guess there's just no accounting for some people's diverse culinary taste, but I have to confess it's nice being married to someone so easy to please when it comes to serving up a down home meal.

The QE II seemed so big when we took it in the 1980s. Next to today's ships it looks small! It is now a hotel, permanently docked, in Dubai.

Falling in Love Again
France Revisited

The first time I traveled to France in 1966, I was overcome with the flush of excitement as I explored the boulevards, monuments, bistros, patisseries and pensions of Paris. The medieval towns, with their cobbled streets and vaulted cathedrals with flying buttresses and stained-glass windows rendered me speechless, and often tearful. But what I remember most about that inaugural trip was falling in love and feeling as though my soul had crept comfortably back into my body.

It began on a boat-train from London to Paris when a beautiful young man, a Turk with a finely chiseled face (the same one I saw in Turkey 47 years later), asked if the seat next to mine was free. We spent the next week together, cruising the Seine, strolling the Champs Elysee, picnicking in the Tuilleries, meandering the Louvre, dining on the Left Bank -- as all young lovers in Paris do.

Many years later, when I traveled through France again, I was no longer an ingenue in search of romance. Still, in a medieval town called Auxerre, I fell in love.

My husband and I had joined friends to explore Burgundy by canal barge, a marvelous way to experience rural France. For seven blissful days we meandered down the Nivernais Canal from Vermenton to Chitres les Mines, all of 30 miles and 45 locks. Each day we glided almost silently down the waterway of the Yonne valley from one medieval village to another in our tri-color little boat with bicycles on the roof, peddling or hiking into town for our daily baguettes and other supplies. Sometimes in the morning we dropped by the village cafe for *croissant* and *cafe au lait* where the locals cheerfully greeted us.

"*Poisson? No poisson!*" one grinning host said to me from behind the counter of his shop one day, red cheeks puffed out, eyes wide with amazement.

"*Non poisson,*" my husband, the French-speaker said, correcting my abysmal accent. "*Croissant!*"

"*Ahl mai oui!*" cried the man then, his eyes squinting in mirth at me. "*Poisson chocolat? Poisson buerre? Poisson miele?*"

Sometimes we explored old village churches and read somberly the long list of "*Enfantes Morte de la Guerre*" -- youth annihilated during the "war to end all wars" -- two, three and four in a family, villages losing an entire generation of their boys.

One day we went to a trout farm, fished out our dinner, and grilled it with fresh parsley and basil offered from the garden of a local farmer. Another time we peddled to *Ferme Misery,* a duck farm, to fetch a picnic of *fois d'gras,* smoked duck, duck pate, fresh bread and homemade rhubarb jam, accompanied, of course, by a bottle of local white wine. In the village of Mailly le Chateau, high upon a hill, the chef from the *Logis de France* greeted us in the square.

"How do you know us?" we puzzled.

"But I saw you at the trout farm, no?" he replied, amazed at the question.

In Clemency, we ate our duck picnic in the shade of an old arched bridge and explored the birthplace of pacifist and writer Romain Rolland. In the evenings we tied up at lovely small villages with names like Colanges, Chevroches, Tannay, and Monceau le Comte to watched the sun set over gin and tonics from the tiny rear deck of our *bateau*. But it was in the ancient hilltop town of Vezalay, and in nearby Auxerre, both famed for their cathedrals, that I fell in love in France again.

We had gone to Vezalay because of its place in history and the stories of its famous basilica. From this ancient stone edifice built in 800 AD the second crusade began in 1164. From here Thomas a

Beckett denounced his king. Here, too, St. Bernard preached and here were said, for a time, to be the bones of Mary Magdalene. This was a place of pilgrimage and high drama and it is awesome still. Along the narrow cobblestone street winding its way up to the great church are flower-festooned shops, restaurants, and art galleries.

One of these galleries displayed the work of Francois Brochet, painter, engraver, sculptor extraordinaire. Drawn by the window display, we entered the shop and were greeted by a man who spoke nearly perfect English. He answered our questions patiently. No, he said, he was not the artist, the artist was an older man. Yes, he nodded, the work was wonderful, especially the elongated sculptures, so full of character and strength. Later, drawn back by the unique carvings, I asked again about the artist while my husband inquired about the town's history.

"Listen," the man said, warming to us. "If you really want to see something special, come back in five minutes." When we reappeared, he locked the door and displayed a sign saying, "Back in 5 minutes." Then he led us to a courtyard in the rear of the shop. From there we were guided down a narrow passage to a set of steps which descended steeply and darkly into a stone abyss in the ground.

"Since you are interested in history, you may like to see this," he said simply. Then he proceeded to show us his painstaking excavations of the quarters in which pilgrims had stayed hundreds of years ago when visiting the holy place on the hill. The cavernous apartments, and his work in bringing them to light, were extraordinary. Gently, lovingly, he showed us carved pieces of pipe heads, shards of dishware, remnants of life among travelers in another time, all of which he had unearthed. Pointing his flashlight toward the ceiling, he explained the system of piped water, the ventilation, the entrances and exits.

"It is slow," he said of his labor of love. "In the summer, there are the tourists, and in the winter, the bats." Then he hesitated and shrugged his shoulders with a smile. "You will forgive me, but I prefer the bats."

When we emerged into the light, he said, "Francois Brochet is my father. He opened this shop forty years ago, the year I was born. My name is Germain. You may remember it because of St. Germain." Then we shook hands, and he presented me with a poster of his father's work, a painting of Vezalay.

Some days later, when our barge trip was concluded, we made our way by car back to Auxerre, a city of narrow winding streets with half-timbered houses, and a magnificent basilica whose vast buttresses are reflected in the river over which it presides. And there, just next to the great church, I saw a plaque at number 5, Rue Cathedral. *"Brochet."* Next to the nameplate, a sign: *"Ouvert 2 - 5 p.m. "* And that is how I came to meet the artist whose powerful work would not release my mind from its grip.

Francois Brochet was a quiet, gracious, elegant man. At seventy-six, he was slender and erect, like his great elongated sculptures. His long hands and fingers were those of an artist. So were his eyes, blue and watery, as though at any moment they would weep for the sorrows of the world. His glasses rested on an equine nose complimented on either side by pink cheeks that rose up on his face like little balls when he smiled. He had a lovely moustache, gray and neatly trimmed, like his thinning hair. I fell in love with him instantly.

I loved him because of his extraordinary gentleness and because of his sensual art and because he did not laugh, nor was he vain, when I said I needed to meet him. I loved him as I imagined he must have been as a young artist, passionate and compelling. For a fleeting moment, I even wished we might have been lovers once. But most of all I loved his soul, because I had glanced, through his art, upon his essence and had seen there, without pretense or guile, a man of special spirit. He did not know, of course, that I felt these things in his presence, that I could not talk for fear of weeping, that I was moved to imagine, Pygmalion-like, that were he to have loved me once, my spiritual beauty might have been created. He only knew that I was among those who admire his work, having come upon his shop, and his son, in Vezelay a few days earlier.

We soon parted. But not before he had escorted us into the courtyard of his home to show us more sculptures. Then, smiling and pointing to the sky above the hedgerow against which loomed the great cathedral of Auxerre, he turned and said, "You see, I do not need to go far for inspiration. The inspiration is here in my own backyard!"

Indeed, Francois Brochet, as it has been all along.

An Italian Romance

If my love for France were visible, like the changing colors of Litmus paper, the tones of my affection would deepen where my heart beats if compared to Italy, a country that pulsates in my veins and feeds my soul. Italy, with its shuttered pastel houses, its spice-scented gardens, its alley sounds, its tempers and scandals, its *duomos* and its tile roofs, its scorching sun, its blue-green seas, its *gigolos* and *bambinos* and mamas lumbering in black, its crumbling facades and pot-holed roads, its street cafes and *trattorias,* is like bells that ring in the night: Italy wakes me with a start to remind me that I am still breathing.

On one journey I found myself overwhelmed by the place again, as though the country I adore were an old lover who had suddenly begun making familiar overtures. First at Stresa, overlooking majestic Lake Maggiore, and then traveling the Riviera's coastline and the fishing villages that drip down the mountains of the Cinque Terre, I felt the hot breath of Italian afternoons on my neck, and yielded once more to its seduction.

In Santa Marguerita Ligure, three kilometers from swish, yacht-filled, Armani-crowded Portofino, I found a two-star hotel whose colorful proprietor beat his fists on the table and shouted in three languages when he was angry. His tirades were admirable. They seemed to relieve him instantly of inordinate stress, like an eruption of Vesuvius.

In the town of Santa Marguerita, real people, like the hotel keeper, sit with dogs at their feet, smoking and sipping Campari soda in piazza cafes. They live above shops that line narrow curved streets, behind gorgeously painted pink, yellow, and green *Trompe l'Oeil* facades of brick and ornate plaster casting. They shout at their kids: *"Guiseppe! Veni qua! Angelina! Piano!"* In the evenings, they stroll along the quayside where local artists flog their work while children drip *gelati* down the front of their shirts. Then they fill the open-air restaurants surrounding the harbor to gorge noisily on pasta and fresh fish.

In a quiet neighborhood cafe, away from the waterfront melee of Sta. Marguerita, I met Roy Cesarini one day, and fell in love for the second time, having recently met the French artist Francois Brochet.

Roy reminded me at once of Brochet: tall, lean, impeccably dressed, genteel. He had the same kind eyes, doleful and full of feeling, and the same pink cheeks holding up his glasses. He, too, had a neatly trimmed moustache. Roy had interceded when a waiter could not make himself understood. "Can I be of assistance?" he asked with only the hint of an accent. And so I came to know his story, and to fall just a little in love with him too.

Roy was not his real name. It was given to him when he was a prisoner of war in England by a chum who had grown so fond of him that he forgot Roy was supposed to be the enemy. Everyone liked Roy, especially Elizabeth Weir. She was the daughter on the farm to which Roy had been sent on work detail. He liked her too. In fact, before long they fell in love. Roy was so special that Elizabeth's mother wasn't unhappy at this turn of events; so special in fact, that he had friends everywhere.

One of them managed to get a message to Elizabeth when Roy was questioned by the authorities. "Don't tell them anything," Roy's message said. "They will say you are collaborating with the enemy." And so, Elizabeth denied that they were "engaged," and Roy denied it, and her mother denied it. But he was sent to Scotland anyway. The letters he wrote to Elizabeth, and the ones she wrote to him, never were received by either of them.

The war years passed, each of them imagining that the other

hadn't written. They lost touch and one day Roy went home to Italy. There he married, had a child, became a cook, then a chef, and then a food services manager. His marriage was good and he was a happy man.

Still, Elizabeth Weir had been his first love, and her memory haunted him. So three years before I met him and heard his story, after his wife died, Roy decided to find Elizabeth. He checked police records and war records and whatever records he could think of, He sent his English friends on similar missions.

Then one day, he got a call. "I found the Weirs!" someone said. Roy went to England, met Elizabeth's brother, and learned that Elizabeth had died two years earlier. "Now I lay flowers on her grave twice a year," he told me.

He paused, then shrugged sadly. "I had a good life," he said, his blue eyes watering, "but she was the first woman I loved, and I don't forget her." Then he bent and kissed my hand. "Madame," he said, "it has been a very great pleasure to talk to you."

I smiled. The pleasure, Roy Cesarini, was all mine.

Romanian pottery

In Search of My Grandmother's Shtetl
A Romanian Pilgrimage

Working briefly in Bucharest some years ago, I couldn't help thinking about the grandmother I'd never met, and my beloved Zayde who died when I was seven. They'd been born in the Ukraine, he near Kiev and she near Odessa. Married young, they had lived a hard life, both before and after emigrating to the United States. What had their early life been like, I wondered, as they struggled to survive in a hostile environment, barely making ends meet? Was this the closest I would ever come to their shtetl, where my grandfather was a tailor and my once-beautiful grandmother lived the life of a lonely wife and mother?

When my colleague in Bucharest said she could arrange a home stay for me at a farm in a northern village, I jumped at the chance. Boarding a train for Suceava where my host family would meet me, I wondered what lay in store.

Bucovina is a timeless place. In the region of northern Romania bordering Moldova, once part of the Ukraine, horse-drawn wagons filled with timber or hay ply the rutted roads, verdant hills dotted with grazing sheep and cows spill into sleepy villages, women in babushkas and black boots carry baskets from market, and religious ritual remains at the center of life. But for the few battered old Dacia cars, the telephone poles, and dim electricity, I could easily have been in the middle of 19th century Eastern Europe, where my Bubbe and Zayde lived before escaping pogroms and making their way to America. Perhaps that is why it did not seem strange that in this faraway place I should feel at once that I had journeyed home.

Suceava, gateway to the famous painted monasteries of Romania, is a grim industrial city located six hours north of Bucharest. Arriving in sooty rain, I was cheered immediately by Daniela Gheorghita and her mother, Marie, who were waiting expectantly for me on the train platform. Dani, a college student in the medieval city of Cluj, spoke fluent English and had traveled home for the weekend to help her mother with my visit. She was petite and pretty and worked hard at accurate translation. "My mother says....." she repeated frequently as I clamored into their vintage Dacia for the long ride home.

Approaching the village, I saw women working in the fields, drawing water from wells, chasing chickens and children in the front yards. I imagined my grandmother's life before she left for the States. Did she wear an embroidered blouse or a babushka I wondered? Did she milk cows and carry a slop pail to the pigs? Did her hands look brown and knurled from hard work? Or was it simply that my host family was so warm and welcoming that instantly I felt part of their lives?

Marie, like her husband Ioan, was a teacher. They lived in a simple house on a hill in the village of Manastirea Humorului, and theirs was the first in the area to offer bed-and-breakfast, a budding enterprise in the New Independent States.

My room was a parlor converted for my visit into a bed-cum-sitting room. One sofa had been opened and made up as a bed, a table and two chairs next to it. A huge ceramic-tiled heater filled one side of the room. The windows were dressed in crisp white lace curtains, to the right of which hung a photograph of Marie as a young woman; to the left was a charcoal drawing of Ioan when he was courting her. In an adjacent room there was a television, and next door, a bathroom with a fine hand-shower, a working toilet, and a sink that spit out brown water.

But the room I came to love was the kitchen, where I soon realized all the living was done. Here, Maria performed miracles with chocolate, cornmeal, cheese, meat and fresh greens.

Her *mamaliga*, the traditional food of Romania some call "cornmeal mush," was the best I have had anywhere. She served it on a wooden board in the adjacent half open shed where guests took their meals, cutting it with a piece of string and sliding it deftly onto plates. Her *ciorba* or sour cream soup was hearty and delicate at the same time, which could also be said of her delicious pastries. I marveled at how all this had been produced in the little room with a cooker, a cupboard and a bed, which I came to realize was where Marie and Ioan sleep.

But then, Marie could do anything. When I asked for milk for my coffee, she jumped up, said *"Da! Da!,"* grabbed a pail from the wall and went off to milk the cow. She got the grass and mud stains out of my white sneakers and made them look like new again before I even know she had taken them. She drove the Dacia like an army sergeant and downed *tuica*, the local plum brandy, with a smile, a shrug and a hearty *"Naroc!,"* the traditional salute to health. Her house was immaculate, her household happy.

I only had to look to her mother to see the stock she was made of. With a twinkle of the eye under her black babushka, she won me over in her kitchen (where she also slept) in the house across the field from Marie's. There, I heard stories of her handsome husband, who defied the Communists when they had no time for Christ, and became a village hero. Dead a year when I met her, she showed me his picture and photos of his funeral, shaking her head sadly. And what a fine man he was dressed in white pants and shirt and a fur trimmed sheepskin vest! They were an extraordinary couple, Dani told me, proud partners and lovers to the end. You could see it in their photographs, and in her gentle pale blue eyes, surrounded by laugh lines, as they moisten in remembrance. Then we talked of Ceausescu times and Gypsies and religious history and politics and by the end of the first evening I spent with her, I had fallen in love with this woman who was my *Bubbe* incarnate.

I'd sensed that from the very first time I saw her in the village on my initial morning there. Dani and I had been walking slowly toward the market square when, like an apparition, an elderly woman emerged from the morning mist. She was carrying a basket filled with goods, her face surrounded by a loosely tied babushka, her apron in place neatly over her long black skirt. Her legs were covered in thick stockings and on her feet she wore sturdy but well-worn black shoes. Suddenly, I was overtaken by the sight of her. My eyes filled with tears. I tried to hide my emotion from Dani but she saw me and gave me a quizzical look.

"She is so like my grandmother," I said, growing weepy. "I feel as if I'm in her presence, as if she is why I was meant to be here."

"She is my grandmother!" Dani said. "Come meet her!"

At once, the woman whose face was so precious embraced me and smiled broadly. Then she said something.

"My grandmother says she is very happy to meet someone from America, and that you are very pretty! She welcomes you to our village."

We waived farewell, promising to meet again that evening. I blew her a spontaneous kiss. Later, when she came through the garden gate to the shed while I was eating, I jumped up and threw my arms around the woman I already loved. Dani grinned at me. "I really like you," she said. "I don't know why, but I feel there is something special going on here!"

· · · · ·

I could have spent all my time just sitting with Marie and her mother in their kitchens, but there was much to see in the region, so each morning Dani and I climbed into the Dacia for the day's excursion. Bucovina's monasteries were built five hundred years ago under the patronage of Stefan cel Mare (Stephen the Great), respected still as both warrior and religious man (despite the fact that he owned Gypsy slaves and could be incredibly cruel to his enemies). They are a mix of Moldovan and Byzantine architecture peppered with "Romanian soul and Christian dogma." Most of them are small with stone walls and wooden roofs, surrounded by living quarters for the black-gowned monks and nuns who offer guided tours. But the truly amazing thing about the painted monasteries is the frescoes that adorn their walls, inside and out. Beautifully colored in reds, blues and greens made of natural dyes, it is a mystery still how these paintings have managed to survive five hundred years of wind, rain and snow. Originally executed to explain the Bible to illiterate peasants who were not permitted to enter the churches, there is a striking similarity among the paintings, always the red river of chaos descending into hell to the right of the doorway, the martyrs making their way into heaven on the left. Veronet is the most famous of the painted monasteries and its *Last Judgment* is considered a masterpiece. Christ sits on the judgment throne surrounded by prophets and martyrs while sinners, Turks and Tartars agonize in Hell's fire and the blessed wait at the gates of Heaven. There are beasts and wild animals, angels, musical instruments, and God Himself sitting above Jesus at the very top of the wall. The church was built in 1488 by Stefan and a copy of his throne sands in the nave. Moldovita is the largest of the painted monasteries and its frescoes are among the best preserved. It boasts, in addition to a *Last Judgment* and *Jesse's Tree* displaying a genealogy of Jesus, a monumental *Siege of Constantinople*. Sucevita is perhaps the most beautiful monastery for its setting. It sits nestled in fortified hills, its white walls shining like a citadel. Sucevita's *Scale of Virtues* depicts the Last Judgment in which souls climb a heavenly ladder of thirty rungs, each one representing both a virtue and a sin.

Driving from monastery to monastery in lush green scenery reminiscent of Scotland or the North of England, Dani sang, talked of student life in Cluj, and told me about her boyfriend who was studying to be a priest. She asked questions about America and computers and popular music. On the way home, we stopped at Marginea, home of Romanian black pottery, and watch a father and son spin their wheels, wet hands shaping a generation of vases and jugs. Then, back home, Marie greeted us with big hugs, smiles, and a glass of *tuica*. After a sumptuous dinner of vegetable *supa* (soup), veal, salad, and sheep's cheese, we drank Turkish coffee together, laughing and talking through Dani's interpretation. Suddenly the gate opened. Grandma had come to join us. I was so happy to see her I let out a cheer. She hugged me and for reasons I am absolutely unable to explain, my eyes again filled with tears.

The next day it poured rain but undaunted, Dani and I set off again. At the small village of Arbore we were treated to a personal tour by the village priest who, Dani said, wanted to marry her aunt many years ago. She turned him down because he was "lazy and not very smart" according to Grandma. There, too, we joined a funeral where the priest was officiating. The body has already been paraded, open casket, through the village, and had been lowered into the grave when we arrived. In a not very somber ceremony, the priest droned on while women in head scarves chatted in whispers and children squirmed, staring at me. The cemetery was crowded with tombs draped in ribbons and plastic flowers, its grounds muddy pools of water. In nearby cars, wreaths of bread were stacked in readiness for post-service socializing.

After we bid farewell to the priest (whom Dani confided she found very attractive, thus launching girl talk and laughter), we took off in search of a coffee, which proved to be another adventure full of burly, unshaven men and a buxom woman chasing Gypsies into a back room while we drank the most exquisite cup of Turkish coffee I've ever had. As we were leaving I suggested that Dani call Marie to say that we were running late but she assured me her mother wouldn't worry despite the bad weather. So off we went, this time in search of a bottle of *tuica* to replace the bottle Ioan had brought back from his mother's village on the day I arrived. I soon realize that *tuica* is something you make, not buy. So arriving back in the village and coming upon Ioan, who had come down the road looking for his cows, we headed up the road to a nearby farmhouse. I waited in the car, rain coming down in buckets, until Dani emerged from the house in gales of laughter. "She doesn't have the key. Her husband locks it up but won't say where it is. We have to come back later!" (This, I learned, was because the farmer's wife had a particular fondness for plum brandy.)

When we finally chugged up to the house, Marie ran out and hugged me hard, frantic with relief that we were safely back. I knew, one mother to another, that we should have called. Then the phone rang. It was the farmer's wife. "Come back," she said. "I have the key!" And off Dani went, returning shortly with two bottles of *tuica*, one especially earmarked for Ioan, who, like the farmer's wife, was an aficionado.

That night, warm in the kitchen, Ioan settled into bed while we three women sat at the table looking through old photo albums. I was amazed by the resemblance between my mother and Marie as younger women. They could have been sisters. And I felt in my soul, as I did on the first day upon seeing Dani's grandmother, that we were deeply, historically connected. Once again, tears welled in my eyes. I had the distinct sense that I was home. I wanted to sit all night in that kitchen, immersed in the magic of the moment, feeling the love that surrounded me.

But morning came and with it gifts and promises of letters and future visits. As we ate a festive breakfast, Grandma appeared, ready to host the one-year memorial for her beloved husband. In her arms she carried the freshly pressed white shirt and pants, the fur-trimmed vest, and the belt she so lovingly beaded for her life partner, as well as her own embroidered dress and fur-trimmed sheepskin vest. The latter garments, the best of all she owned, she presented to me for dressing up in so that we could record my visit with photographs proving that I was indeed part of the family. Then there ensued all manner of excitement and laughter, and when I emerged from my room fully garbed, cheers and applause. We assembled in the back yard, a veritable alpine field, and took turns snapping photographs. Then, tearfully and with great hugs all around and promises of a reunion, Grandma joked, "I'm coming to America with the cows and the chickens!" Once again I climbed into the Dacia with Dani as we set off for Suceava, the sun sparkling upon a now familiar and much loved setting.

At the train station, I hugged "my Romanian daughter" farewell, tears flowing yet another time, and sent her on her way home – to where the heart is – and where a mother and grandmother, who had become part of me, waited. I wondered if we would ever meet again. Then I vowed that, somehow, sometime, we would. We were, after all, family.

Dani now lives with her husband (who is not a priest) in Chicago where she works as a CPA. Ioan has passed away. Marie made her first visit to America in 2017. Grandma is still feeding the cows and chickens.

These earthenware artifacts are typical of what you see in Romanian homes, along with embroidered cloths and clothes. My friend in Bucharest gave them to me when we worked together. My Suceava family dressed me up in the traditional wedding dress worn by Marie's mother at her wedding as I was leaving. They tried to gift me with the gorgeous outfits but of course, I refused such generosity. One of my treasured pictures is of the day I stood in the fields and were photographed dressed for a Romanian wedding.

Gypsy Girl in Bucharest

In a vacant, half-built fountain on the Calea Victoriei,
where plumes of water ought to be prancing up and down
Like proud ballet dancers, debris gathers instead,
The detritus of a nation sloughing off its dubious past.
There, listless, you sit on the cement ledge,
Rapturously inhaling glue from a soiled plastic bag,
As if it were oxygen keeping you alive.
Your deep brown eyes are dull, lifeless,
Like your hair, and your bare feet, the color of mud,
Emerge from beneath a flowered skirt,
Shabby and tattered, like the red sweater
You wear on a sweltering day in June.
You are all of six, maybe seven.
One day, I wonder, will this fountain
Be finished, and will its waters flow
Amid shade trees, cool and restorative?
And will you be there, red ribbons in your hair,
Reciting poetry like the next Papusza?

Papusza was a Romani poet who was excommunicated by her community for writing about the life of Gypsies.

Sacre Couer

Paris Blues

There is something ludicrous about standing on the Pont Neuf asking yourself why you're there. The question implies, at the very least, that your senses have become dangerously dulled, or that you are *nouveau riche,* an overindulged ingrate. Most people would give anything to stand on that iconic bridge overlooking the Seine. They'd salivate for the opportunity to stroll from there to a sidewalk café where, sipping a glass of *vin blanc,* one can watch the Parisian parade. What wouldn't they forfeit to gaze into the eyes of the Mona Lisa at the Louvre, to stroll down the Champs Elysee, or to wander the Boulevard St. Michel?

I've been lucky enough to have done all that and more: I've grown weepy at Rodin's "The Kiss," marveled at Monet's wall of lilies at the Orangerie, listened to chamber music in the stained-glass magnificence of St. Chapelle. I've eaten at La Coupole, seen Carmen at the Paris opera, walked through the Sorbonne, the Bourse, and the cemetery at Montmarte. I've shopped at Au Bon Marche and in boutiques off the Boulevard Hausmann. I've even fallen in love in Paris. These were all first-time experiences -- but there is only one first time.

Paris was glorious during my initial foray in 1965. Matrons in imitation Chanel suits glided through the Tuilleries to meet friends at fashionable bistros wearing matching leather pumps and handbags. Students on the Left Bank, cigarettes dangling from pouty lips, argued politics in bookstores and brooded in the Metro. Men in berets carried home the evening baguette, often on bicycles.

On my first visit to the city of Edith Piaf, the Moulin Rouge, and Yves Montand there were still French francs, delicious *prixe fixe* dinners, and prams pushed by nannies. In that pre-pyramid, pre-Pompidou Centre time when no such atrocities scourged the landscape, I stayed in a *pension* on Rue Victor Hugo that looked like a World War II bordello. I had croissant and café au lait for *petit dejeuner* served by a waiter in a black vest and trousers covered by a long white apron.

On that first trip, I cried at the sight of the Eiffel Tower and the Arc d'Triomphe. I took the Metro from Notre Dame to the Louvre, from Sacre Coeur to Montparnasse, from Place de la Concorde to St. Chapelle, from the Marais to Menilmontant. I walked until I could walk no further, soaking in the unspeakable beauty of a city without equal. I wondered if I would ever again see this extraordinary place so full of history, romance, and magnificent architecture. I vowed I'd give anything to experience, just once more, the twinkling lights of Paris bathing lovers along the banks of the river in warm twilight as *bateaux* sailed by. And with each subsequent visit, I discovered something new and wonderful: Place des Vosges, Harry's Bar, the famed bookstore Shakespeare & Co., the Picasso Museum.

The gods were indeed good to me, for I've visited Paris regularly during the past forty years and I do not take lightly that blessing.

But on my recent trip I felt, for the first time, like a jilted lover. I asked myself terrible questions: Why did I come back? What should I do now that I have explored, numerous times, Parisian treasures? What am I supposed to do here, now, this time?

I asked myself an even more ominous question: Is it possible for an inveterate traveler to lose the thrill of reprise? Is there such a thing as traveler's ennui? Do I need larger fixes and only new places to feel again the thrill of people and place?

I lay awake for three nights in a *pied a'terre* on Rue Temple, these inquiries gnawing at me. In the newness of another place I had just visited I was intrigued, curious, culturally alert – but not charged in the way that Paris had always excited me. I was chilled to think that it may never be possible to feel again that excitement in this most beautiful of cities.

Perhaps the problem was Paris itself, which seemed to be sagging under its own weight. The streets weren't as clean as I recalled. Congestion was worse. More Roma begged at the train station amidst noisy political protests; a man tried conning me with stories of a lost wedding ring. The Champs Elysee was now devoid of classy boutiques having been replaced with the travesty of McDonalds and globalized shops. The price of a coffee was prohibitive and yet the streets were clogged with people.

I felt like a mother whose children are grown and leading their own lives: She loves them deeply, unconditionally; it would break her heart never to see them again. But sometimes when they reveal things she cannot understand, she's sad, disappointed, worried. She longs for their innocent days when they were vibrant and beautiful, and for the love that beat so fiercely in her own young heart that she wept because of it.

I would feel utterly deprived not to see Paris again – as despondent as if I were never to travel to new venues. I appreciate how lucky I've been that work and wanderlust have taken me to so many faraway places.

But the fact is I stood on a bridge in Paris and wondered what I was doing there. That is as troublesome a question as I have ever asked. So I will not return to the jeweled city until I can answer that nagging question: What am I doing here? I will not go back without the kind of overwhelming enthusiasm that drew me there the first time.

Anything less would be a travesty.

Land o' Lakes
England's Glorious North Country

"I can quite see why the English like trekking through cow dung in the pouring rain," I wrote cheerfully to a friend from England's Lake District. "It kind of grows on you." And indeed it does. But Dorothy Wordsworth painted a much more poetic picture in 1802, a year after she and brother William moved into Dove Cottage, Grasmere:

> "There was the gentle flowing of the stream, the glittering lively lake, green fields without a living creature to be seen on them, behind us a flat pasture with cattle feeding...a dog's bark now and then, cocks crowing, birds twittering, the snow in patches at the top of the highest hills..."

Except for the tourists in summer season, little has changed in the nearly two centuries since the poet's sister, a gifted writer herself, recorded her impressions. As soon as the sun came out, we saw exactly what she had written so rapturously about in her now-famous Journals.

The Lake District, five hours drive northwest of London on the M6, is one of the most spectacular landscapes in Europe. Its verdant hills and mountains, shimmering waters, and narrow lanes opening into Lilliputian villages conspire to surprise and delight. Add a variety of good venues for eating or sipping Best Bitter in dark-beamed, brass decorated pubs, sprinkle with some of the friendliest people England has to offer, local craft shops, charming accommodation, and you have the makings of a wonderful holiday, even if the climate can be a tad touchy. If you are a walker, you will love the area even more, thanks to numerous guidebooks and ordinance maps that lead you to hikes of varying length and difficulty.

Although relatively small by North American standards, the Lake District is divided into north and south, or upper and lower regions. Grasmere, Rhydal and Hawkshead, closely associated with the Wordsworths, form the center of the more popular south or lower region. Headquartered in the Windermere/Bowness area, the only lake with motor boats and water sports, you can strike out for any one of numerous sites.

We chose Coniston village, four miles from Hawkshead and eight miles from the center of Ambleside, for our lodging. Famous for its Old Man mountain, the village is perhaps less picturesque than some, but also draws fewer tourists in high season. It is a gorgeous walk or drive from there to any other points of interest

One of the attractions near Coniston is Brantwood, home of John Ruskin, 19th century philosopher, artist, and social activist. A man ahead of his time except when it came to women writers, Ruskin is alleged to have influenced such greats as Tolstoy and Gandhi. The eccentric Ruskin predicted social security, a national health system, unions, and the women's movement. His home, which sits perched atop a hill overlooking Coniston Water and the village once drew visiting greats. Today it is a museum, bookshop, and restaurant -- the Jumping Jenny -- a fine place for scones and tea or a light meal.

Nearby, the village of Hawkshead offers two splendid 18th century pubs, good shops, and gentle village lanes. It is also home of the grammar school and the small church attended by Wordsworth. Starting a walk from here, you might traverse sheep-inhabited fields and hills, wind your way through stiles and gates, and struggle up and down farmland to glimpse Tarn Hows, much as William and Dorothy did long ago.

But sooner or later you will head for the main Wordsworth attraction in the Lake District, Grasmere's famous Dove Cottage, managed by the Wordsworth Trust. It is heavily visited by lovers of British Romanticism and less literary tourists alike. Here, enthusiastic, knowledgeable guides are on hand to take you through, pointing out furniture, artifacts, and pictures in the small, cozy house which bring the Dove Cottage days alive. Don't miss the room Dorothy wallpapered with newspapers for the children of William and Mary and be sure to ask why she chose to miss the wedding of her beloved brother to her best friend. After touring the house, browse through the museum, excellent for gaining an historical, social and regional context. Then cross the road and walk through the village full with shops, cafes, and galleries. Be sure to stop in the churchyard to see the graves of Wordsworth, his wife Mary, Dorothy, and beloved daughter, Dora.

Between Grasmere and Coniston, both good starting points for hearty hiking, lies the small, picturesque village of Elterwater from which many walkers begin, perhaps so they can return at the end of a tiring trek to the excellent and well-frequented Britannia Pub, with its outdoor tables and hanging gardens. A typical walk from this embarkation point might take you along the clear, rippling waters of the river, past Thrang Farm, to the old village of Chapel Stile, a center of the Langdale quarries many years ago. From there, you will cross a number of fields offering wonderful views of the Langdale valley on your way back to the village.

In the northern region, Derwentwater and Ullswater dominate the scene and provide a dramatic and perhaps bolder landscape. Here the mountains are taller and closer offering spectacular hiking trails for the experienced climber. As in the south, guest houses, country hotels, and bed'n'breakfast facilities are plentiful. Boating excursions are available as they are at Windermere and Coniston. Keswick (home of Coleridge). Cockermouth (birthplace of the Wordsworths) serves as the center of commerce, as Kendal and Ambleside do in the more southerly region. Keswick also offers hiking equipment rentals and live theater during the summer season.

In one of her journals dated 20 January 1798, Dorothy wrote, *"After the wet dark days, the country seems more populous. It peoples itself in the sunbeams."* Reading that passage, the two hundred plus years that divided us seemed to slip away. Like Dorothy, I reveled in the natural beauty of the Lake District, and its continuing tranquility. In spite of the rain, I would like to have walked here with her, in her beloved north country, stopping perhaps, to sip tea and talk of poetry. Like her roving spirit, I will surely return.

CAIRO MOSQUE

Middle East

"There's always tomorrow."
ANON.

Dubai Desert Wish

Against my better judgement I await the driver who will take me from the lobby of my hotel to an evening in the desert near Dubai, city of concrete, chrome and glass. I know that I've signed on for a typical tourist excursion that includes racing over sand dunes in a specially designed vehicle, riding a camel and getting your hands decorated with henna if you so wish. But I have only one layover day in Dubai and I figure that dinner in the desert under the stars is worth the cost of the trip.

The driver, who bears a striking resemblance to a young version of Libya's late dictator Muammar al-Qaddafi, greets me wearing men's traditional long white robe known as a dish-dash and a headscarf, or keffiyeh, held in place by a braided red cloth encircling his head. We are joined by a French woman and her young son and a young woman from South Africa, who climb into the back seat leaving me to ride shotgun with Qaddafi.

This is fortuitous because I get to talk to him like the feminist and journalist that I am. I ask him questions about the landscape as we set out on our one-hour journey and about his country's culture. As he relaxes into the conversation, which my companions seem to be enjoying, I tell him laughingly who he reminds me of. He thinks it's funny too. Then I ask about his family.

His wife, he tells us, was killed in a car crash, leaving him with three children, one of whom is a little girl. They all live with his parents now. It's a tragic story that makes me sad. I ask about her, and about their life together in such a conservative culture. Was yours an arranged marriage? I ask. Of course. Did she wear an abaya and hijab? Of course. Was she permitted to go out by herself? Not necessary. Did he think she would have liked more independence? No.

I take a risk and deepen the conversation. Qaddafi, I realize, thinks I'm crazy the more we talk, but to his credit, he continues engaging with me. "Do you think your wife, and other women like her, ever long for more in life than simply being their husband's cook, maid, laundress, sexual vessel, mother of their children?" I explain to him that I've just come from Somaliland where women are chattel. They have no voice, no right to their own bodies, no personal possessions, no way to be people; they are simply property, deprived of everything but survival, if they're lucky.

"No," he says, adding, "She got to sit in the front of the car, just like you."

I can't stop thinking about his wife. I wonder what she might have been like if she'd been born somewhere else. I wonder if she and I could have talked honestly if we'd ever met.

I explain to Qaddafi that in my country, his wife might be called a victim of her culture. "Maybe you're a victim too," I suggest. "Maybe you would have been enriched if she'd had more freedom to be who she was in her heart." He looks at me like I'm nuts.

We arrive at the desert and Qaddafi dutifully starts our high speed, terrifying sand dune dips and swerves. We beg him to stop but he thinks we are having fun. When we convince him we really want to forfeit this part of the trip, he relents and takes us to the campsite, where we forgo camels and henna and are seated on carpets for dinner under the stars.

On the trip back to the city, I notice that Qaddafi has removed his keffiyah, relieved, it seems to me, that he can drop the facade that is part of a job he wishes he didn't have to do. This time I ask about his daughter.

She is eight years old and completely enveloped in the traditional life they lead. "What do you think she would like to be when she grows up if she could choose?" I ask. Qaddafi looks at me like I'm totally ridiculous. "What if she could go to school, maybe become a teacher or a nurse, or even a doctor?" I continue. "Think about it. She's probably full of life. Don't you want her to be all that she dreams of?"

For some reason I feel a fierce attachment to this unseen child. I care about her, just as I feel sad for her mother, and all the other females like them. I think Qaddafi is probably a good man in a bad culture. I really want to reach him.

"Listen," I say. I tell him about the work that I do to help make the lives of women and girls better. I explain western ideas about human rights, women's rights, freedom and autonomy. I talk about living the fullest life possible as God's gift and blessing. I can't be sure but maybe, just maybe, I've planted a seed.... "I'm telling you," I smile. "I'm going to be on your shoulder as that little girl grows up! I'm going to keep whispering in your ear about her. I won't go away so watch out! I'm always going to be there for her!"

When he drops us off at the hotel, Qaddafi smiles at me. I extend my hand and he actually shakes it. I am glad I have gone to the desert in a dune buggy. It's an experience I don't forget. Perhaps Qaddafi remembers it too.

It is several years now since I was in Dubai. I still think about that little girl and I still whisper in Qaddafi's ear. I like to think he hears me as he watches his daughter dance to her dreams. I like to imagine that he takes joy in seeing the young woman she is becoming. It's a long shot, I know, but hey, a girl can dream at any age, can't she?

I often think about that little girl, and wonder if her father thinks of me as she grows older. You don't always know when you have made a difference in someone's life.

The Wailing Wall

Israel

When the sun rises and sets in the ancient city of Jerusalem a lavender hue of such peacefulness envelops the landscape that it becomes difficult to imagine the violence that has always dominated its history. In those pink-blue moments of calm daybreak and in the restfulness of twilight, I tried to imagine what it would have been like to have lived in the time of the Canaanites and Christ, to have endured invasions by Roman legions, Crusaders, and Turks, to have been evicted time and time again, as a Jew, from one's homeland, to have felt the terror of door to door fighting during the Six Day War of 1967, after which it was said that every family in the city wore black for a month because no home was left untouched by the carnage. And in my quiet moments, I tried to understand the enormous emotion and conflict I felt as I visited the land of my ancestors.

One day, I stood on a Jerusalem street corner with the Women in Black, a group of Israeli and Arab women who for years demonstrated peacefully every Friday afternoon for an end to the violence between their peoples. I'd met Lila, one of the organizers, at a women's conference in New York. She took me with her on my first Friday in Israel. A large, imposing woman with auburn hair, she reminded me that the two forces dominating everything in Israel are politics and religion.

"There's an election coming up," Lila said. "We hope fervently that a new Labor government will behave as if it has power. We want desperately to see a reordering of priorities in this country. After all, we are burdened like so many others by debt, social problems, and the absolutely ridiculous policies of a long-term conservative government."

I am ashamed to admit how terrified I felt at the prospect of joining the Women in Black. I'd heard stories of what could happen if you stood in symbolic black waving peace placards. Vitriolic verbal attacks were the least of it. What really frightened me was the possibility of physical abuse and the idea of objects being hurled from passing cars and buses.

Sure enough, as I stood with the women, a man shouted from across the street, "Whores of Israel! Bitches! Sluts!"

At that, six angry teenage boys with *yarmulkes* on their heads and prayer shawls around their necks hurled stones at us. "Kill them! Traitors! Arafat's lovers!"

Women doing their *shabbas* shopping walked around us, their faces portraits of disdain. Children clutched their mothers' hands as if we were witches. From a bus, people shook their fists at us and screamed words we couldn't hear.

The internal anguish I felt after my first week in Israel was unresolved by having stood so briefly with women whom I had hoped would strengthen my own visceral conviction. Had I been able to spend more time with Lila, perhaps she could have helped me find expression for the emotions roiling inside me. But the encounters I was having in that tiny, complex country were only deepening my inner turmoil and there seemed no relief.

One source of that turmoil was the age-old battle for a beleaguered piece of land, and what I brought to it as someone with a Jewish heritage. "Go to Israel," my Jewish friends had told me over the years, "and you will see. You will feel something incredible, and you will be moved in ways that you can never understand unless you have been there." They were right. I should not have been so surprised to feel it, even as a secular Jew of the Diaspora.

As I stood over the Galilean hills and the Golan Heights, just beyond Mt. Hermon to where Syria and Lebanon lurked, I looked down upon the village that has endured sporadic terrorist attacks for years and where not long before my visit a group of children had been systematically executed. I spent a night on a kibbutz and saw first-hand what a people had made of the barren land. I stood on top of Masada and wondered what it must have been like to be among the 960 Jews who committed mass suicide rather than become Roman slaves. And I went to Yad Vashem, where I gazed in silence upon the single shoe of a child, preserved in remembrance of the million and a half children who perished in Nazi Germany. Is it any wonder that if you tell an Israeli the brutality must stop they will remind you that unless you have been an Israelite you cannot understand?

Women are not the only ones in black in Israel. There are also the Hasidim, the ultraorthodox sect of religious Jews whose beliefs and lifestyle offend many modern Israelis, and who caused me anguish. In their long black coats, beards and hairlocks hanging from beneath thick black hats, they are called "parasites" by some who are angry that their children are exempted from military service. For me, they represented something else: the institutionalized oppression of women that seemed to go unnoticed in Israel, even by most women.

"Shall I tell you what I think of feminism?" one tour guide asked me. "I would rather be free in my home to be revered as the center of my family. Who wants to work outside and then come back at night to do all the work in the house as well?"

"But shouldn't that be changed? Why not share the work, as a family?"

"Somebody has to lead and somebody has to follow. That's the way it is. It's tradition, and you can't change it."

"But it's not about tradition!" I argued. "It's about oppression and patriarchy!"

"Back off," my gentile husband said. "You'll create an international incident." He joked with the guide about what a zealot I can be and tried to divert my attention to the Wailing Wall. But there I saw women praying five deep in the hot sun while on the other side of a dividing screen the men stretched out in the shade along the major portion of Judaism's most sacred symbol. When women had tried to pray on that side not long before, chairs were thrown at them, along with hideous invectives.

Suddenly a man rushed at me, screaming. "What is he saying?" I asked our guide.

"He says you should cover your shoulders."

"But it's 100 degrees out!"

I wore a sundress that reached my ankles but left my shoulders exposed. The idea that a man was shouting at me about my dress was infuriating. Then a woman approached me. I thought she was an activist who wanted my support but she began to question me.

"Do you light the Sabbath candles?" I shook my head no.

"But it is our duty! We women must keep alive the traditions of the home."

Then, pointing to a group of women swaying five-deep at the Wailing Wall, their heads completely covered in the hot sun, she asked, "Why don't you go to touch the wall?"

"I will touch it when I can do it over there," I said, pointing to the long shade of the men's most sacred side. "I will touch it when you are not considered polluted and forced to leave your marriage bed when you are menstruating. I will touch it when I can touch the Torah."

Never had I felt so lonely in a crowd as I remembered Virginia Woolf's words: *"As a woman, I have no nation. As a woman, I want no nation. As a woman, the world is my nation."*

Later, in the King David museum, I cringed at an exhibit entitled *Man and His Kitchen*. Where was women's contribution to Jewish history? Why were all the streets named after men? Where were women's voices in the *Jerusalem Post*? How could it be that in one tourist brochure alone there were sixteen ads for "efficient escorts" and "gracious girls" in a land that so revered its own mothers?

Slowly my anger abated, but not my confusion. Not my

conflicted political convictions. I deplored the pain of Jewish suffering through the ages, and felt genuine empathy for the Arab minority, now so oppressed. How could I know what I would feel if I had lived in the tortured and exquisite holy city where in the name of religion so many have been exiled and brutalized?

Perhaps if I'd had more time in the oasis offered by the Women in Black, if I'd made friends with Lila's circles, I would have had a clearer sense of Israel's political dilemma and its relation to women. But all I could feel was bewildered. I was haunted and hopeful at the same time. I was moved by two cultures I could not understand, enraged by yet another example of unchallenged misogyny, and heartsick at the victimization of innocent people. How was I to reconcile all that?

The trip to Israel was a difficult one, but I'm glad to have gone when it was safe and most of the country was accessible. Since that visit, as a journalist, I have often condemned Israel's oppression of the Palestinians living in the occupied territories. I've taken a lot of criticism for that from family, friends and strangers. I continue to wonder, sadly, how a people who have suffered as much as we Jews have can treat others so badly.

The Late, Much Loved Rula Quawas

Jordan

A Post-Feminist Era? Not By a Long Shot

They sit in a semi-circle, fully attentive. Some wear hijab, looking like Botticelli-painted nuns. Others reveal their hair, perhaps a headscarf wrapped loosely around their necks. Some are married and mothers, some are single, one is a foreign student earning her Ph.D. studying art as social commentary among Middle Eastern women. A few are struggling to find their way to feminism in a Middle East context while others celebrate their arrival into the world of like-minded women. They are studying for a master's degree at the University of Jordan in Amman, where I was invited to speak about the history of the women's movement in America and beyond.

The young women gazing at me remind me of something I have known since I became engaged in, and committed to, feminism: The world is full of feminists, fledging or fully developed. They reside in every continent and community and likely have been there for a long time, although we may not have called them that in their day. They remind me too of women I met in Nairobi at the final UN Decade for Women conference in 1985, some who came knowing they would be severely punished when they returned home, and yet they came, 14,000 strong.

They remind me of women I met in Beijing ten years later at the Fourth World Conference on Women, some of whom came with male chaperones, and yet they came, 40,000 strong. They remind me of women who came to give testimony, to offer analysis through the lens of gender, to speak truth to power, to inspire and advise others.

Women in the thousands – each representing many more from their communities - came to these places far away from home to address issues of poverty, violence, human rights, the environment, economic security, peace, justice and more. They came because as one feminist said, "It is clear that the world we live in is driving us mad by limiting our possibilities and insisting on our second class status." They came to declare that "We are here, there and everywhere, and we are not going away."

The women I met in Jordan reminded me of the diversity of feminists and "feminisms," and of the ways in which all feminists make a difference. Laila al-Atrash, for example, is a novelist and media figure recognized by the Arab Human Report as a writer who has influenced her society in meaningful ways. Her works have been incorporated into university curricula and adapted as movies.

Rula Quawas, the professor of American Literature and Feminist Theory who invited me to Jordan, founded the Women's Studies Center at the university in 2006 and served as its director for two years. "I look at the classroom as a site of resistance," she says. "We discuss, debate, raise awareness. We need to ensure that grassroots women know what is going on and that they are no longer silent or silenced. It is essential they be part of the fabric of society," says the beloved teacher. Four of her students recently produced a documentary video about sexual harassment on the campus of their university. It was considered an outrage by many people. Dr. Quawas and her students were threatened, but their courage opened a dialogue that never would have occurred had she and her students not brought the matter to light.

Rawan Ibrahim, an academic in social work who attended high school in Vermont, is researching the stigmatization that many orphans face in Jordan, especially the circumstances of those born out of wedlock. She works to change attitudes and provide social services to this vulnerable population. She also works to support the Jordanian government's effort to deinstitutionalize children through the development of the first formal foster care program in the region.

Then there is Abeer Alshroof, a young woman who with her

husband is active in an initiative designed to help orphans and underprivileged families secure basic necessities. "One of our main purposes is to see that the children continue their education instead of having to work in order to help their families," Abeer says. "We want the children to know that they be whatever they want and that poverty will not stand in their way."

The students in Rula Quawas's class are following in the footsteps of these feminist role models. They are learning from the wisdom, intellect and courage of the women who have gone before them. They are growing into their own feminism, one that is sensitive to gender, culture, and the wider world in which they live. That's why one of them, Leen Arkhagha, wrote a poem encouraging other young women to resist oppression and to embrace a vision of what their future can be instead of yielding to tradition. It includes these lines:

"It does break my heart after all,
That you have chosen to torture your soul
And pull away from the person you are,
Only leaving another bruise and scar.

Will you forever abandon the magic you master?
Have you not thought of what would happen hereafter?"

It's a sentiment that every woman in Nairobi or Beijing would understand. It's also a call to budding feminists everywhere, especially those in a classroom it was my privilege to visit in Jordan.

I met my friend, Rula Quawas, when she was teaching in Vermont on a Fulbright Scholarship. Our paths crossed again at a conference in Boston not long after she had returned home. Jordan's leading feminist scholar and activist, she invited me to Amman to guest lecture in her women's studies classes. It was my second trip to Jordan so instead of visiting Petra and all the historic sites, I was able to spend quality time with Rula and her friends. She passed away suddenly at the age of 57 a year after I was there.

NAVAJO HANDCRAFTS

North America

"You might as well expect rivers to run backwards as any man [sic] born free to be contented penned up."

CHIEF JOSEPH

Shadows and Stars

> It seems to me that the shadows are of supreme importance in perspective.
>
> LEONARDO DA VINCI

Key Largo is in a word, retro -- a throwback to the 1950s. You might not realize it on a drive-through to Key West, but you get it if you stop overnight. You feel it staring at the *African Queen*, the actual boat in which Bogie and Hepburn made cinematic history. (The boat is unmistakable with its canopy and the boiler Bogey kept banging to keep her moving.) You sense it stopping in the late afternoon at the Caribbean Club where bearded guys with tattoos play pool and drink Coors surrounded by Bogie and Bacall pictures from the movie *Key Largo*. If this doesn't do it, try sun-downers at the Sheraton, a flamingo-pink pseudo-tropical getaway that shouts for pedal pushers and ruffled off-the-shoulder halter tops. Key Largo is definitely a 1950s kind of place.

We were in the mood for it when we pulled in for the night at The Blue Lagoon, post-war cottages nestled between the Gulf of Mexico and U.S. Route 1. The guidebook billed it as a "resort run by caring hosts who make mom-and-pop lodges worthy of your patronage." It was no resort, but it was pleasantly tropical. Driving into lush, overgrown gardens randomly surrounding the grounds with colorful bougainvillea and assorted orchid-like flowers was promising.

The woman on duty, Mary Beth, was friendly. But Lazlo, the proprietor, was hardly my idea of "pop." Deeply tanned, his Hawaiian shirt seductively open half-way down his chest, his square face chiseled as romance novels boast, he was remarkably handsome. His blue-gray eyes and equine nose were offset by a perfectly shaped mouth and straight, square teeth.

Salt-and-pepper hair added to his good looks.

"Is this your daughter?" he asked my husband, as I approached Lazlo's pickup truck after we'd registered.

For a nanosecond I thought he was serious. Then I got angry: Lazlo had played with my ego and made me feel stupid. People named Lazlo, guys who had escaped Hungary in 1956, were supposed to be like Victor Lazlo in *Casablanca*, suave and chivalrous, not ridiculous or insulting.

Suddenly Mary Beth appeared. "I'm wearing your shirt," she said, taunting Lazlo, cigarette in hand. "You put it in the give-away bag, but I got it out." Then she said, "He was going to toss it and it's a perfectly good shirt." She drew on her cigarette, fingering Lazlo's blue denim shirt. "You wouldn't think he's my boss, the way I talk to him."

Lazlo was telling my husband about his German neighbors. I don't know what triggered the conversation. Then, looking at me, he said, "You're Jewish, aren't you? You know what they did last April? They celebrated Hitler's birthday! Can you imagine!" He smiled conspiratorially.

"Remarkable," I said.

Mary Beth smiled at Lazlo as she drifted toward the office. She was clearly in love with him; her compulsions were such that she was incapable of hiding it.

The sun cast long shadows across the gardens. A chill permeated the air. I entered the cottage we had rented for the night. It was reminiscent of places my parents had rented on vacations before there were Holiday Inns. The kitchen had a porcelain table and two chairs in front of a window with Venetian blinds. Plastic flowers adorned the table. A tea towel hung from the refrigerator door. A coffeemaker and toaster sat on the Formica counter. In the bathroom, a paper mat with a map of Florida lay in front of a shower covered by a mildewing plastic curtain. Two skimpy towels hung from a towel bar above the toilet. Miniature Ponds soaps lay next to plastic cups covered in Saran Wrap. Yellowing wallpaper peeled away from the sink. In the main room, a television mounted on a shelf presided over a double bed made with overly laundered sheets. An open closet hosted naked wire hangers above a luggage rack. Two rattan chairs stared vacantly at each other across the room. Through screened Jalousie windows, a breeze moved faded print curtains. I wondered if Bogie and Bacall had digs like this when they were filming.

I went to the office. Mary Beth was eating spaghetti from a styrofoam container, watching TV. I fingered the brochures in a rack looking for a seafood restaurant.

"What can I do for ya?" she asked. She recommended Alabama Jack's, a vintage barge restaurant specializing in crab cakes, country-western music and clog dancing.

"Can you imagine Lazlo wantin' to throw this shirt out?" she asked, smoothing it down over her breasts. I thought she must have been pretty once, even though her teeth were crowded and her face was sun-lined now.

"Don't forget about the comet!" Mary Beth said, jumping up. "Should be real clear soon. A friend o' mine is comin' over with a telescope."

The Hale-Bopp Comet had been making nightly appearances and was spectacular, even to the naked eye. So we fixed gin-and-tonics, grabbed sweaters and binoculars, and headed for the waterfront with other guests who were drifting toward the boat dock. Two French guys and a couple from South Africa had staked out the deck chairs. An elderly man and woman sat on a swing hanging precariously from beneath a thatch-roofed sunshade. We stood on the concrete jetty huddling against the chill. Waves rippled into the jetty and seagulls swooped into them like kamikazis. The sky turned pink, then purple. Mary Beth's friend arrived with his telescope. Mary Beth wandered onto the scene. Lazlo had disappeared.

Just before pastel hues faded into darkness, Hale-Bopp appeared. Its hazy glow looked like a star covered by thin cotton, a tail trailing at the end. It was amazing through binoculars, which we shared because Mary Beth's friend never invited anyone to look through his telescope. Then everyone talked about where they were from and what they had seen in Florida. Afterwards we dispersed into the night.

After dinner, when we lay in the too-soft bed with the faded sheets, my husband whispered, "This place gives me the creeps."

The next morning when we drove out Lazlo was talking to some people. He waved. We didn't see Mary Beth.

Driving north, we passed the Caribbean Club. It looked like any other shack by the road. I hardly noticed the sign for the *African Queen*. The Sheraton stood, imperious, like any other over-priced hotel. The malls along U.S. 1 could have been on any strip in America. There was nothing distinctive about Key Largo.

Except maybe Bogie and Bacall, or Lazlo and Mary Beth.

A Soft Adventure for the Hale and Hearty

We are three women in our fifties in search of "soft adventure." At least that's how the week-long outdoor trip to the Canadian Rockies is billed. We will be riding, hiking, rafting, and more, according to the brochures, and we are advised to get in shape before arriving. We are also asked to fill out an extensive medical history and to sign a liability waiver. In spite of the clean beds and hot showers that await us at Goat Mountain Lodge at day's end, this hardly sounds soft to me. Besides, I've known my traveling companions since we were all ninth graders together.

One of them is a Girl Scout leader and can do anything. The other is an avid hiker and kayaker. They both play tennis regularly. I, on the other hand, brush my teeth for exercise. Still, a week in the snow-capped Rocky Mountains sounds too good to miss, so putting aside my trepidation, I depart on a sunny, hot July day, duffel bag packed for every possible contingency and climate.

Arriving at the airport in Calgary, we meet our smiling and energetic driver, Leanne, and our companions for the week. They include a lawyer couple celebrating their anniversary, a dad and his three teenage sons, a woman who is an expert in flora, her daughter, and her two grandchildren.

Outside of realizing immediately that one of the two kids is going to be very annoying, our four hour drive to Golden, British Columbia, is promising. We spot mountain goat, mountain sheep, a coyote, two elk, and something small and furry along the roadside. Arriving at the Lodge, we spot a black bear on the road before being greeted by an amiable young staff, headed by

Aaron, a young man with an Amish-style beard. Crystal, who serves dinner and sees to everyone's needs in the sweetest, most innocuous manner, takes us to our cabin, which is smaller than a breadbox but does have a private bath. We settle in, crack open the vodka and tonic, and enjoy the first of seven gourmet dinners, tucking in early for the challenges ahead.

The next morning, Doug and Sandy, proprietors of the lodge, join us for a huge breakfast which features the best oatmeal I've ever eaten. (The secret, it seems, is walnuts and maple syrup.) We pack our lunches, fill our backpacks with snacks, water, sweaters, and rain gear, and head out for the longest hike of the week, a five-mile trek through verdant forest and damp woods.

The Rockies are in the midst of an almost unprecedented heat wave, and the humidity is a killer. The mosquitos are so thick we are literally swallowing them. There is no way to shed our long sleeves and jeans, and besides, it is raining enough to need outer protection. The annoying kid whines a lot, which we begin to realize is genetic. But the air smells like perfume, Ruth's instruction in plant life is impressive, and despite the fact that I feel like I'm wearing Saran Wrap in a Turkish bath, I am deeply proud of my stamina. We trudge on. After lunch on a log, we trudge on some more, our faces dripping sweat, rain, and mosquito repellant. At the end of the day, I am soaking wet and exhausted, but cheerful. I have just accomplished something no one would believe me capable of: I have kept up with the best of them. Still, the cozy lodge is a welcome relief. It's rustic, log cabin decor and huge stone fireplace are just the thing, and Noel, the cook, serves up an amazing three-course meal that leaves us oohing and aaahing long after the creme brulee has been devoured.

Day two is riding day and by now we have the routine down: Eat more than you thought possible for breakfast, pack a hearty lunch and snacks, stash plenty of water and always the rain gear in your back pack, and be ready on time. (Today we will have a cookout lunch.) For once, I have a leg up. I have taken a few riding lessons so I feel comfortable when I meet my horse, Misty. Jim and his son Jared, who live near New York City, aren't so sure about their horses, and for good cause, it turns out. Jim's horse absolutely will not leave the corral on this hot morning, and it takes Leanne, a seasoned horsewoman, to show him who's boss, by which time Jim has decided to spend the day in the hot tub. Jared soldiers on until his horse is stung by a bee and takes off into the woods, alarming the other horses, who break ranks. Jared has the presence of mind to jump off and somehow, order is restored. Jared walks the rest of the trail, a gorgeous trek alongside and through cold rivers green with silt and gently rushing little whitecaps. We stop for lunch at a campsite where our guide cooks huge sausages over an open fire, then nap before retracing our steps back to the lodge.

Wednesday brings what Doug calls "the high point." I call it the moment of truth. We are being helicoptered up to 7,000 feet to hike the high alpine meadows of a nearby mountain. Ever since signing onto this trip, my greatest trepidation has been about flying in a glass bubble through mountain terrain, not once but twice. (It's a round trip journey.) Since I find flying in anything traumatic and unnatural, helicopters hold a special place in the chambers of my brain where fear resides. I've dreamed about this moment. I've told myself that I don't have to do it. I've decided that it is my day for the hot tub. But I'll be damned if I'm going to wimp out now. So garnering all the emotional strength I have, I clamber into the six-seater, grasp my friend's hand on one side, the knee of the lawyer on the other, and warn the pilot through my helmet microphone that he has a very nervous flyer on board.

Fortunately, my mike doesn't work, because as soon as we lift off, I am thoroughly enthralled. I love it! The views are stupendous, the mountains make me feel like I'm not really all that far from the ground, and besides, our pilot, Don, could set this baby down on a dime. (He nearly has; he once landed on two logs.) On the way back, I fight my best friend, the Girl Scout, for the front seat. She wins, which is probably a good thing. I hadn't realized that up there, even the floor is glass.

Invigorated, we decide to go canoeing that evening in the hopes of spotting a mother moose and her two cubs that the lawyers saw while fishing the day before. Our guide for the evening is Wayne, a big, burly, bearded guy who knows these parts like the back of his hand. His wife, Pat, comes along with a picnic dinner. We glide around Lake Susan in the evening light, the lake growing smoother as the light dwindles from blue to pink to gold-flecked lavender. No moose appear, but there are loons and beaver dams and the sound of birds, and the snow-capped mountain backdrop is something out of an MGM epic.

On the way back to the lodge, Wayne lets us in on local politics (which he says are ruining the environment) and then launches into an editorial about how soft our adventure really is. He says he hikes up the mountain from the bottom- never takes the helicopter- and that what we're doing is nothing compared to real, rugged outdoor life.

"Wayne," I say, "you are looking at three women who will soon turn 60. The whole world thinks we're hot stuff, and you're calling us wimps? I don't think so!"

Pat gives me a high five and doubles over laughing. "He needed that!"

"Honey, they all need that!" I say, and now we are all in stitches. Wayne shoots Pat a look that says, "Them girls are something else, huh?" He tries for a rebuttal, but it's a lost cause. We are not letting him get away with anything, and besides, we tell him, if he doesn't behave himself, Pat is spending the night with us. When we get back and tell Jim what Wayne said, he is shocked. "Is he nuts?" Jim asks rhetorically. "You women are great! Listen, I'll handle Wayne. You give him to me for one day in New York. I'll just drop him off on 42nd Street with one subway token and let *him* have a soft adventure!" By now, Wayne has fired us up for the remainder of trip, and from what we hear, he can't stop talking about "them ladies up at the Goat Mountain Lodge!"

Now that we're pumped, a morning hike and a rafting afternoon seem like child's play until our Australian guide, Rob, tells us we'll be rafting fours (out of a possible five). Having rafted threes before, my stomach regresses to pre-helicopter status, but I try to remain calm in the face of the alarming safety talk because my friend, Jean, is blanching visibly. Besides, I know that when I panic I can just fall into the boat and close my eyes, which is how I tend to spend most of my serious rafting time. It's a cold, wet, wild and wonderful ride and we manage not to lose anyone before Jean and I opt out of the four/five part of the trip. Emma-the-Girl-Scout carries on, however, and ends up, we later learn, with Rob in her lap while a man flies overboard. (Everyone remained calm and did the right thing, Rob assumed command, and the lost passenger was rescued, oar in hand.)

On our last day, we hike to the foot of a glacier for a spectacular view of what looks like a blue-white claw frozen in time. Rushing rivers sweeten the air. Animal prints and scat in the mud tell us that we have missed a bear not long ago. The sky is crystal clear blue, complimenting the variations of green that reach up to meet it. We lounge by the river soaking in the exquisite beauty of this magic kingdom while Aaron takes the diehards further up the mountain. Then we all head back for a farewell barbeque, enhanced by champagne that Jim has laid on, which flows until the last game of scrabble and gin rummy has been won. Aaron plays guitar and we all sing. Reluctantly, we say goodnight, promising to trade addresses and keep in touch.

In the morning, my friends and I return to wearing "real" clothes, blow-drying our hair, and applying a bit of makeup. At the Calgary airport, we all hug, laugh about Wayne, and say things like "we'll never forget it." I confess that I have "a dirty little secret: I actually hate hiking." But no one bats an eye, because I did it anyway. I rode the waves and I flew in a glass bubble. I swallowed mosquitos and made friends with a horse. I didn't worry when one of my shins turned a most unattractive shade of yellow, because I fell out of a helicopter, or banged into a tree while riding, or smashed into some rocks while hiking, or perhaps all three. I proved that you have to be pretty strong to survive soft adventure.

I'm sure everyone on the trip would agree, and I like to think that Wayne would too.

Images of Alaska

Green lights dancing in a northern sky,
While native storytellers spin tall tales
And totem poles smile ancient secrets.
At sunset, Denali – The Great One –
Casts shadows on a vast tundra expanse,
Masking caribou, moose, and bear among the berries.
Sitka spruce, silvered by night skies, glisten,
And calving glaciers crash cavalierly into the sea.
Belugas, orcas, and humpback cavort
Gleefully in their underwater domain,
Benny Benson's gold-star flag flapping in the wind.
As flight planes come to rest at the water's edge,
The Columbia ferry crawls up the Inside Passage,
And in Talkeetna, at the Fairview Inn,
A stranger plays honky-tonk in the bar.
Meanwhile, blue-eyed, bearded Bill Owens,
In maroon suspenders and an ivory bear tiepin,
Takes a seat at Blondie's café,
An Anchorage legend at eighty-eight.
"It's a crazy story!" he begins,
Launching his life story.
Like everything else in Alaska, he's larger than life
In a land frozen in time.
This is truly the last great frontier.

Everglades

Alligators sunning on a rock,
A silly, sinister, toothy grin
Barely shrouding ancient
Contempt for the world,
While siblings slither
Into murky water.
Swoops of color
From a profusion of birds,
Some silent, others singing,
A family of otters cavorting
In the swamp, mindless
Of the much and mire
Amid which primordial fish
And minnow swim.
A woodpecker knocks out
Staccato sounds, high and hidden.
Reeds and grass and water lilies,
And endless species that stir among them
Here in this netherworld, the trick is
To keep your eyes open, low and high,
To walk, slow and open, to listen
Amid the silences for host sounds
From this steamy, secret, long ago place,
Where crocs are king, and a lone owl
Keeps the haunting nightly vigil.

Signs of Vermont

Here, between *frost heaves* and a *narrow bridge*,
Amid church reminders that ask --
If God seems absent, guess who moved? --
Among *Flea Markets* and *Pick Your Own* pumpkins,
Here, where *Sabra Field* and *Simon Pearce* reign,
Perhaps there are *Fresh Eggs*, or *Quilts*, or *Syrup Ahead*!
In this land of *moose* and deer, and
Spirit of Health holistic healing,
where a *Coop* offers only *all natural* foods,
and where *Main Street* meets *Mountain Road*,
Where *Ben and Jerry's*, or *Green Mountain Coffee*
and *Cabot cheese* are on offer at the *Country Store*,
Where *Pottery* and *Antiques* mix with *Welding*
and *Wood for Sale*, here
May Peace Prevail on Earth, and may we all
Experience Deceleration.

Misty Mountain Night

As though a godly cataract had descended on the world
    in solitude of night,
blinding us to life's midnight minutiae,
a steamy cloak of gray enshrouds the view
    outside my bedroom.
Wrapping itself around the mountain, fog dips down
in stubborn density, and lies upon the meadow,
    thick, unyielding, bold.
I like to watch its glow, its lucid obscurity, its teasing
    swirls of possibility.
I love its slightly sinister aura, its hint of magic tales.
In this fanciful kingdom, where nothing else stirs,
    save thin air, and me,
where time is useless and known only to gnomes,
who can say what will reveal itself with morning's warmth.
    When the veil lifts,
who will know what fairies came to call?

Winter Curse in New England

The nor'easters came regularly that year,
Fierce and voracious, as if on a schedule.
Worse than any I could remember,
Arctic chills wrapped blowing winds
Around us like nettled cloaks,
And walls of snow blew sideways, as
Lace curtains blowing in an open window,
Or laundry drying on a summer clothesline.
Plows went up and down, up and down,
Spreading salt and sand on slick roads,
While we brought in wood from the stockpile
To keep the fire in the wood-burning stove alive.
It dragged on and on, that whiteout winter.
Even the New England natives talked about it,
Feeling trapped, like Alaskans or Igloo-ed Inuits
In far northern climes. After a time, even the
Children grew tired of sledding and snowshoeing
And grownups said it was time to hang up their skis.
From November to March that crystal dust fell and flew
Around us, while we tried to wait patiently for the sight
Of crocuses and daffodils again.
The nor'easters came regularly that year,
And it was not an easy time for some.
Still, we knew the days would lengthen,
the snow would melt,
The scent of spring would return.
When it did, we were glad.
"That was one long winter," we said,
Once it was over. One long winter indeed.

Day Four in the Land of Enchantment

Day four and we have been one more day driving,
Through fog and rain and flat terrain and
Hillbilly music offered up with fervent hopes
That we will find ourselves in Christ.
Interstate 40 is an endless vast ribbon road,
Punctuated by the semi-skylines of Memphis
And Little Rock and Oklahoma City,
Alternating with strip towns of
Waffle Houses and Days Inns that fade into one,
And where waitresses look like they could do with
A night's sleep, if not a battered women's shelter.

Time loses meaning, except that the days drone on
Into one stiff joint after another, and sometimes
We get hungry or stop to sleep. But it is worth it.
Every last boring, homogeneous, macadam mile of it,
Once we get to Tucumcari and turn onto Highway 104 north.

For there, in the pink-blue light of New Mexico,
In that special, magical glow that I've only seen
Once somewhere else, in Vermont, I think,
At the end of a bone-biting, snow-cold day,
There is the gift. The solitude. The quietness.
The purity of unblemished sky. The width and breadth
Of clarity, broken only by mesas and bramble bush,
And an occasional trailer or pickup truck in the distance.

This is the reason we do it. The peacefulness.
The portrait to left, right and center.
The geological wonder of it. The awesome godliness.
The Indian thing and Georgia O'Keefe and Ansel Adams.
Just to be part of that, my God!

It's worth the trip, it is,
And I will do it again and again,
For one more glimpse of red rock,
Green scrub vista, one more curved
Peak of pleasure, one more sunburst on sandstone,
One more day in the land of enchantment.

Global Perspectives In Poetry

All the Starving Children

Their eyes are everywhere,
The children for whom I ate
green peas when I was young.
Their eyes are everywhere,
Staring at me from dark hollow pools
of despair.

In Mexico,
They sprawl on the pavement,
Claiming scraps of newspaper
for home.
Bony fingers stretch out
like splayed chicken feet.
It's one o'clock in the morning,
But they are wide-eyed,
And their eyes are everywhere.

In Bangladesh,
They buzz around my car,
Like flies on mucous-filled noses
and dry lips. Their hands
have that same withered
habituated crook,
Inverted, paralyzed,
And their eyes are everywhere.

In Somalia,
They drag themselves,
Collapsing in the dust like tumbleweed
blown in by non-existent breezes.
Their eyelids droop down, concealing glazed pupils,
And still,
Their eyes are everywhere.

Their eyes are everywhere....
Forcing me to avert mine.

Getting Religion

I went to the remnants of the Berlin Wall,
Stood at the foot of the Brandenburg Gates,
Crossed the barren border of Checkpoint Charlie,
And, weeping in chill wind for all that had happened there,
I found religion.

I saw the simple burial ground of Geza Gardonyi,
Folk hero of Hungary who told their tale of liberation,
I walked the streets of Buda, Pest and Eger,
where hideous acts of history made me question
the essence of humanity, and still,
I found religion.

I visited the land of Vaclav Havel and Smetana's "Ma Vlast",
And watched cheerful queues of Czechs anxious to view their heritage
on the day ancient crown jewels were shown,
I pressed my face against an iron fence To see the jumbled graves
of the Prague Ghetto, and there too,
I found religion.

It wasn't in the great Cathedrals, Where cold cavernous spaces
drip gold, and icons gazing heavenward ignore beggars near the knave,
Nor in the Gothic grandeur of Tyn Church, nor in the Baroque splendor
of St. Vitus and St. George. Neither monastery nor chapel could claim it.

I found it instead in the humble face of the waiter in East Berlin,
And in the eager eyes of a hotel hostess who finally had a passport.
I saw it in the kind moustached smile of an old man playing accordion
on the Charles Bridge, and in the boy who spoke perfect
English, selling Russian souvenirs to new tourists under the bronze
majesty of Jan Huss.

I rejoiced in it in the beer halls and in the wine cellars,
and in the shops, museums, and theatres.
I celebrated its pulse in Hungarian laughter
and its pathos in Czech poetry and hungry human connection.
I found religion in Eastern Europe, holy, holy,
And its name is Freedom.

I Listen and My Heart is Breaking

I listen to the women of Rio,
When the speak of street children murdered,
And my heart is breaking.

I listen to the women of Chernobyl,
Tell of childish faces grown old and lifeless,
And my heart is breaking.

I listen to the women of Bophal,
Whisper the grotesqueness of deformity and disease,
And my heart is breaking.

I listen to the women on the Solomons,
Giving testimony to jellyfish babies born without limbs,
And my heart is breaking.

I listen to the women of Manila,
Mourning the prostitution of their daughters,
And my heart is breaking.

I listen to the women of Addis Ababa,
Describing empty stomachs and drought,
And my heart is breaking.

I listen to the women of Cyprus,
And Ireland and Sri Lanka and South Africa,
I hear conflict's pain, and my heart is breaking.

But also,

I listen to the Madres, and Women in Black,
And African mamas. I listen to young women
Of Asia, and the Pacific Rim. I listen
To the female voice of North Africa,
And the Middle East and Eastern Europe,
And I hear the power of Everywoman, Everywhere.

Then, I rejoice. I hope. I take heart.

I wrote this poem after attending the 1985 UN Decade for Women conference in Nairobi, Kenya. Sweet Honey in the Rock set the poem to music.

Aboriginal Man

Brown skinned and broad faced,
Your eyes clouded with wisdom, age,
And most likely fatigue and sorrow,
You tell us tales of Uluru, how the scars
And pock marks came to be on the huge
Monolith, sacred to your ancient people.
The fury of the snake woman, you say,
Rent the rock. "You can believe it or not.
That's the way it was, I'm telling you true."
You know everything about plants and rocks
And desert animals, how they can give life,
Or take it away. I know nothing of such things,
And least of all, the pain of your ancestors,
Whose spirits wander still, even as white men,
Oblivious, scar your sacred rock
In the name of conquest.

Beyond The Veil

Sisters of the chador, my heart weeps to see you
in the silenced, somber blackness of non-being.
I shudder at the hiss of your oppression,
I grieve for the sound of your tears,
stifled behind guarded gates in the medieval landscape
of captivity. I cringe at the poverty of your soul.
What can I offer you, Maidens, Mothers, Crones,
Who might have given so much, were essence
not squeezed from you by terrorists and oppressors
of this, and other times?

Only this --

So long as one of you remains sheathed
and silenced, veiled and voiceless,
tethered and terrified,
all of us, sisters, fight for your freedom.
We stand for you, we speak on your behalf,
We occupy tables denied to you.
We remember. And know this:
We will never relinquish you to shadowed humanity.
We are with you, and you are with us
And we shall, all of us, emerge from the darkness together.

Queen Maeve's Grave

Oh, green, green, green
The velvet path to your resting place
On high, 'neath the circle of stone
That crowns you.
Green, as only Eire can be,
Moist, fragrant, defiant green,
As the glint in your eye must have been
When you stood tall and proud
To lead the way. Majestic Maeve,
In solitude then, as now,
Three thousand years hence.
Look down upon the
Green, green, green of your land.
We know you still.

Queen Maeve was an Irish warrior queen born in 50 BC – if, indeed, she was real. Her grave can be visited in Sligo, Northern Ireland.

Epilogue

Longings

There was a time when I thought all longing would cease,
When I would no longer yearn for flowers and velvet and love,
A time when I would have had my fill of surprises
and daydreams and fantasied journeys,
A time when I would say, "I have reached my fullness.
I need no more, see?" Silly, silly me.

End Matter

Acknowledgments

"Khartoum Nights" first appeared in *Croning Tales*, Elayne Clift, OGN Publications, 1996.

"Three Days in Luang Prabang," "Visions of Vietnam," and "Sadness in Cambodia" first appeared in *ACHAN: A Year of Teaching in Thailand*, Elayne Clift, Bangkok Books, 2007.

"This is Thailand, Silly!" first appeared in www.boloji.com December 2008.

"Shadows and Stars" first appeared in *Melusine: Women in the 21st Century*, March 2010.

"Iceland: Nice Place to Visit but Would You Want to Live There?" first appeared in *Senior Voice*, Sept. 2013

"Counting Cats in Zanzibar" first appeared on www.go60.us/travel-logs/item/1224-counting-cats-in-zanzibar-reflections-on-travel-through-a-7th-decade-lens, February 2014

"A Cook, A Driver, and a Train Station" first appeared in *Railonoma: Unforgettable Train Stories*, Anupama, Ed., Good Time Books Pvt. Ltd, New Delhi, 2014

Dubai Dream first appeared in www.go60.us in January 2017.

The following poems first appeared in *Demons Dancing in My Head*, Elayne Clift, OGN Publications, 1995:
  "I Listen and My Heart is Breaking"
  "And Still the Women Weep"
  "Getting Religion"
  "For Mikreta"

The following poems first appeared in Other People, Other Lands, Elayne Clift, OGN Publications, 1999:

"Aborgine Man"
"Queen Maeve's Grave"
"Tienanmen Square"
"Day One in the Land of Enchantment"
"Everglades"
"Images of Alaska"
"Gypsy Girl in Bucharest"

Photo Credits

Unless otherwise noted all photos by Elayne Clift. Used with permission

page 7: lion, image by designerpoint on Pixabay

page 40: Masai Warrior, Juliya Shangarey/Shutterstock.com

page 70: Emerald Buddha, JPSwimmer, commons.wikimedia.org

page 86: Angkor Wat, image by sharonang on Pixabay

page 91: Caribbean, Image by PublicDomainPictures on Pixabay

page 98: Panama Canal, image by artes2franco on Pixabay

page 117: tortoise, image by fe31lopz on Pixabay

page 119: old Havana, image by frejka on Pixabay

page 141: Tower Bridge, image by fotofan1 on Pixabay

page 146: Cappadocian town, image by Hans on Pixabay

page 160: Stockholm, image by monikawl999 on Pixabay

page 164: Oslo opera house, image by office8 on Pixabay

page 174: Pigeon Square, Boris Stroujko/Shutterstock.com

page 206: Iceland, image by 12019 on Pixabay

page 214: QE 2, Tim Dyer, creativecommons.org/licenses/by/3.0/

page 240: Sacre Couer, image by 271277 on Pixabay

page 249: mosque, image by 680451 on Pixabay

page 254: Wailing Wall, image by EvgeniT on Pixabay

About the Author

Elayne Clift, M.A., a Vermont Humanities Council Scholar, is an award-winning writer and journalist, a writing workshop leader, and a lecturer. Her work has been widely anthologized and appears in numerous publications internationally. A regular columnist for the *Keene* (NH) *Sentinel* and the *Brattleboro* (Vt.) *Commons*, and a reviewer for the *New York Journal of Books*, she has written for various magazines and periodicals. Her novel, *Hester's Daughters*, a contemporary, feminist retelling of *The Scarlet Letter*, appeared in 2012 and her award-winning short story collection, *Children of the Chalet*, was published by Braughler Books (2015). www.elayne-clift.com.

www.ingramcontent.com/pod-product-compliance
Lightning Source LLC
Chambersburg PA
CBHW070736170426
43200CB00007B/545